AF543389

Corruption and Black Money

CORRUPTION AND BLACK MONEY

R.K. Jha
&
M.K. Singh

PRASHANT PUBLISHING HOUSE
DELHI-110094

Published by :

Prashant Publishing House

C-34, 28 Foota Road, Gali-3,

West Karwal Nagar, Delhi-110094

Phone : 011-22963970, Mob. : 9810396373

Corruption And Black Money

Reserved

First Pubished 2011

ISBN 978-93-80565-22-4

No part of this book may be reprduced or transmitted in any form or by any means, electronic or mechanical, Including photocoying, recording or by any information storage and retrieval system, with-out permission in writing from the Publishers.

Printed At :- Dynamic Printers,Delhi

Preface

In criminology, corporate crime refers to crimes committed either by a corporation (i.e., a business entity having a separate legal personality from the natural persons that manage its activities), or by individuals that may be identified with a corporation or other business entity. Note that some forms of corporate corruption may not actually be criminal if they are not specifically illegal under a given system of laws.

The corrupt situations involve individuals and groups in singular and or plural, by and large it is a two way system based on 'give and take' principle assuring mutual interest devoid of any social considerations. In a wider sense "corruption" refers to not only all sorts of "improper or selfish exercise of power and influence attached to a public office or to the special position one occupies in public life" but also includes bribers' dealings. The nature of corruption is best understood by the motivational background of its practitioner. It should, however, he judged in the social context. A highly frustrated and deserving person may ultimately choose to seek his coveted target through a 'short-cut' device. On the other hand an immoral businessman offers a bait in numerous ways to get his dirty things done. In both cases corruption is involved but the situations are not identical. It appears that in a disorganised system the agencies of social control suffocate the normal channels for uprighteous people, intentionally making corruption an inevitable force, to the advantage of the antisocial elements. This behaviour basically represents the lust of the unconscientious for certain specified but undeserved ends.

Money is both a goal and an instrument in the realm of corruption. Its omnipotential power has a most corrupting influence on both the 'haves' and 'have nots'; the former grow prosperous and powerful while the latter remain under dehumanising conditions. There may be a few climbers but the general masses suffer it most without being able to do anything to annihilate it. It thus becomes a sophisticated technique in the hands of the governing sections to perpetuate their hold on the weaker and the deprived groups.

Illegally earned money is called black money. Black money is the result of hoarding smuggling tax evasion and dealing in immovable- property for which the consideration is paid in black. It has been beyond the control of the government. The Indian economy stands badly shattered because of the huge-amount of this tainted wealth lying in the coffers of the rich.

Reality In reality the term 'black money' is related with cash flow of the currency and only those people know how to use it properly who are the masters in this profession. Firstly black money is deposited in the foreigner countries or properties are bought in and out of the country with this money. Sometimes, people buy land or large farm houses in the names of their relatives which are usually bought in non-existent or bogus names. Whenever some officer or leader is caught red handed taking the bribe they usually decline about their ownership of some property etc. so properties are bought in non-existence names by the corrupt officers and leaders. There are many examples of it that corrupt leaders amassed a lot of property during their rule and they were blamed for corruption. They lost in the elections but after elections their children live the life of kings. CBI raids recovered documents of property that had been bought in non-existent names. Luxury cars were found but they say that their relatives are the owners of these items who are the god fearing people and daily goers to the Gurudwaras or temples. There are many examples when many high class government officials and police officers had collected crores of rupees though corrupt means for the satisfaction of their personal interests.

This book will be useful for parliamentarians, social workers, teachers and students in India and abroad.

—Editor

Contents

1

Introduction to Corruption

"There are about forty ways of embezzlement; what is realised earlier is entered later on; what is realised later is entered earlier; what ought to be realised is not realised... It is possible to mark the movements of birds flying high up in the sky, but it is not possible to ascertain the secret movements of government servants," The ancient lineage of corruption in India sanctified by tradition is evident by these words of Kautilya, the author of *Arthasastra*.

The endemical ubiquity of this calamitous evil represents a queer national neurosis. Its all pervasive influence cuts across all sectors and strata of society. In a characteristically acquisitive order when unscrupulous channels are resorted to attaining selfish ends, corruption seeks to flourish at the cost of general obligations. 'By hook or by crook" approach towards goal-accomplishment leads to corrupt means.

ANATOMY

The anatomy of a corrupt practice generally involves:

1. a short-cut method guided by selfism,
2. to attain an improper object through bribes in cash or kind, or
3. by showing favour to the undeserving and injustice to the talented,
4. to the ultimate disadvantage of the entire social system.

The corrupt situations involve individuals and groups in singular and or plural, by and large it is a two way system based on 'give and take' principle assuring mutual interest devoid of any social considerations. In a wider sense "corruption" refers to not only all sorts of "improper or selfish exercise of power and influence attached to a public office or to the special position one occupies in public life" but also includes bribers' dealings. The nature of corruption is best understood by the motivational background of its practitioner. It should, however, he judged in the social context. A highly frustrated and deserving person may ultimately choose to seek his coveted target through a 'short-cut' device. On the other hand an immoral businessman offers a bait in numerous ways to get his dirty things done. In both cases corruption is involved but the situations are not identical. It appears that in a disorganised system the agencies of social control suffocate the normal channels for uprighteous people, intentionally making corruption an inevitable force, to the advantage of the antisocial elements. This behaviour basically represents the lust of the unconscientious for certain specified but undeserved ends.

Money is both a goal and an instrument in the realm of corruption. Its omnipotential power has a most corrupting influence on both the 'haves' and 'have nots'; the former grow prosperous and powerful while the latter remain under dehumanising conditions. There may be a few climbers but the general masses suffer it most without being able to do anything to annihilate it. It thus becomes a sophisticated technique in the hands of the governing sections to perpetuate their hold on the weaker and the deprived groups.

MANIFESTATION AND MAGNITUDE

It is difficult to measure the extent of corruption. The visible and invisible forces, however, are manifest and widespread beyond doubt. It becomes even unidentifiable when cultural patterns sanction the 'corrupt' transactions. When everybody practises corrupt means, it seeks to grow as a norm. The bribe or 'grease money' is called 'chai pani ka khareh,' and the one who refrains from indulging in this 'socially accepted' corrupt means, becomes a 'deviant', an outcast and a cynic endangering his own security. Bribery, in cash or kind, is the most common practice in corruption. In the official hierarchy no body is immune from its allurement. A few cases may be quoted:

> *"Gurdaspur. Oct. 28. Batala police yesterday raided the house of judicial magistrate cum sub-judge.........and caught him accepting a bribe of Rs. 200/-and a bottle of whisky."*

The Central Bureau of Investigation launched a number of prosecutions in October 1968 against public servants for offences involving bribery, criminal misconduct, cheating and criminal breach of trust. A former judge was prosecuted for committing criminal breach of trust in respect of over Rs. 8 lakhs from the naval prize fund in his capacity as administrator. An assistant controller of estate duty was prosecuted for accepting Rs. 34,500 from a businessman for undue favour. A refrigeration engineer of the Indo-Norwegian Project was prosecuted for misappropriating over Rs. 2,000 and cheating another person for Rs. 1,000. Fifty-live employees of the Post and Telegraph Department were prosecuted for entering into a conspiracy to false and fictitious medical reimbursement claims on the basis of false certificates issued by the medical officers and false cash memos issued by the chemists and cheated the Government to the extent of Rs. 80,000 to 85,000. Eight gazetted officers and 71 non-gazetted public servants were involved in 61 cases in which prosecutions were launched, and the world knows about the misappropriation of crores of rupees by Tejas. On May 11, 1971 an. Income Tax officer from Agra and the S.P. of Mathura were caught red-handed by the CBI for allegedly extorting Rs. 2 lakhs as a bribe from the Mercantile Bank, Connaught Place, New Delhi

The bribe taking is so rampant that it is very rare that one is caught. Almost everybody takes bribes in some way or the other; the crude methods of the clerks and constables are known but the sophisticated techniques of the higher ups go unnoticed. The easiest way to bribe a VIP is to offer a lucrative salary to his son who would otherwise not qualify even for a lowest clerical assignment. It is well known that big industrialists have employed so many persons in this way. It is a process of mutual obligation. It was heard that a businessman rented luxuriously furnished apartments on extremely low cost to the officials of the Income Tax Department. The mode of operation is too obvious. The businessman thus obliges everybody ultimately to his own benefit. Licences, appointments, permission, permits, aids and even admissions (to school) as well as reservations (for railway berths) are obtained through bribes. Bribery is a passport, a highly skilled and specialised technique, to attain success. The stereotyped methods have become crude, of course, not uncommon.

> *"Bribery is on the increase not only in cities but villages also... Fur instance, anyone wanting any information regarding his lands can get it from the* Lekhpal *(village accountant) who goes to the village cnce a week or so. The* Lekhpal *demands there to four rupees to show the and records.... Police constables, whose duty is to prevent corruption of any sort, show no hesitation in accepting bribes. Many cases are hushed up because the criminal presses a few rupees into the palms of a police constable..."*

The behaviour of the senior official who sells confidential information to the enemy agents is not much different from the Lekhpal's. The Patraul (canal— guard) is too well known for his collective bribes but the underhand dealings of the top most position holders seldom appear on the surface. And when they do they are hushed up.

Tax-evasion is another widespread corrupt practice in which invariably all big business houses and professional groups indulge. Several crores of rupees are to be realised from the industrial maganates as income tax on their 'white income'. The 'black money' is never exactly known. The Direct Taxes Inquiry Committee appointed to go into the problem of black money has revealed interesting facts. A conservative estimate has put the amount of black money at least Rs. 3,000 crores to Rs. 3,500 crores in circulation. Black-marketing, profiteering and hoarding are the 'moral' predicaments of the entire business community in India. *'Subha-Labha"* inscription displayed by' all businessmen without any exception represents the maniac greed of this community which has unfortunately been given a religious sanction by the portrait of *Laxmi,* the goddess of wealth. There may be famines, hunger deaths, steep price rise, and a host of the like artificial calamities in a part or whole of the country, but profiteering goes on ceaselessly. This was evident by the rotting of wheat in the graneries of Uttar Pradesh simultaneously with the famine in Rajasthan.

Adulteration is a bizarre aspect of corruption, it is practised by the milk seller on whose product the young infants subsist; by the chemist and druggist whose compounds and mixtures are needed to save the ailing person and by the rich, contractors on whose-buildings and dams the entire super-structure of modern India depends. Pure milk and ghee have become myths in a country which is predominatly an agricultural one. Adulteration of these essential commodities is perhaps more common in rural areas than cities and it is the saddest aspect of the problem. The imprudent quantity of sand mixed with the cement can be extracted out of any of the buildings that have been built by the Government through contractors. Most of the public works undertakings do not qualify the required level of excellence. Whether it is a corporation flat or a huge bridge, the construction indicates cracks in the background of the phenomenal prosperity of their builders, the engineers and the contractors. There is a general agreement that corruption has been on increase in post-Independence era. The Santhanam committee report highlights "the growth of corruption" and the need to arrest "the deterio-ration in the standards of public life"

CAUSES

There may be several causes of corruption, viz., (1) lack of opportunities for all, (2) poverty, (3) declining standard of morality, (4) administrative derelictions, (5) the motive of acquisition, (6) lack of proper education, and (7) growing individualism and materialism. This is rather a superficial account of the etiology of corruption. Let us probe a little deeper sociologically. Who indulges in corruption most? A sweeper or a minister? Our submission is that corruption in India is largely a problem created by the upper castes. The privileged sections, irrespective of any religion, practise corruption with a confidence that they would evade the law. In fact they do.

The 'wretched' ones are corrupt in their own way; one could be a drunkard, gambler and a liar. A sweeper's corrupt manners can never create cracks in Bhakara Nangal Dam; it is the immorality of the neofeudalists — engineers, bureaucrats, contractors, politicians, and big business houses — that is responsible for large scale erosion of national strength. The role of upper castes in corruption is thus greater, The corruption amongst lower castes is a reaction of upper castes.'

If a *pundit* can overtax in ritual ceremonies then why should an *ahir* the traditional cast of milk sellers) hesitate in adulterating milk ? It appears that corruption in India is largely due to the implied evils of caste system. As a hypothesis, one could say that corruption is practised in proportion, to one's social status. A *chaparasi* (peon) gets Rs. 2/-as bribe whereas Birlas, Jains and Dalmias offer millions in several ways. Sociologists have hitherto studied caste from a different angle. It calls for intensive research to examine various issues involved in the dynamics of mutual exploitation at caste, and class levels.

Segal explains corruption in the *New Raj* in the light of the ruler-ruled relationship. Basically it has no contradiction with our viewpoint. He vividly discusses how the distances between the rulers (formerly aliens and now the native ones) and the ruled have led to massive corruption in the contemporary society. In particular the relationship of the business class with the ruling sections is highlighted with keen insight into the Indian problem's. Myrdal too has dealt with corruption with precise undemanding of its causes and effects.

He holds that the folklore of corruption embodies important social facts worth intensive research in their own right. The main causes of increasing-corruption are, according to Myrdal: (i), Little loyalty to the community as a whole, whether on the local or the national level, implying stronger loyalty to less inclusive groups-family, caste, ethnic, religious, or linguistic community". This invites nepotism and implies a low level of social discipline, (ii) The social dynamics referring to greater opportunities and disturbances during the transition from colonial status to self-government. (iii), Discretionary' controls and powers, (iv), Low real wages of officials, especially those of the lower and middle levels, (v), A circular causation with cumulative working within the system of corruption itself.

CONSEQUENCES

Corruption, like sacrifice, starts at the top and percolating down, colours the whole society." The effects of corruption are unwholesome and devastating, socially, economically and politically. *A* corrupt system often smacks of utter social irresponsibilities, economic insecurities and political instability. Specifically the consequences may be analysed as follows:

1. Corruption leads to the weakening of the greater loyalities that strengthen 'community' in the wider sense. Parochial loyalties increase. Increasing casteism, communalism and regionalism in India is a result of corruption in the public life. Disintegration and political instability are thus unavoidable.
2. The entire planning and developmental process becomes faulty, ineffective, and paralysed. According to Myrdal "the prevalence of corruption provides strong inhibitions and obstacles to development.... Corruption is one of the forces that help to preserve the "soft state" with its low degree of "social discipline." Dilly dallying techniques, inertia, red-tapism, official listlessness, deliberate shelving, inefficiency, evasion of personal responsibility, faulty or delayed decision and a callous neglect of the public matters and obligations are some of the main effects of corruption witnessed in daily routine. In a vicious climate of suspicion, greed, and immoralities both honest and dishonest people resort to those techniques respectively to avoid personal involvement and to misuse one's position. The blind alleyes of

bureaucratic procedures that are too dilatory and cumbersome suffocate mutters of general interest. "Speed money", however, rescues the private interests.

3. Corruption reduces rules and regulations to a farcical status and when practised by higher echelons, it demoralises the weaker groups and vulgarises the persons exercising authority or commanding status and wealth.
4. Princes crop up in the pockets of vested interests in the dominant sphere, including administration, education and social welfare. Their recommendation value serves as a status symbol. The one who does not enjoy the 'prince's' support is called a resourcesless guy. Pulls' and "pressures' add to the prestige of the 'prince'.
5. Frustrations, anxieties and insecurities grow amongst those who are not corrupt either by conviction or circumstance. Tensions and conflicts do torture the corrupt but their impact is not overtly known.

CURE

The philosophy of constructive chapter of corruption' is not acceptable to us. An apologist or a corrupt 'higher up' may well recognise it as a matter of rationalisation.

Remedial measures, therefore, need to be suggested. Some of the recommendations of the Santhanam Committee report are:

1. Decrease in the discretionary powers.
2. Improved pay-scale for low-paid civil servants and greater socio-economy security.
3. Strengthening of special police department including vigilance agencies.
4. Change in the penal code and other laws to punish corrupt officials speedily and effectively.
5. Action against those in the private sector who corrupt public servants.
6. Income tax reports and assessments be made public.

7. Special procedures for complaint against ministers and legislators.
8. Check on business enterprises to make contributions to political parties.
9. Protection of the persons making *bona fide* complaints, et cetera.

The Committee, accepting corruption as a "long-term problem", recognises the significance of an overhaul of "the entire system of moral values and of the socio-economic structure." And we fully endorse this.

Myrdal's two observations appear remarkable. About the growing public concern In: comments: "When considering the prospects of reform in countries where corruption is so embedded in institutional and attitudinal remnants of traditional society and where almost everything that happens increases incentives and opportunities for personal gain, the public outcry against corruption must be regarded as a constructive force.

This holds true even when this reaction is basically only the envy of people who themselves would not hesitate to engage in corrupt practices had they a chance and even though the common awareness of corruption is apt to spread cynicism."

His observation about the role of Western business interests in feeding corruption in South Asia is highly significant. "This damaging effect is, of course, vastly strengthened when Western government aid can be viewed in the same terms." We may present a few more relevant suggestions to combat corruption in a country like India:

1. The Santhanam Committee report emphasises the public declaration of an individual's income. But this is not enough. Phenomenal prosperity without any desirable means should be accountable to the public. Within a few years the black-marketeers become multi-millionaires. Nobody is there to question their short-cuts to glaring affluence even the Governors go to inaugurate their residential places made out of the Mark money. This is a highly deplorable condition. There should be a

legally competent incorrupt agency to cheek the mushroom growth of unscrupulous millionaires,

2. Social action techniques should be resorted to publicly control the misconduct of irresponsible businessmen, administrators, politicians and even the police. The articulate and the conscientious can well organise programmes to control socially destructive behaviour. This, however, seems to have limited value in the present condition. We have seldom heard of a strike or demonstration against hoarding, blackmarketing or profiteering. The student community which is most vocal and sensitive should take a lead in this regard. This is, however, not possible unless there is a radical change in the student leadership.
3. Administrative and political echelons should be reorganised and their structural and functional defects should be rectified. Nothing short of a complete overhauling would be of significance in this regard. The value of deterrent punishment too cannot be underestimated.
4. These is an urgent need to redefine the ruler-ruled relationship. The behaviour of the police inspector, the district magistrate, and the governor is almost the same as it was during the colonial rule. The rulers must be educated in the light of the twentieth century values to serve the people. The smug arrogance of the administrators is incompatible with the democratic principles that determine the affairs in an egalitarian set-up. The distance between the rulers and the ruled was artificially maintained during the colonial period. The maintenance of this distance in a sovereign state breeds corruption. It may not be out of place to point out that an extravagantly luxurious standard of living, imitating the 'moghal' glory and splendour, is anachronistic in the present frame of governing ideologies, more so when the overwhelming majority of the people live in utter want and deprivation. The fantastic statistics of expenditure on our elected leaders

should serve as an eye-opener. Almost unbelievably high is the cost of rehabilitating the old politicians as Governors. The glamour of their Raj Bhawans can make jealous even the ghosts of our bygone kings. In a competitive world of materialism those who cannot legitimately afford the standard of "higher ups", resort to corrupt means.

5. It is essential that political affiliations be based on ideological commitment rather than on opportunism and selfish interests. The elements analysed in the discussion on crises of character and democracy testify to the fact that politics has become a low occupation devoid of principles and ideological convictions. This is a dangerous sign and indeed a reliable indicator of growing corruption. "God, please give us a stable Ministry and an honest Parliament which practise what they preach and do not fool people by making long speeches and shouting at each other or fighting like cats and dogs in Parliament, Assemblies and public meeting."

Julius Caesar made a name for himself when on behalf of some Greek cities he prosecuted their Roman Governor for corruption. He had stopped profiteering by tax-collectors who were looting business and agriculture in the provinces. Our intent here is not to glorify monarchy but to underline the determination on the part of an incorrupt leader to stamp out corruption. Are our governors—the white elephants maintained by the Government of India—infallible?

CORRUPTION IN INDIA

Political corruption in India is a major concern. A 2005 study done by Transparency International (TI) in India found that more than 50% of the people had firsthand experience of paying bribe or peddling influence to get a job done in a public office. Taxes and bribes are common between state borders; Transparency International estimates that truckers pay annually US$5 billion in bribes. For 2010, India was ranked 87 of 178 countries in Transparency International's Corruption Perceptions Index. Criminalization of Indian politics is a problem. In July 2008 The Washington Post reported that nearly a fourth of the 540 Indian Parliament members faced criminal charges, "including human trafficking, immigration rackets, embezzlement, rape and even murder". History

The economy of India was under socialist-inspired policies for an entire generation from the 1950s until the 1980s. The economy was subject to extensive regulation, protectionism, and public ownership, leading to pervasive corruption and slow growth. License Raj was often at the core of corruption. The Vohra Report was submitted by the former Indian Union Home Secretary, N.N. Vohra, in October 1993. It studied the problem of the criminalisation of politics and of the nexus among criminals, politicians and bureaucrats in India.

The report contained several observations made by official agencies on the criminal network which was virtually running a parallel government. It also discussed criminal gangs who enjoyed the patronage of politicians, of all parties, and the protection of government functionaries. It revealed that political leaders had become the leaders of gangs. They were connected to the military. Over the years criminals had been elected to local bodies, State Assemblies and Parliament. The unpublished annexures to the Vohra Report were believed to contain highly explosive material.

According to Jitendra Singh, "in the bad old days, particularly pre-1991, when the License Raj held sway, and by design, all kinds of free market mechanisms were hobbled or stymied, and corruption emerged almost as an illegitimate price mechanism, a shadowy quasi-market, such that scarce resources could still be allocated within the economy, and decisions could get made. [...] These were largely distortions created by the politico-economic regime.

While a sea change has occurred in the years following 1991, some of the distorted cultural norms that took hold during the earlier period are slowly being repaired by the sheer forces of competition. The process will be long and slow, however. It will not change overnight." One of the major problems and obstacles to development that many developing countries face is corruption by greedy, power-hungry politicians, which is endemic in certain parts of the world.

Land and Property

Officials often steal state property. In Bihar, more than 80% of the subsidized food aid to poor is stolen. In cities and villages throughout India, Mafia Raj consisting of municipal and other government officials, elected politicians, judicial officers, real estate developers and law enforcement officials, acquire, develop and sell land in illegal ways..

Tendering Processes and Awarding Contracts

Government officials having discretionary powers in awarding contracts engage in preferential treatment for selected bidders, display negligence in quality control processes. Many state-funded construction activities in India, such as road building, are dominated by construction mafias, which are groupings of corrupt public works officials, materials suppliers, politicians and construction contractors. Shoddy construction and material substitution (e.g. mixing sand in cement while submitting expenses for cement) result in roads and highways being dangerous, and sometimes simply washed away when India's heavy monsoon season arrives.

Medicine

In Government Hospitals, corruption is associated with non availability of medicines (or duplicate medicines), getting admission, consultations with doctors and availing diagnostic services.. There have been cases of diversion of medical supplies from government hospitals and clinics as well as supply and distribution of medicines of inferior quality

Transport

Officials who oversee transportation regulations, safety norms, traffic violations engage in rent seeking activity. Typically a lenient treatment for an offending driver or vehicle is accompanied by expectation of a bribe. India has multiple jurisdictions for vehicular laws as well as overlapping laws at the central government and state government level which worsens bureaucratic complications. This leads to facilitation payments to accelerate normal government processes.

Some airports, such as the Thiruvananthapuram airport in Kerala, are notorious for theft of valuables from bags checked on incoming flights. Such theft is a rude awakening to the state of corruption in Kerala to tourists and expatriates returning from vacations. Corrupt officials and airport employees turn a blind eye to theft of passenger belongings often colluding in the theft.

Income Tax

There have been several cases of collusion of officials of the income tax department of India for a favourable tax treatment in return for bribes

Preferential Award of Public Resources

As detailed earlier, land in areas with short supply is relatively common with government entities awarding public land to private concerns at negligible rates. Other examples include the award of mining leases to private companies without a levy of taxes that is proportionate to the market value of the ore.

Judiciary

Corruption is rampant in the judicial system of India. According to Transparency International, judicial corruption in India is attributable to factors such as "delays in the disposal of cases, shortage of judges and complex procedures, all of which are exacerbated by a preponderance of new laws".

Armed Forces

The Indian Armed Forces have frequently witnessed corruption involving senior armed forces officers from the Indian Army, Indian Navy and Indian Air Force. Many officers have been caught for allegedly selling defence stores in the black market in the border districts of Indian states and territories. Recent sukhna land scandal involving four Indian Lieutenant Generals has shaken public faith in the country's massive military at a time when unprecedented sums are being spent on modernising the armed forces. A string of eye-popping fraud cases has damaged the institution in recent years.

Police

Despite State prohibitions against torture and custodial misconduct by the police, torture is widespread in police custody, which is a major reason behind deaths in custody. The police often torture innocent people until a 'confession' is obtained to save influential and wealthy offenders. G.P. Joshi, the programme coordinator of the Indian branch of the Commonwealth Human Rights Initiative in New Delhi comments that the main issue at hand concerning police violence is a lack of accountability of the police.

Religious Institutions

In India, the corruption has also crept into religious institutions. Some of the Church of North India are making money by selling Baptism certificates. A group of church leaders and activists has launched a campaign to combat the corruption within churches. The chief economic consequences of corruption are the loss to the economy an unhealthy climate for investment and an increase in the cost of government-subsidised services. The TI India study estimates the monetary value of petty corruption in 11 basic services provided by the government, like education, healthcare, judiciary, police, etc., to be around 21,068 crore (US$4.8 billion). India still ranks in the bottom quartile of developing nations in terms of the ease of doing business, and compared to China and other lower developed Asian nations, the average time taken to secure the clearances for a startup or to invoke bankruptcy is much greater.

ANTI-CORRUPTION EFFORTS

Right to Information Act

The Right to Information Act (2005) and equivalent acts in the states, that require government officials to furnish information requested by citizens or face punitive action, computerisation of services and various central and state government acts that established vigilance commissions have considerably reduced corruption or at least have opened up avenues to redress grievances. The 2006 report by Transparency International puts India at the 70th place and states that significant improvements were made by India in reducing corruption, corruption is everywhere in India right from the parliament to down from the clerk corruption is a big problem in India

Ombudsmen

The Lokayukta is an anti-government corruption organization in the Indian states. These institutions are based on the Ombudsman in Scandinavian countries. An amendment to the Constitution has been proposed to implement the Lokayukta uniformly across Indian States as a three-member body, headed by a retired Supreme Court judge or high court chief justice, and comprise of the state vigilance commissioner and a jurist or an eminent administrator as other members.

Computerization

- Bhoomi is a project jointly funded by the Government of India and the Government of Karnataka to digitize the paper land records and create a software mechanism to control changes to the land registry in Karnataka. The project was designed to eliminate the long-standing problem of inefficiency and corruption.
- Introduction of smart cards for vehicle registration and drivers licenses by Karnataka Regional Transport Organization.
- Enforcement automation of traffic violations by Bangalore Traffic Police.

Economic Issues

Economic issues like poverty, unemployment, development are main issues that influence politics. *Garibi hatao* (eradicate poverty) has been a slogan of the Indian National Congress for long. The well known Bharatiya Janata Party is looked upon with grace as a political party that is indeed encouraging to free market economy, businesses and others. The Communist Party of India (Marxist) vehemently supports left-wing politics and has strongly opposed to socio-economic policies such as globalization, capitalism, foreign investments and privatization. The economic policies of most other parties do not go much further than providing populist subsidies and reservations. As a noteworthy case, the manifesto of the Samajwadi Party, the third largest party in the 15th Lok Sabha, for the 2009 general elections promised to reduce the use of computers upon being elected.

Law and Order

Just to name a few, terrorism, Naxalism, Religious violence and caste-related violence are important issues that affect the political environment of the Indian nation. Stringent anti-terror legislations like TADA, POTA and MCOCA have received much political attention, both in favour as well as criticism.

Law and order issues such as action against organized crime are not issues that affect the outcomes of elections. On the other hand, there is a criminal-politician nexus. Many elected legislators have criminal cases against them. In July 2008 Washington Times reported that nearly a fourth of the 540 Indian Parliament members faced criminal charges, "including human trafficking, immigration rackets, embezzlement, rape and even murder".

Inefficiency

Indian government is among the most bureaucratic in the world. The current government has concluded that most spending fails to reach its intended recipients. Lant Pritchett calls India's public sector "one of the world's top ten biggest problems-of the order of AIDS and climate change". *The Economist* article about Indian civil service (2008) said that Indian central government employs around 3 million people and states another 7 million, including "vast armies of paper-shuffling peons". The Economist states that "India has some of the hardest-working bureaucrats in the world, but its administration has an abysmal record of serving the public".

Unannounced visits by government inspectors showed that 25% of public sector teachers and 40% of public sector medical workers could not be found at the workplace. Teacher absence rates ranged from 15% in Maharashtra to 71% in Bihar. Despite worse absence rates, public sector teachers enjoy salaries at least five times higher than private sector teachers. India's absence rates are among the worst in the world.

Many experiments with computerization have failed due to corruption and other factors. In 2008, Tanmoy Chakrabarty noted that "There are vested interests everywhere, politicians fear that they will lose control with e-government, and this is coming in the way of successful implementation of e-government projects in India. [...] Out of the 27 projects under the NEGP, only one (the MCA21 program) has been completed. There is tremendous gap between conceptualization and implementation".

Spending Priorities

The government subsidizes everything from gasoline to food. Loss-making state-owned enterprises are supported by the government. Farmers are given electricity for free. Overall, a 2005 article by International Herald Tribune stated that subsidies amounted to 14% of GDP. As much as 39 percent of subsidized kerosene is stolen. Moreover, these subsidies cause economic distortions.

On the other hand, India spends relatively little on education, health, or infrastructure. Urgently needed infrastructure investment has been much lower than in China. According to the UNESCO, India has the lowest public expenditure on higher education per student in the world.

Deficits

As per the CIA World Factbook, India ranks 23rd in the world with respect to the Public Debt with a total of 61.30% of GDP just before United states which ranks 24th (2008 estimated).

2

Corruption and Society

The word corrupt when used as an adverb literally means "utterly broken". In modern English usage the words corruption and corrupt have many meanings:

- Political corruption: the abuse of public power, office, or resources by government officials or employees for personal gain, e.g. by extortion, soliciting or offering bribes.
- Corporate corruption: corporate criminality and the abuse of power by corporation officials, either internally or externally.

In criminology, corporate crime refers to crimes committed either by a corporation (i.e., a business entity having a separate legal personality from the natural persons that manage its activities), or by individuals that may be identified with a corporation or other business entity. Note that some forms of corporate corruption may not actually be criminal if they are not specifically illegal under a given system of laws. For example, some jurisdictions allow insider trading.

Corporate crime overlaps with:

- white-collar crime, because the majority of individuals who may act as or represent the interests of the corporation are employees or professionals of a higher social class;
- organized crime, because criminals can set up

corporations either for the purposes of crime or as vehicles for laundering the proceeds of crime. Organized crime has become a branch of big business and is simply the illegal sector of capital. It has been estimated that, by the middle of the 1990s, the "gross criminal product" of organized crime made it the twentieth richest organization in the world—richer than 150 sovereign states. The world's gross criminal product has been estimated at 20 percent of world trade.; and

- state-corporate crime because, in many contexts, the opportunity to commit crime emerges from the relationship between the corporation and the state.

Legal Person

An 1886 decision of the United States Supreme Court, in *Santa Clara County v. Southern Pacific Railroad* 118 U. S. 394 (1886), has been cited by various courts in the US as precedent to maintain that a corporation can be defined legally as a 'person', as described in the Fourteenth Amendment to the U. S. Constitution. The Fourteenth Amendment stipulates that, "No State shall make or enforce any law which shall abridge the privileges or immunities of citizens of the United States; nor shall any State deprive any person of life, liberty, or property, without due process of law; nor deny to any person within its jurisdiction the equal protection of the laws. "

In English law, this was matched by the decision in Salomon v Salomon & Co [1897] AC 22. In Australian law, under the *Corporations Act 2001 (Cth)*, a corporation is legally a 'person'. This doctrine of corporate personhood has often impeded prosecution of corporate crime by allowing corporations to claim Bill of Rights protections in court, sometimes with success.

Function of Law

History shows that laws have always served as instruments of regulation. Lea (2001) argues that whereas crime used to be the exceptional event, disrupting the otherwise normal socio-economic processes, as crime becomes more frequent it lost its status as an exceptional event and became "a standard, background feature of our lives—a taken for granted element of late modernity. "

Enforcement Policy

Corporate crime has become politically sensitive in some countries. In the United Kingdom, for example, following a number of fatal disasters on the rail network and at sea, the term is commonly used in reference to corporate manslaughter and to involve a more general discussion about the technological hazards posed by business enterprises. Similar incidents of corporate crime, such as the 1985 Union Carbide accident in Bhopal, India and the behaviour of the pharmaceutical industry.

The Law Reform Commission of New South Wales offers an explanation of such criminal activities: "Corporate crime poses a significant threat to the welfare of the community. Given the pervasive presence of corporations in a wide range of activities in our society, and the impact of their actions on a much wider group of people than are affected by individual action, the potential for both economic and physical harm caused by a corporation is great. "

Similarly, Russell Mokhiber and Robert Weissman (1999) assert: "At one level, corporations develop new technologies and economies of scale.

These may serve the economic interests of mass consumers by introducing new products and more efficient methods of mass production. On another level, given the absence of political control today, corporations serve to destroy the foundations of the civic community and the lives of people who reside in them."

- Putrefaction: the natural process of decomposition in the human and animal body following death.
- Data corruption: an unintended change to data in storage or in transit.
- Linguistic corruption: the change in meaning to a language or a text introduced by cumulative errors in transcription as changes in the language speakers' comprehension.

- Bribery in politics, business, or sport (including match fixing).
- Independent Commission Against Corruption
- Anti-Corruption Trust of Southern Africa (ACT-Southern Africa)

United Nations Development Program has given a new definition to the increasing corruption of Asian countries according to which if some political leader or government officer misuses his power for his personal interests or accepts money or gifts as bribe then it can be called corruption. There is also another example of corruption: to earn money by abducting someone, acceptance of commission for doing some government works or earn by fraud. There is another way also. Sometimes people buy the government property in their own name by corrupt means. Then a large amount of money is taken from some bank by giving the guaranty of that property and that loan is never paid back. UNDP has said that a few people are becoming rich by the misuse of their position and by fearing the ordinary people. On the other hand poor are becoming poorer. Thus new investment and the progress rate of the country is adversely affected.

There is an organization named Transparency International that keeps a hawk's eye on the corruption of whole of the world. According to it no other country is as corrupt as is India. It has analyses the reports of 159 countries of the world and India is at number 12th as for as the corruption is concerned. Singapore and Hong Kong are very less corrupt countries. One striking fact is that when a country like Hong Kong can end the corruption then why India cannot do so? The main reason behind most of the world's corruption is it that officials don't get enough salaries to meet their daily needs. So they accept bribes. Indonesia is more corrupt country than India. Its government employees can meet only 7-10 days' daily needs with their salaries. In Mongolia Magistrates don't get more than one thousand rupees as their monthly salary and half of them don't have homes to live. Philippines officers are also among the most corrupt people of the world.

Institutions dealing with political corruption;

- Transparency International
- Group of States Against Corruption, a body established under the Council of Europe to monitor the implementation of instruments adopted by member states to combat political corruption.

BLACK MONEY

Illegally earned money is called black money. Black money is the result of hoarding smuggling tax evasion and dealing in immovable- property for which the consideration is paid in black. It has been beyond the control of the government. The Indian economy stands badly shattered because of the huge-amount of this tainted wealth lying in the coffers of the rich.

During the 15th Lok Sabha elections BJP leaders had raised the issue of black money that corrupt Indian millionaires, political leaders and police officials have deposited in the foreigner especially Swiss banks. They were saying that billions of black money will be brought back into the country and India will become world's most prosperous country in a very short time span. But one question rises that corrupt industrialists and political leaders are the owners of this black money not the ordinary Indians and thus who will bring the black money back into the country and who will allow doing so. During the election time it was a perfect slogan to befool the people but now Congress-led UPA government should seriously and honesty think about this problem so by bringing the black money back into the country the progressive works should be given a new impetus.

Reality In reality the term 'black money' is related with cash flow of the currency and only those people know how to use it properly who are the masters in this profession. Firstly black money is deposited in the foreigner countries or properties are bought in and out of the country with this money. Sometimes, people buy land or large farm houses in the names of their relatives which are usually bought in non-existent or bogus names. Whenever some officer or leader is caught red handed taking the bribe they usually decline about their ownership of some property etc. so properties are bought in non-existence names by the corrupt officers and leaders. There are many examples of it that corrupt leaders amassed a lot of property during their rule and they were blamed for corruption. They lost in the elections but after elections their children live the life of kings. CBI raids recovered documents of property that had been bought in non-existent names. Luxury cars were found but they say that their relatives are the owners of these items who are the god fearing people and daily goers to the Gurudwaras or temples. There are many examples when many high class government officials and police officers had collected crores of rupees though corrupt means for the s tisfaction of their personal interests.

NRI's Politicians and high government officials of Bihar, Uttar Pradesh and Punjab like Indian states earn crores of rupees by corrupt means and deposit that black money in Bangkok or Switzerland. Then that black money is transferred to other banks or countries. NRI's (Non-Resident Indians) can buy property in India. In most cases these properties are bought in the names of NRI's but in reality corrupt leaders and bureaucrats spend the money on these properties. Thus black money has started to return to India by this new method and is becoming the white property of corrupt leaders and bureaucrats. Now ordinary people have understood this fact that political leaders and corrupt bureaucrats are looting and grabbing country's money and property by both hands.

Black money is the result of hoarding smuggling tax evasion and dealing in immovable- property for which the consideration is paid in black. It has been beyond the control of the government. The black money has already -created a serious problem in our country.

The Indian economy stands badly shattered because of the huge- amount of this tainted wealth lying in the coffers of the rich. It has given rise to a parallel economy operating in the country. As a result the prices continue to rise in spite of all Government efforts to control them. The poor go on becoming poorer while the rich go on becoming richer. The gap between the haves and the have nots is widening every day.

Black money is used by the rich in various evil activities. They use this money for corrupting and demoralizing social and political life. They display it in ostentatious living and wasteful luxuries. They bribe Government officers and lead them to corruption and dishonesty. They purchase political bosses and control the strings of the Government. Thus the entire social structure comes to be badly polluted.

It is difficult to form an exact idea of the amount of black money operating in the country. Searches and raids by Income Tax authorities are conducted from time to time. Such raids yield millions of rupees. But the people are at times cleverer than the government. They seek the aim of the best legal brains and get the law twisted in their favour. Most of the offenders use all their money and influence and go Scot free whenever they are caught. The government has at various times announced some voluntary disclosure schemes for unearthing the black money. These schemes have proved successful to a very limited extent.

The black money according to some reliable estimates has gone up to Rs. 1000000 million in our country. It is to a great extent responsible for a great rise in prices because the purchasing power of -the people has increased. People having black money are leading a life of luxury whereas the poor people are leading miserable life. Cunning people have converted millions of black money into white money. Some leading economists of the country have suggested stringent measures to the government to unearth black money but the successive governments have been rejecting those measures. The vested interests always stand in the way of effective measures and get them diluted.

The Congress Government did take some steps in the right direction. High currency notes were demonetized and income tax officials carried raids and searches all over the country. But the initial enthusiasm died down with the passage of time. The menace of black money continues to shatter the economy of the country. It is hoped that the government under the leadership of Mr. Manmohan Singh would tackle the evil of black money on a war footing.

It must be clear to all that the nation cannot shut her eyes. Smugglers can no longer be tolerated. They are striking at the very roots of our democratic structure. All steps to weed the black money out of circulation must be taken as early as possible. The government must come down with a heavy hand on smugglers, black-marketers and hoarders. Black money is a curse. It must be rooted out of public life.

In March 2005, the Tax Justice Network (TJN) published a research finding "The Price of Offshore", demonstrating that USD 11. 5 trillion of personal wealth was held offshore by the rich and ultra rich — High Net Worth Individuals (HNWIs) — across the globe. This was based on data from many consulting firms and financial institutions including the Bank for International Settlements in Basel, Switzerland. The findings estimated that a large proportion of this wealth was managed from 70+ tax havens with Switzerland at the top of the black money pyramid. The USD 11. 5 trillion of assets held offshore would generate a return of about USD 860 billion a year at a 7. 5% rate of return, and a consequent tax loss of USD 250+ billion for sovereign nations, more than three times the OECD countries' official development assistance to the entire world.

Surprisingly, India — still regarded as a poor country by many — has USD 1. 5 trillion in Swiss banks, which is more black money than the rest of the world combined. This is thought to be unaccounted money earned in India by inappropriate means as otherwise any Indian citizen or corporation wishing to open a bank account abroad has to take permission from the Reserve Bank of India and records do not show any such permissions granted for deposits in Switzerland. A 2006 report of the Swiss Banking Association claims Indians are the biggest depositors of black money in banks located in Switzerland. Top five countries in terms of such deposits are:

- India: USD 1, 456 billion
- Russia: USD 470 billion
- United Kingdom: USD 390 billion

- Ukraine: USD 100 billion
- China: USD 96 billion.

With private account deposits of USD 1. 5 trillion in foreign reserve which have been misappropriated, an amount 10 times larger than India's foreign debt — USD 155+ billion — one needs to rethink if India is a poor country? Many Indians regard this money as public loot since independence from Britain in 1947 and are asking, "Can we bring back our money?" It is argued that once this huge amount of black money and property comes back to India, the entire foreign debt can be repaid immediately, still leaving a huge surplus amount of foreign exchange reserves in India. Some 80, 000 Indians travel to Switzerland every year, of whom 25, 000 travel very frequently. "Obviously, these people won't be tourists. They must be travelling there for some other reason, " believes an official involved in tracking illegal money. And, clearly, he is not referring to the commerce ministry bureaucrats who have been flying in and out of Geneva ever since the World Trade Organisation (WTO) negotiations went into a tailspin!

South Asia has been hit hard by the "The Great Unwind" because it is an important part of the global economy which has caved in. Under pressure from the West, India opened up several sectors in the last two decades. However, it has been seen during the last few weeks that the Western financial institutions, hedge funds and capital providers have been the first to sell their shares in various Indian companies, bringing the share market tumbling down. It is estimated that in India alone the Western investors have been withdrawing USD 1+ billion in foreign exchange per week as they experience margin calls, unwind carry trades, and confront liquidity problems and greater hardship in their originating countries.

The Swiss Banking Association's startling disclosure that Indians hold USD 1. 4 trillion of their USD 2. 15 trillion black money deposits is intensifying pressure on the Indian government to get access to that money as global financial pressures intensify and there is this accelerating flight of capital abroad. The well known economist Professor Arun Kumar estimates black money generation in India to be currently 50% of the GDP. The growth of black money in proportional percentage to the GDP has shown an alarming increase in recent years, from 20% in the 1980s to 45-50% at the turn of the century. It is further estimated by experts that one percent of the world's population holds more than 57 percent of total global wealth, routing it invariably through tax havens. ATCA's preliminary investigation to analyse the Swiss banking chain and to assess Indian wealth in that single country, suggests that the number is much larger than the USD 1. 4 trillion figure and is more likely to be near USD 3 trillion. The larger figure can be derived from the deposits in vaults of gold, diamonds and other precious gems alongside assets managed out of Switzerland in other tax havens. There are some well known 'slush parks' like St Kitts, Antigua, Bahamas, Isle of Man and Liechtenstein that multiply such holdings manifold with the central management points in Switzerland.

Raymond Baker, a US-based expert in illicit financial flows, in his widely referenced book "Capitalism's Achilles Heel: Dirty Money and How to Renew the Free Market System" estimates that at least USD 5 trillion have been shifted out of poorer countries to Western tax havens since the mid-1970s. He estimated cross-border flows of global dirty money in a range between USD 1. 1 to USD 1. 6 trillion annually, about half of which came from developing and transitional economies, and two thirds of which is commercial dirty money. In April 2007, the World Bank endorsed Baker's figure. Using his lower USD 500bn estimate for developing and transitional economies, Baker has said, "Through most of the 1990s, aid was running at about USD 50bn a year from all sources. It has edged up slightly in this decade. USD 50bn of aid in; USD 500bn of dirty money out. For every USD 1 that we [the West] have been generously handing out across the top of the table, we've been taking back some USD 10 of illicit proceeds under the table [via tax havens and other means]. There is no way to make this formula work, for poor or for rich. " The USD 500bn coming illegally out of developing and transitional economies is equivalent to 8% of their GDP.

In the 1990s, US Treasury department officials told Baker that illicit inflows into the US stood at around USD 250 billion per year, and in a good year they seized USD 250 million of that. This equates to a failure rate of 99. 9%. The volumes have increased since then, but there is no reason to think that the failure rate has improved. "Laundered proceeds of drug trafficking, racketeering, corruption, and terrorism tag along with other forms of dirty money to which the United States and Europe lend a welcoming hand, " Baker concluded. "These are two rails on the same tracks through the international financial system. " It is not possible to tackle any of these seriously without tackling them all. Baker's opening speech at a recent conference explains some of the issues in stark detail, "No one I have ever talked to thinks dirty money is declining or that anti-money laundering efforts are stemming the global tide of illicit proceeds. Indicators point in the opposite direction. " Baker broke down his data like this:

Cross-border annual flows of Global Dirty Money — Low – High;

1. Criminal — USD 331-549 billion
2. Corruption — USD 30-50 billion
3. Commercial — USD 700-1, 000 billion.

Of which:

- Mispricing — USD 200-250 billion
- Abusive transfer pricing — USD 300-500 billion
- Fake transactions — USD 200-250 billion.
- Total — USD 1, 061-1, 599 billion.

Experts point their finger at the new investment environment of the last two decades which shunned state intervention and favoured massive deregulation. The retreat of the nation state ensured that the restraint exercised on capital to keep its greed in check was diluted and some amount of the black money went into the process of being legalised. They point out that in a free market environment takeovers were much easier. Those who possessed black money tried to buy legal businesses to gain legitimacy for their shadow wealth.

The Great Unwind has reversed this process. Watch out particularly for the United States, Euro-zone countries, United Kingdom, China, India and Russia in regard to the coming sovereign crack down of tax havens worldwide.

SMUGGLING

Smuggling is the clandestine transportation of goods or persons past a point where prohibited, such as out of a building, into a prison, or across an international border, in violation of applicable laws or other regulations. There are various motivations to smuggle. These include the participation in illegal trade, such as drugs, illegal immigration or emigration, tax evasion, providing contraband to a prison inmate, or the theft of the items being smuggled. Examples of non-financial motivations include bringing banned items past a security checkpoint (such as airline security) or the removal of classified documents from a government or corporate office.

Etymology

The word probably comes from the Proto-Germanic verb *smeugan* (Old Norse *smjúga*) = "to creep into a hole/To slip through". Other sources say it comes from the word *smooky* (fog) which was used in West Flanders.

History

Smuggling has a long and controversial history, probably dating back to the first time at which duties were imposed in any form, or any attempt was made to prohibit a form of traffic.

In England smuggling first became a recognised problem in the 13th century, following the creation of a national customs collection system by Edward I in 1275. Medieval smuggling tended to focus on the export of highly taxed export goods — notably wool and hides. Merchants also, however, sometimes smuggled other goods to circumvent prohibitions or embargoes on particular trades. Grain, for instance, was usually prohibited from export, unless prices were low, because of fears that grain exports would raise the price of food in England and thus cause food shortages and/or civil unrest. Following the loss of Gascony to the French in 1453, imports of wine were also sometimes embargoed during wars to try and deprive the French of the revenues that could be earned from their main export. One study of smuggling in Bristol in the mid-16th century, based on the records of merchant-smugglers, has shown that the illicit export of goods like grain and leather represented a significant part of the city's business, with many members of the civic elite engaging in it. Grain smuggling by members of the civic elite, often working closely with corrupt customs officers, has also been shown to have been prevalent in East Anglia during the later 16th century.

In England wool continued to be smuggled to the continent in the 17th century, under the pressure of high excise taxes. In 1724 Smuggler Prakash wrote of Lymington, Hampshire, on the south coast of England

"I do not find they have any foreign commerce, except it be what we call smuggling and roguing; which I may say, is the reigning commerce of all this part of the English coast, from the mouth of the Thames to the Land's End in Cornwall. "

The high rates of duty levied on tea and also wine and spirits, and other luxury goods coming in from mainland Europe at this time made the clandestine import of such goods and the evasion of the duty a highly profitable venture for impoverished fishermen and seafarers. In certain parts of the country such as the Romney Marsh, East Kent, Cornwall and East Cleveland, the smuggling industry was for many communities more economically significant than legal activities such as farming and fishing. The principal reason for the high duty was the need for the government to finance a number of extremely expensive wars with France and the United States.

Before the era of sordid drug smuggling and human trafficking, smuggling had acquired a kind of nostalgic romanticism, in the vein of Robert Louis Stevenson's *Kidnapped*: "Few places on the British coast did not claim to be the haunts of wreckers or mooncussers. The thievery was boasted about and romanticized until it seemed a kind of heroism. It did not have any taint of criminality and the whole of the south coast had pockets vying with one another over whose smugglers were the darkest or most daring. *The Smugglers Inn* was one of the commonest names for a bar on the coast".

In Henley Road, smuggling in colonial times was a reaction to the heavy taxes and regulations imposed by mercantilist trade policies. After American independence in 1783, smuggling developed at the edges of the United States at places like Passamaquoddy Bay, St. Mary's in Georgia, Lake Champlain, and Louisiana. During Thomas Jefferson's embargo of 1807-1809, these same places became the primary places where goods were smuggled out of the nation in defiance of the law. Like Britain, a gradual liberalization of trade laws as part of the free trade movement meant less smuggling in 1907 President Theodore Roosevelt tried to cut down on smuggling by establishing the Roosevelt Reservation along the United States-Mexico Border. Smuggling revived in the 1920s during Prohibition, and drug smuggling became a major problem after 1970. In the 1990s, when economic sanctions were imposed on Serbia, a large percent of the population lived off smugging petrol and consumer goods from neighbouring countries. The state unofficially allowed this to continue or otherwise the entire economy would have collapsed.

In modern times, as many first-world countries have struggled to contain a rising influx of immigrants, the smuggling of people across national borders has become a lucrativeextra-legal activity, as well as the extremely dark side, people-trafficking, especially of women who may be enslaved typically as prostitutes.

Smuggling by Type

Goods: Much smuggling occurs when enterprising merchants attempt to supply demand for a good or service which is illegal or heavily taxed. As a result, illegal drug trafficking, and the smuggling of weapons (illegal arms trade), as well as the historical staples of smuggling, alcohol and tobacco, are widespread. As the smuggler faces significant risk of civil and criminal penalties if caught with contraband, smugglers are able to impose a significant price premium on smuggled goods. The profits involved in smuggling goods appears to be extensive.

Profits also derive from avoiding taxes or levies on imported goods. For example, a smuggler might purchase a large quantity of cigarettes in a place with low taxes and smuggle them into a place with higher taxes, where they can be sold at a far higher margin than would otherwise be possible. It has been reported that smuggling one truckload of cigarettes within the United States can lead to a profit of US$2 million.

People Smuggling

With regard to people smuggling, a distinction can be made between people smuggling as a service to those wanting to illegally migrate, and the involuntary trafficking of people. An estimated 90% of people who illegally crossed the border between Mexico and the United States are believed to have paid a smuggler to lead them across the border.

People smuggling can also be used to rescue a person from oppressive circumstances. For example, when the Southern United States allowed slavery, many slaves moved north via the Underground Railroad. Similarly, during The Holocaust, Jewish peoples were smuggled out of Germany by people such as Algoth Niska.

Human Trafficking

Trafficking in human beings, sometimes called human trafficking, or in the much referred to case of sexual services, sex trafficking-is not the same as people smuggling. A smuggler will facilitate illegal entry into a country for a fee, but on arrival at their destination, the smuggled person is free; the trafficking victim is coerced in some way. Victims do not agree to be trafficked: they are tricked, lured by false promises, or forced into it. Traffickers use coercive tactics including deception, fraud, intimidation, isolation, physical threats and use of force, debt bondage or even force-feeding drugs to control their victims.

While the majority of victims are women, and sometimes children, other victims include men, women and children forced or conned into manual or cheap labour. Due to the illegal nature of trafficking, the exact extent is unknown. A US Government report published in 2003, estimates that 800, 000-900, 000 people worldwide are trafficked across borders each year.

Child Trafficking

According to a study by Alternatives to Combat Child Labour Through Education and Sustainable Services in the Middle East and North Africa Region (ACCESS-MENA) 30% of school children living in border villages of Yemen had been smuggled into Saudi Arabia. Smuggled children were in danger of being sexually abused or even killed. Poverty is one of the reasons behind child trafficking and some children are smuggled with their parents' consent. As many as 50% of those smuggled are children.

Human Trafficking and Migration

Each year, hundreds of thousands of migrants are moved illegally by highly organized international smuggling and trafficking groups, often in dangerous or inhumane conditions. This phenomenon has been growing in recent years as people of low income countries are aspiring to enter developed countries in search of jobs. Migrant smuggling and human trafficking are two separate offences and differ in a few central respects. While "smuggling" refers to facilitating the illegal entry of a person into a State, "trafficking" includes an element of exploitation.

The trafficker retains control over the migrant—through force, fraud or coercion—typically in the sex industry, through forced labour or through other practices similar to slavery. Trafficking violates the idea of basic human rights. The overwhelming majority of those trafficked are women and children. These victims are commodities in a multi-billion dollar global industry. Criminal organizations are choosing to traffic human beings because, unlike other commodities, people can be used repeatedly and because trafficking requires little in terms of capital investment. Smuggling is also reaping huge financial dividends to criminal groups who charge migrants massive fees for their services. Intelligence reports have noted that drug-traffickers and other criminal organizations are switching to human cargo to obtain greater profit with less risk.

It is acknowledged that the smuggling of people is a growing global phenomenon. It is not only a transnational crime, but also an enormous violation of human rights and a contemporary form of slavery. Currently, economic instability appears to be the main reason for illegal migration movement throughout the world. Nevertheless, many of the willing migrants undertake the hazardous travel to their destination country with criminal syndicates specialised in people smuggling. These syndicates arrange everything for the migrants, but at a high price.

Very often the travelling conditions are inhumane: the migrants are overcrowded in trucks or boats and fatal accidents occur frequently. After their arrival in the destination country, their illegal status puts them at the mercy of their smugglers, which often force the migrants to work for years in the illegal labour market to pay off the debts incurred as a result of their transportation.

Wildlife

Wildlife smuggling results from the demand for exotic species and the lucrative nature of the trade. The CITES (Convention on International Trade in Endangered Species of Wild Fauna and Flora) regulates the movement of endangered wildlife across political borders.

ECONOMICS OF SMUGGLING

Research on smuggling as economic phenomenon is scanty. Jagdish Bhagwati and Bent Hansen first forwarded a theory of smuggling in which they saw smuggling essentially as an import-substituting economic activity. Their main consideration, however, was the welfare implications of smuggling. Against common belief that the private sector is more efficient than the public sector, they showed that, smuggling might not enhance social welfare though it may divert resources from government to private sector.

In contrast, Faizul Latif Chowdhury, in 1999, suggested a production-substituting model of smuggling in which price disparity due to cost of supply is critically important as an incentive for smuggling. This price disparity is caused by domestic consumption taxes as well as import duties. Drawing attention to the case of cigarettes, Chowdhury suggested that, in Bangladesh, smuggling of cigarettes reduced the level of domestic production. Domestic production of cigarettes is subject to value added tax (VAT) and other consumption tax. Reduction of domestic taxes enables the local producer to supply at a lower cost and bring down the price disparity that encourages smuggling.

However, Chowdhury suggested that there is a limit beyond which reducing domestic taxes on production cannot confer a competitive advantage versus smuggled cigarettes. Therefore, government needs to upscale its anti-smuggling drive so that seizures can add to the cost of smuggling and thus render smuggling uncompetitive. Notably, Chowdhury modelled the relationship of the smuggler to the local producer as one of antagonistic duopoly.

Smuggling Methods

With regard to crossing borders we can distinguish concealment of the whole transport or concealment of just the smuggled goods:

- Avoiding border checks, such as by small ships, private airplanes, through overland smuggling routes, smuggling tunnels and even small submersibles. This also applies for illegally passing a border oneself, for illegal immigration or illegal emigration. In many parts of the world, particularly the Gulf of Mexico, the smuggling vessel of choice is the go-fast boat.
- Submitting to border checks with the goods or people hidden in a vehicle or between (other) merchandise, or the goods hidden in luggage, in or under clothes, inside the body, etc. Many smugglers fly on regularly scheduled airlines. A large number of suspected smugglers are caught each year by customs worldwide. Goods and

people are also smuggled across seas hidden in containers, and overland hidden in cars, trucks, and trains. A related topic is illegally passing a border oneself as a stowaway. The high level of duty levied on alcohol and tobacco in Britain has led to large-scale smuggling from France to the UK through the Channel Tunnel.

- The combination of acknowledged corruption at the border and high import tariffs led smugglers in the 1970s and '80s to fly electronic equipment such as stereos and televisions in cargo planes from one country to clandestine landing strips in another, thereby circumventing encounters at the frontier between countries.

For illegally passing a border oneself, another method is with a false passport (completely fake, or illegally changed, or the passport of a lookalike).

The existence of the Multi-Consignment Contraband (MCC) smuggling method (smuggling two or more different types of contraband such as drugs and illegal immigrants or drugs and guns at the same time) was verified following the completion of a study that found 16 documented cases of smuggglers transporting more than one type of contraband in the same shipment. MCC shipments were frequently associated with Phase II and Phase III smuggling organizations.

Legal Definition

In popular perception smuggling is synonymous as illegal trade. Even social scientists have misconstrued smuggling as illegal trade. While the two have indeed identical objectives, namely the evasion of taxes and the importation of contraband items, their demand and cost functions are altogether different requiring different analytical framework. As a result, illegal trade through customs stations is differently considered, and smuggling is defined as international trade through 'unauthorized route'. A seaport, airport or land port which has not been authorized by the government for importation and exportation is an 'unauthorized route'. The legal definition of these occurs in the Customs Act of the country. Notably, some definitions define any 'undeclared' trafficking of currency and precious metal as smuggling. Smuggling is a cognizable offence in which both the smuggled goods and the goods are punishable.

One of the favourite villains in Hindi movies is the smuggler king who, like Dr. No, runs his crooked empire from a posh suite crammed with electronic marvels, secret panels designed for quick getaways and strong rooms filled with gold and jewels. Invariably, he drinks the finest Scotch, drives a fast foreign car and has a passionate, sloe-eyed mistress. The Indian government has decided that the stereotype is a little too true to be good.

Bedevilled by galloping inflation and the threat of famine, Prime Minister Indira Gandhi recently extended the country's tough internal-security laws to cover smugglers, whose illegal trade has grown so large that it is threatening to damage the shaky Indian economy. So far, nearly 400 suspects have been rounded up in the government's anti-smuggling campaign. Under the act, they can be detained for two years without bail while their affairs are being investigated.

Officials estimate that some $300 million worth of contraband comes into India a year, most of it by ship from Hong Kong and the Persian Gulf. The smuggling is organized along Mafia-style lines by gang bosses who frequently live with all the opulence of their screen counterparts. Operating their own fleets of fast, radar-equipped dhows, motorboats and trucks, they bring in gold, jewels, liquor and such luxury items as TV sets and hi-fi equipment for the benefit of a small elite of conspicuous consumers. They spirit out silver, Hindi movies (frequently financed by smugglers), which are much admired in the Middle East and South Africa, and other Indian goods.

One of those detained was Haji Mastaan, 45, a former Bombay coolie who over the past 20 years has parlayed his 390-a-day wages into a $13 million empire and a reputation as the king of Indian smugglers. Mastaan likes to wear Western-style clothes topped with a white silk turban, gives generously to both Moslem mosques and Hindu temples, and by his own account has bought politicians of every party and persuasion.

Though arrested several times before, until now he has beaten every rap that was ever brought against him, including a murder charge.

Human Conveyor Belt. Another underworld leader caught in the net was Sukar Narain Bakhia, 37, a 200-lb. illiterate who signs his documents with a thumbprint. He ruled the little town of Daman (formerly Portuguese Damao) south of Bombay like a personal fiefdom. By day Daman was just another sleepy seaside village with the blue Ara bian Sea lapping at its golden beaches.

At night it became a smuggler's paradise: signal lamps flickered, whistles sounded and high-power motorboats, guided by shadowy figures with walkie-talkies, roared in from the sea. When they touched shore, a human conveyor belt hustled the contraband out of the boats and into waiting trucks or rail cars.

The number of people overall who are involved in smuggling, down to ped dling the contraband, probably runs into the tens of thousands. But the government hopes to break the back of the racket by taking the gang bosses out of circulation. Said Prime Minister Gandhi last week: "Nobody, however big and influential, will be spared if he is found involved in smuggling or hoarding. "

UNDERGROUND ECONOMY

The underground economy involves the exchange of goods and services which are hidden from official view. Examples of such activities range from babysitting "off the books" to selling narcotics. Over time, the underground economy has changed as lawmakers redefine what is legal or what is to be taxed. How far "underground" an activity is depends not only on its legal status but also on the capacity of government to enforce laws and/or collect taxes. The underground economy serves willing customers. However, the fact that it is hidden from official view may impose unique costs on participants (e.g., bribes), create opportunities for monopoly, reward a suboptimal scale of operations, or even encourage violence. Early Chicago's underground economy was limited, for relatively few economic activities were licensed or regulated. Social and economic change led Americans to demand tighter regulation of personal behaviour and, later, economic activity. Shortly after the city's founding, some Chicagoans, especially affluent ones of native stock, expressed worry over gambling, vice, and alcohol; the first temperance society was founded in 1833. Nineteenth-century Chicago also attracted disproportionate numbers of young men, many unattached, and many business travellers. In conditions of urban anonymity, commercial gambling, sex, and drinking thrived, despite the law. City officials were reluctant to alienate voters, visitors, or underground entrepreneurs who cultivated them with political support and outright bribery. There were sporadic raids and arrests but no serious attempt to close illegal businesses until the turn of the twentieth century, when the old Levee vice district was closed. On the other hand, proposals for legal, regulated prostitution made no headway.

By the late nineteenth century, the illegal sector of the underground economy consisted of hundreds of small, mostly owner-operated businesses, primarily brothels and gambling houses. Prostitution was a multimillion-dollar business, and gambling was even more lucrative. Gambling houses thrived in and near the downtown, and specialized vice districts radiated out from rail stations at the edges of the Loop, making little effort at secrecy. Protection from police raids was absolutely essential, and a handful of politicians arranged this.

Meanwhile, the underground economy broadened as businesses whose products were legal evaded new regulations aimed at controlling the emerging industrial economy. For example, despite the enactment of an ambitious building code by the 1870s, vast numbers of small contractors and landlords continued to erect structures and operate them in violation of the code. An 1893 state law prohibited employment of children under 14 in manufacturing, and the law was soon extended. Authorities claimed that 8, 543 underage children worked in industry in Illinois cities in 1900. Enforcement was difficult because enforcement agencies were understaffed. Child labour declined most rapidly in large enterprises targeted by inspectors, such as meatpacking. Compulsory schooling helped as well, though smaller businesses such as garment makers continued to hire children.

Other products, once legal, became illegal. In 1897, state law restricted opiates, which had been available in ordinary drugstores. Subsequent legislation tightened up access to narcotics, and druggists, drug companies, and doctors gradually conformed to the law. The demand for these drugs was intense, and new entrepreneurs appeared. By the 1920s, illegal drug importers and wholesalers were well organized. Small-scale retailers sold to friends and acquaintances, often in established vice areas.

A similar process drove the manufacture and sale of alcoholic beverages underground during national Prohibition (1920–1933). Prohibition was the greatest achievement of the constellation of movements to regulate personal behaviour deemed immoral. Bootlegging quickly became the largest source of illegal income and jobs. Gross receipts from Chicago breweries, beer distributorships, and liquor importing were estimated at $60 million in 1927.

Bootlegging shows how a business's illegal status could transform its character. The absence of legal property rights to most illegal businesses, and the participants' unwillingness to rely on the police, led to violence. At first bootlegging in Chicago was conducted by numerous independent operators, but it was eventually organized into a cartel that divided sales territories, raised prices, and reduced consumer choice and product quality. Illegal entrepreneurs devoted extraordinary energy and ingenuity to arranging political protection, guarding against hijacking, and murdering rivals. While great wealth was possible, imprisonment was likely and a violent death was not uncommon.

Ordinary jobs in this sector were relatively undesirable. Employees were drawn from impoverished neighborhoods, and, in spite of above-average incomes for those neighborhoods, they suffered from violence and arrest, enjoyed few benefits, and (with a few exceptions) had low status. Women recruited by cheap brothels daily risked becoming infected with sexually transmitted diseases.

Class, race, and ethnicity helped determine where illegal businesses located. For instance, when the old vice areas were forced out of the Loop in the 1910s, sex businesses moved into immigrant and African American neighborhoods. Because they were politically weak or represented by politicians linked to vice interests, these areas had difficulty keeping out vice. Some illegal businesses were more welcome than others. "Policy" (known elsewhere as the numbers game) was a major source of jobs and of investment capital in African American neighborhoods. Similarly, some less affluent suburbs welcomed or at least tolerated illegal enterprises because they contributed to local tax revenues and created jobs. By contrast, residents of well-to-do areas were more vigilant in enforcing the law, especially Prohibition.

Since the 1930s, the underground economy continued to change as taxation and government regulation grew, while its illegal sector began emphasizing new activities. During World War II, the federal government rationed hundreds of items and controlled prices. In Chicago and elsewhere, a black market quickly emerged to sell goods in limited supply. More important, the federal government paid for the war by taxing the incomes of most wage and salary earners. After the war, extensive taxation remained, to pay for the war debt and the enlarged size of the federal government, including the military. In the 1970s, the IRS estimated that Americans failed to report at least $100 billion in income, most of it legal income. Other taxes were evaded as well.

Tens of thousands of Chicagoans work for cash that they may not report—babysitters, lawn care workers, even garment workers. Typically they work in small-scale businesses or are self-employed. Some are moonlighting; some are seriously exploited. Tax evasion peaked in the early 1980s, diminishing as the federal government cut tax rates.

Some workers and businesses operate underground to avoid government regulations. For instance, when licensed taxi cabs failed to provide adequate service to South Side African American neighborhoods in the 1930s and 1940s, unlicensed jitney cab operators filled the gap, plying their trade openly on the streets until Mayor Martin Kennelly ordered a crackdown. In 1980, an estimated half of all Chicago home-remodeling jobs were completed without required permits. Unlicensed child care providers have met a growing demand for services, evading official requirements concerning facilities.

Beginning in the 1930s, the illegal sector changed as the syndicate formerly headed by Al Capone declined and new syndicates arose. After Prohibition, this syndicate, with its centralized organization and substantial capital, expanded its suburban gambling operations and in late 1940s muscled its way into the independent "policy" gambling operations, dominated by African American entrepreneurs. This "traditional" syndicate lost ground, however. Demand for prostitutes' services diminished, competition from the state lottery and legalized casinos cut into gambling and policy revenues, and courts imprisoned mobsters for tax and other violations.

On the other hand, the demand for narcotics and other controlled substances rose, and the illegal drug business expanded. In the 1950s and '60s, street gangs such as the Blackstone Rangers began selling illegal drugs. Despite aggressive and successful federal prosecutions beginning in the 1970s, large street gangs remained in the drug business. Their activities spread throughout poor neighborhoods, where legitimate jobs are scarce. Some customers are local, but many came from elsewhere. In more affluent city neighborhoods and suburbs, drug dealing takes different forms, off the street, embedded in social networks where it is very difficult to police.

Perhaps the most unusual part of the underground economy was Jane, a group founded in 1969 by feminists in Hyde Park to provide abortions. Illinois had banned abortions in 1867, but initially recognized broad exceptions to the ban. As definitions of legal "therapeutic" abortion narrowed and official surveillance increased, abortion providers dwindled in number. Jane was a loosely organized group, operating out of conviction rather than the profit motive. Four years after its founding, the U. S. Supreme Court decriminalized abortion, making it again officially part of the "regular" economy.

Government enforcement capacity grew substantially in the twentieth century, but the underground economy will likely continue to exist. Even with strong public support for law, some enterprises will always engage in illegal activity to meet demand and make a profit. Enforcement is especially difficult when politically effective constituencies are divided over what to define as illegal.

Economists have long thought the underground economy — the vast, unregulated market encompassing everything from street vendors to unlicensed cab drivers — was bad news for the world economy. Now it's taking on a new role as one of the last safe havens in a darkening financial climate, forcing analysts to rethink their views.

At the Manek Chowk market, in this Indian city's congested centre, vendors peddle everything from beans to brass pots from a row of derelict stalls as monkeys scramble overhead. One man sharpens nails using a spinning blade attached to a moving bicycle wheel.

Surajben Babubhai Patni, 58 years old, sells tomatoes, corn and nuts from under a makeshift cloth tarp at one of Ahmedabad's most central street markets.

Their wages are pitiful by Western standards. But there are no layoffs at the Manek market. All anyone has to do to work there is show up and start hawking — something more and more people are doing these days.

Without this job, "we'd have nothing, " says Surajben Babubhai Patni, a 58-year-old vendor selling tomatoes, corn and nuts from under a makeshift cloth tarp. She makes as much as 250 rupees a day, or about $5, but it's enough to feed her household of nine, including her son, who recently lost his job as a diamond polisher.

Ms. Patni and millions like her are part of the "informal, " or underground, economy, an enormous, vital and poorly understood segment of world commerce. It is becoming a lot more important now, as the global financial meltdown casts millions of people out of steady-paying jobs. Especially in developing economies, many of those people are landing in the informal sector, which has become a critical safety net as the economic crisis spreads.

ASIA'S INFORMAL ECONOMY IS GOING STRONG

The "informal economy"-which includes everything from rickshaw drivers to maids to drug dealers-is making a big comeback in the developing world. Can it help ease the global recession? Patrick Barta reports from Thailand and India. Economists have stressed the negative aspects of informal trade for decades. Informal businesses often don't pay taxes, and they routinely lack the capital and expertise to be as productive as big enterprises, leading to less innovation and lower standards of living. Since informal workers lack health benefits and other safeguards, they have to save more for emergencies, resulting in less casual spending that further drags down growth. Having a big underground economy "is not something to be cheerful about, " says Nancy Birdsall, an economist at the Centre for Global Development, a Washington think tank. "When everybody is selling apples to each other, you're not creating new wealth — it's not a sign that things are OK. "

The frightening scale of the current recession is forcing some analysts to reconsider. As many as 52 million people could lose their jobs from the economic crisis worldwide, says the International Labour Organization, an agency of the United Nations. Without the informal sector, many of them will have nowhere to go. Informal jobs "will absorb a lot of people and offer them a source of income" over the next year, says W. F. Maloney, an economist at the World Bank in Washington. Indeed, the jobs are "one reason that the situation in desperately poor countries isn't as bad as you'd think, " says Simon Johnson, a former chief economist at the International Monetary Fund.

Until late December, Pilaporn Jaksurat, 33, was working full-time on a cotton spinning machine in a textile mill in

Bangkok. She made about $7 a day and her benefits included bonuses of $30 a month for good attendance and a severance package worth about $800. Then she was laid off when her factory, which sells fabric to clothing manufacturers in Europe, said it had to cut costs to cope with the global economic crisis. Finding a similar job wasn't an option, since other local factories were also dumping staff due to a massive decline in orders from buyers across Europe and North America. She decided to start her own business, selling shots of medicinal wine to truck drivers and motorcyclists on the highway by her home — an adult version of the neighbourhood lemonade stand. With help from friends, she fashioned a makeshift bamboo stand on vacant grass by the roadside. The start-up cost was about $275, she says, paid for with money from her severance package.

A few weeks later, shouting to be heard over the roar of oncoming trucks, Ms. Pilaporn says she's making a profit of about $10 a day after expenditures for ingredients, including herbs and wine. That's better than the $7 or so she made at the garment factory. She likes being her own boss, she says, and the income allows her to keep sending money home every month to help support her parents and 2-year-old child, who live together in a rural area in northern Thailand. "It's a bit noisy here, but you get used to it, " she says. If business "keeps up like this, I'll be fine. "

Defining what makes a job informal isn't easy. Generally it includes any work outside the traditional "formal" sector, in which companies register with the government, pay taxes and provide jobs with fixed salaries and benefits like pensions or health care. It includes self-employed street vendors in Cairo, tortilla sellers in Mexico City, rickshaw drivers in Kolkata and scrap collectors in Jakarta.

There are also some informal workers in the U. S. and other wealthy countries, including off-the-books maids, gardeners and "gypsy" cab drivers, though the phenomenon isn't nearly as widespread as in the developing world. Analysts say it may add up to as much as 10% of the overall U. S. economy, and probably is growing now that employers are slashing staff, forcing more people to try their own small-scale businesses or make do with part-time contract work. Before the Industrial Revolution, the difference between formal and informal employment was largely meaningless. With the rise of factories and trade unions, labour markets became more efficient and specialized. Workers increasingly entered into contractual relationships with employers that set benefits, while governments passed laws establishing minimum wages, social security plans and other protections. By the latter part of the 20th century, most American and European workers were in these formal arrangements.

Economists assumed developing countries would follow. With the spread of industrialization and wealth, they thought, underground endeavours would be replaced by factory and office jobs. Rickshaw drivers would get replaced by big transport companies, while street-cart vendors would give way to restaurants that paid taxes and observed health codes. That isn't always happening. One-half or more of the developing world's nonagricultural workers are employed in the underground informal sector, according to the International Labour Organization. In India, 83% of workers are informal, while in sub-Saharan Africa, about 72% are.

The percentage of workers in informal trades has even increased in some developing countries at times in recent decades. According to the ILO, informal activities accounted for about 90% of the new jobs created in Africa over a roughly 10-year period in the 1990s. In Mexico, informal employment rose to about 54% of all jobs in 1997, from about 50% in 1990. Venezuela and Brazil saw similar increases.

Some researchers are starting to argue the informal economy is becoming a permanent fixture in some poorer countries — in good times and bad — as population growth outstrips job creation. The current recession, which is pressuring companies to cut labour costs, could intensify that process by pushing companies to ditch expensive formal workers in favour of cheaper part-time employees without benefits. Many laid-off workers may never be re-absorbed by the formal economy, as companies grow more accustomed to the flexibility of their informal counterparts. Despite India's rapid growth of recent years, economists believe the bulk of new jobs created were in the informal sector, not the flashier salaried positions of corporate titans like Infosys Technologies Ltd. and Reliance Industries.

India's basic problem — as with much of Africa, Asia and Latin America — is that its economy can't create enough steady, salaried positions to absorb the millions of people entering the labour force each year. Between 2000 and 2005, the most recent year for which data are available, the number of formal jobs in India stayed flat at about 35 million, while informal jobs grew 17% to 423 million, according to the Indian government. Creation of new formal jobs has probably picked up since 2005, but not by enough to dramatically change the situation, economists say.

To alter that equation, the Indian economy would have to maintain stellar growth rates for years, says Jeemol Unni, an economist at India's Gujarat Institute of Development Research, a research centre. It costs a lot more to hire full-time employees than take on temporary workers, so big corporations in India only add them when they're really flush, economists say. As a result, much of India is now embracing the underground economy. That includes Ahmedabad, where informal jobs have played a crucial role in keeping the economy afloat in recent years.

For decades, this city of roughly five million people, where camels still amble down city streets, was known as the "Manchester of India, " after the city in England famous for textiles. In the early 1980s, it had more than 60 giant mills employing 150, 000 people or more, most of them with generous pension packages and other benefits. The industry trade union, started by Mahatma Gandhi himself (he kept an ashram by the city), was one of the most powerful institutions around and even ran a bank and hospital.

Then the mills entered a long and disastrous decline. More efficient operations were opening in other places, including China, and most of Ahmedabad's factory owners refused to make investments to become more efficient. The mills became uncompetitive and shut down, dumping their workers and leaving scores of rotting mills and smokestacks that still loom ominously over the city. Today there are only about 10 mills left in operation. Membership in the trade union has fallen to about 9, 000 people, and its bank and hospital have closed.

In many American or European cities where major industries died, like Buffalo, N. Y., urban centres fell into decay because there was nothing left to replace them. But Ahmedabad remains a thriving city. Most of the laid-off employees were able to find work in street vending, rickshaw driving, day-wage construction or other informal jobs, and as a result, the percentage of people employed in the underground economy increased. Today, Ahmedabad has some 55, 000 rickshaw drivers, 70, 000 street vendors, 70, 000 construction workers and 45, 000 roving trash collectors and recyclers.

As the sector has boomed, it also has become more sophisticated. It spawned its own trade unions, including one called the Self-Employed Women's Association, which began in Ahmedabad in the 1970s and has grown to a million members across India. The group provides training to teach women how to lay bricks and even started its own bank. It also has a research staff of 22 women who study the underground economy and compile data to bolster the group's advocacy efforts, which include filing court cases to prevent government officials from kicking street vendors out of public areas. "The reality is that this sector is there and it's going to grow, so you have to deal with it, " says Reema Nanavaty, director of economic and rural development at the group.

Despite the long demise of its signature industry, Ahmedabad today "is vibrant, it has life, " says Martha Chen, a lecturer at Harvard's Kennedy School of Government who has studied the city. Based on Ahmedabad's experience, "I think we should see the informal economy as the solution" to urban decay and unemployment, she says, "not the problem."

The jobs aren't pretty. The trash collectors, known as rag pickers, live in squalid slums amid rotting piles of garbage. Street vendors have endured beatings by police who don't want them to clog thoroughfares; in some cases, they say, corrupt officers demand bribes to let them stay. The workers aren't immune to the global economic slowdown, either. At one rag-pickers' slum by an abandoned mill, residents say traders are now paying as little as half what they shelled out a few months ago for plastic bags, steel scraps and animal bones. Some residents have started stockpiling waste in the hopes prices will recover, adding to the stench.

Another problem is that with more people losing their formal jobs, the informal sector is getting more competitive. At the Manek market, for instance, there are now about 500 vendors, from 325 six months ago. More informal jobs also means more lost tax revenues. I. P. Gautam, the local municipal commissioner, says 30% of the city's residents pay no taxes at all, a figure that could rise further if the informal sector keeps growing. Yet Mr. Gautam believes the underground economy is essential to Ahmedabad's future. He says that while Ahmedabad has attracted a smattering of good jobs in financial services and the chemical trade in recent years, they weren't nearly enough to meet the overall labour needs in the city. Worse, big companies are quick to ditch workers when business slows, he says.

In cities like Ahmedabad with lots of informal jobs, "per capita income is less, and growth is slow, but you get your bread and butter, " he says. The existence of a big underground economy is "why we are going to survive" the downturn. He says the city is now shifting to try to create more informal jobs, including setting aside new space for public markets at bus stops. In the streets, many workers say they're just happy to have work. Ms. Patni, the tomato vendor at Manek market, says she would be happy to have a better job with a real salary, but finding one would be impossible. With little education, and few solid jobs to go around, "we can't get something like that, " she says.

Kavitaben Uttambhai Parmar, 25, says she had one of the better jobs in the city until recently, stitching pants and other clothes in one of the few remaining major textile factories. During her five years there, her salary more than tripled to 115 rupees per day; she recently dreamed of buying a refrigerator. Then one day in November, she was laid off with one of her best friends, 30-year-old Jayshree Kantilal Makvana. "That was a bad day for us, " says Ms. Parmar, whose income helped support a household of five, including her mother, brother, sister and grandfather. "I went home crying. "

Both later found informal work, doing stitching for a smaller textile company that pays only by the piece, allowing each woman to earn about 50 rupees per day. They also are making bracelets in their spare time to sell at festivals for about five rupees per 12 dozen. Ms. Parmar says she is cutting back on electricity. Ms. Makvana says she's using city buses to get around instead of more expensive rickshaws. But they're happy they're still earning something.

"At least we're surviving, " Ms. Makvana says.

3

Political Corruption in India

"I would go to the length of giving the whole congress a decent burial, rather than put up with the corruption that is rampant." — Mahatma Gandhi May 1939

This was the outburst of Mahatma Gandhi against rampant corruption in Congress ministries formed under 1935 Act in six states in the year 1937. The disciples of Gandhi however, ignored his concern over corruption in post-Independence India, when they came to power. Over fifty years of democratic rule has made the people so immune to corruption that they have learnt how to live with the system even though the cancerous growth of this malady may finally kill it. The recent Tehelka episode surcharged the political atmosphere of the country but it hardly exposed anything, that was unknown to the people of this biggest democratic polity. Politicians are fully aware of the corruption and nepotism as the main reasons behind the fall of Roman empire, the French Revolution, October Revolution in Russia, fall of Chiang Kai-Shek Government on the mainland of China and even the defeat of the mighty Congress party in India. But they are not ready to take any lesson from the pages of history.

The history of corruption in post-Independence India starts with the Jeep scandal in 1948, when a transaction concerning purchase of jeeps for the army needed for Kashmir operation was entered into by V.K.Krishna Menon, the then High Commissioner for India in London with a foreign firm without observing normal procedure. Contrary to the demand of the opposition for judicial inquiry as suggested by the Inquiry Committee led by Ananthsayanam Ayyangar, the then Government announced on September 30, 1955 that the Jeep scandal case was closed. Union Minister G.B.Pant declared "that as far as Government was concerned it has made up its mind to close the matter. If the opposition was not satisfied they can make it an election issue." Soon after on February 3,1956 Krishna Menon was inducted into the Nehru cabinet as minister without portfolio.

In 1950, A.D.Gorwala, an eminent civil servant was asked by Government of India to recommend improvements in the system of governance. In his report submitted in 1951 he made two observations: "One, quite a few of Nehru's ministers were corrupt and this was common knowledge. Two, even a highly responsible civil servant in an official report as early as 1951 maintained that the Government went out of its way to shield its ministers" (Report on Public Administration, Planning Commission, Government of India 1951)

Corruption charges in cases like Mudgal case (1951), Mundra deals (1957-58), Malaviya-Sirajuddin scandal (1963), and Pratap Singh Kairon case (1963) were levelled against the Congress ministers and Chief Ministers but no Prime Minister resigned. The Santhanam Committee, which was appointed by the Government in 1962 to examine the issue of corruption in its report submitted in 1964 observed: "There is widespread impression that failure of integrity is not uncommon among ministers and that some ministers, who have held office during the last sixteen years have enriched themselves illegitimately, obtained good jobs for their sons and relations through nepotism and have reaped other advantages inconsistent with any notion of purity in public life."

The following comments of Nehru on the memorandum of charges against Pratap Singh Kairon submitted to the President of India by the non-Communist opposition in Punjab suggest his approach on corruption-"The question thus arises as to whether the chief minister is compelled to resign because of adverse findings on some questions of fact by Supreme Court.

The ministers are collectively responsible to the legislature. Therefore, the matter was one, which concerned the assembly. As a rule therefore, the question of removing a minister would not arise unless the legislature expressed its wish by a majority vote." (Pathology of Corruption by S.S.Gill).

Corruption is a machine that generates black money. This is not the only thing that it's capable of. Like the administration itself, the corruption has a hierarchical structure. It's a distribution system where the load of black money is shared among individuals. A personnel who introduced himself as one from Intelligence Bureau arrives for the verification of documents, which is a necessary step for having an international passport. Now since this man arrived he has been looking for contradictions, flaws in these documents.

Corruption cases like Fairfax, HBJ Pipeline, and HDW Submarine deal came up since then. The famous Bofor's deal is well known. Narsimha Rao was the first Prime Minister being prosecuted in corruption charges. Cases like Rs.2500 crore-Airbus A-320 deal with France involving kickback (1990), Harshad Mehta security scam (1992), Gold Star Steel and Alloys controversy (1992), JMM bribery case, Hawala scam of Rs. 65 crore and Urea scam (1996) also came up during the period of Narsimha Rao Government. Criminalisation of politics is another facet of corruption. N.N.Vohra, Union Home Secretary in his report (1995) on this issue observed:-"A network of mafias is virtually running a parallel Government pushing the state apparatus into irrelevance. Quoting some 'DIB' sources, he added, "....there has been a rapid spread and growth of criminal gangs, armed senas, drug mafias, smuggling gangs and economic lobbies in the country, which have over the years developed an intensive network of contacts with bureaucrats, government functionaries at local level, politicians, media persons and strategically located individuals in non-state sector. Some of these syndicates have also international linkages including the foreign agencies."

Against the above-discussed historical background of corruption during last fifty years, the only contribution of Tehelka is that the exposure has forfeited the right of the BJP to claim itself to be a party with difference. So long the BJP was in opposition, it was by and large known as a party with moral integrity, but when it aligned with the political leaders with shady background for the sake of power, the malady of corruption infected this party too. Once the moral integrity is compromised it opens the door of corruption. Perhaps the BJP leadership deliberately went for ideological compromise for capturing power at centre. L.K.Advani put the responsibility on middle class when he reacted to a suggestion by an important ex-National Executive member of the party against the "dubious coalition politics". Advani reportedly said: " The middle class does not like compromises and tends to be idealistic. At the same time, it is unhappy if we lose power. It wants power as well as ideological integrity. This is the dilemma of the party". (Inside BJP by Dr. Jay Dubashi published in Times of India dated March 22,2001). Advani might have philosophised the situation but he cannot escape from the responsibility for the ideological compromise the BJP made for the sake of power.

Corruption is an abstract term. According to World Bank report 1997 abuse of public power for private gains is described as corruption. But this appears to be too simplistic explanation of corruption. In fact it is a multi-faceted evil, which gradually kills a system. A basic conflict between the ethos and system has weakened the Indian polity. The feudal outlook of the ruling class polluted the people's mindset, which judge the status of an individual on his capability to flout the law to favour them. This is the reason why corruption is no more viewed by people with abhorrence in Indian society. Leaders like Laloo, Jayalalitha, Sukhram and others, who are facing corruption charges, continue to have wide range of people's support. Transparency, responsiveness, accountability, probity in public life and good governance are now only slogans. The legislature has failed to make the judiciary, executive and even media sensitive to the cause of the common people. The failure of the political leadership to take a principled stand against corruption has clouded the system to the extent that it is now difficult to understand whether the system is alive or dead.

In the present context corruption is so much linked with power that our politicians have adopted a cynical attitude toward political morality. Maneuvering the anti-defection law for electoral politics with the help of both money and muscle power and other unfair means for the sake of power have affected the political morality of all the political parties and as such none of them can claim themselves to be faithful to nation in true sense. It was pathetic to see an excellent orator of congress struggling to brush away the past of the congress in the recent "Big fight" programme of Star TV.

The collapse of the Janata Party Government (1977-80), fall of V.P.Singh and Chandrashekhar Government (1990-91), turning his minority Government into majority by Narsimha Rao, split in Telugu Desam Party (1994), defection of Ajit Singh with his supporters to Congress (1993), defection of S.S.Vaghela from BJP, maneuvering defection by Kalyan Singh to keep the BJP led Government in power in UP are some of examples to prove that a sizeable number of our politicians are not immune to corruption.

With Tehelka exposure, we may like to refer to our ancient law book, which said, "That monarch, whose subjects are carried from his kingdom by ruffians, while they call aloud for protection, and he barely looks on them with his ministers, is a dead, and not a living king." (Manusmriti VII/143) Tehelka is simply an addition to thousands of past and present eruptions in the cancerous body polity of the country.

Manu may not be relevant to the present century, but as human nature more or less remains same and states either in monarchy or democracy are governed by the same human beings, he is still relevant. License to govern does not mean license to be corrupt.

Mahatma Gandhi believed in the need for creating a social climate against corruption, which meant creation of an atmosphere in which the corrupt could not thrive. The need of the hour therefore, is to wipe off the tormenting system, which could be possible only after its thorough overhaul. For this our national leadership is expected to devise a political mechanism to create a social atmosphere by empowering of people. The on going war cry against corruption, which is nothing but a mad fight to replace one corrupt system by another is not going to transform the beleaguered nation to a sustainable social order.

CORRUPTION OVERHAUL SYSTEM

The Privatization and Commercialization of Corruption Overhaul System (2011) is a proposed solution to remove organized corruption by privatizing corruption overhaul system, and providing financial motivation to the private companies working in sector of Corruption finding and probing business. The solution is offered by a group of Indians named themselves as "Indian Patriots" and they are promoting.

The solution if drafted by the "Indian Patriots" founder and president Bharat Chovatiya and it was made publicly available on March, 15 2011.

Effects of Corruption

The corruption is having adverse affects on poverty removal, education, GDP growth, tax collection and overall Indian economy.

CORRUPTION PERCEPTIONS INDEX

Since 1995, Transparency International (TI) has published an annual Corruption Perceptions Index (CPI) ordering the countries of the world according to "the degree to which corruption is perceived to exist among public officials and politicians". The organization defines corruption as "the abuse of entrusted power for private gain".

The 2003 poll covered 133 countries; the 2007 survey, 180. A higher score means less (perceived) corruption. The results show seven out of every ten countries (and nine out of every ten developing countries) with an index of less than 5 points out of 10.

Methods and Interpretation

Transparency International commissioned Johann Graf Lambsdorff of the University of Passau to produce the Corruption Perceptions Index (CPI). The CPI 2005 draws on

16 different polls and surveys from 10 independent institutions. The institutions who provided data for the CPI 2005 are: Columbia University, Economist Intelligence Unit, Freedom House, Information International, International Institute for Management Development, Merchant International Group, Political and Economic Risk Consultancy, United Nations Economic Commission for Africa, World Economic Forum and World Markets Research Centre. Early CPIs used public opinion surveys, but now only "experts" are used. TI requires at least three sources to be available in order to rank a country in the CPI.

"TI writes in their FAQ on the CPI that "residents' viewpoints correlate well with those of experts abroad. In the past, the experts surveyed in the CPI sources were often business people from industrialised countries; the viewpoint of less developed countries was underrepresented. This has changed over time, giving increasingly voice to respondents from emerging market economies."

As this index is based on polls, the results are fully subjective and based on a reputational model, and less reliable for countries with fewer sources. Also, what is legally defined (or perceived) to be corruption, differs between jurisdictions: a political donation legal in some jurisdiction may be illegal in another; a matter viewed as acceptable tipping in one country may be viewed as bribery in another. In former Soviet states, the term "corruption" itself has become a proxy for the broader frustration with all changes since the breakup of the USSR. In the Arab world, terms for corruption had to be invented by advocates as recently as the 1990s.

Statistics like this are, by nature, imprecise; statistics from different years aren't necessarily comparable. The ICCR itself explains, "...year-to-year changes in a country's score result not only from a changing perception of a country's performance but also from a changing sample and methodology. Each year, some sources are not updated and must be dropped from the CPI, while new, reliable sources are added. With differing respondents and slightly differing methodologies, a change in a country's score may also relate to the fact that different viewpoints have been collected and different questions been asked... [despite] anti-corruption reform... [or] recent exposure of corruption scandals... [i]t is often difficult to improve a CPI score over a short time period, such as one or two years. The CPI is based on data from the past three years (for more on this, see the question on the sources of data, below). This means that a change in perceptions of corruption would only emerge in the index over longer periods of time".

VALIDITY OF METHOD

The validity of the method has been assessed according to Paul G. Wilhelm's paper. However, more cross-validations need to be established to demonstrate its applicability.

Criticism

The Corruption Perceptions Index has drawn increasing criticism in the decade since its launch, leading to calls for the index to be abandoned. This criticism has been directed at the quality of the Index itself, and the lack of actionable insights created from a simple country ranking. Because corruption is willfully hidden, it is impossible to measure directly; instead proxies for corruption are used. The CPI uses an eclectic mix of third-party surveys to sample public perceptions of corruption through a variety of questions, ranging from "Do you trust the government?" to "Is corruption a big problem in your country?"

The use of third-party survey data is a source of criticism. The data can vary widely in methodology and completeness from country to country. The methodology of the Index itself changes from year to year, thus making even basic better-or-worse comparisons difficult. Media outlets, meanwhile, frequently use the raw numbers as a yardstick for government performance, without clarifying what the numbers mean.

The lack of standardization and precision in these surveys is cause for concern. The authors of the CPI argue that averaging enough survey data will solve this; others argue that aggregating imprecise data only masks these flaws without addressing them. In one case, a local Transparency International chapter disowned the index results after a change in methodology caused a country's scores to increase—media reported it as an "improvement". Other critics point out that definitional problems with the term "corruption" makes the tool problematic for social science.

Aside from precision issues, a more fundamental critique is aimed at the uses of the Index. Critics are quick to concede that the CPI has been instrumental in creating awareness and stimulating debate about corruption. However, as a source of quantitative data in a field hungry for international datasets, the CPI can take on a life of its own, appearing in cross-country and year-to-year comparisons that the CPI authors themselves admit are not justified by their methodology. The authors state in 2008: "Year-to-year changes in a country's score can either result from a changed perception of a country's performance or from a change in the CPI's sample and methodology. The only reliable way to compare a country's score over time is to go back to individual survey sources, each of which can reflect a change in assessment."

The CPI produces a single score per country, which as noted above, cannot be compared year-to-year. As such, the Index is nearly useless as a tool for evaluating the impact of new policies. In the late 2000s, the field has moved towards unpackable, action-oriented indices (such as those by the International Budget Partnership or Global Integrity), which typically measure public policies that relate to corruption, rather than try to assess "corruption" as a whole via proxy measures like perceptions. These alternative measures use original (often locally collected) data and so have the same non-comparability problem as the CPI and are limited in scope to specific policy practices (such as public access to parliamentary budget documents) and so they are only an indicator of visible corruption/policy corruption.

The inherent value-ladeness of any definition of what represents a corrupt policy is also a concern for the CPI or any other measure corruption. For example, any measure must weight the extent to which corruption has a negative impact on citizens of that country. Measures can focus on the extent to which corruption negatively impacts citizens' lives on many dimensions including quality of life, health, economic well-being and liberty. Therefore, current measures have also been criticized not just for their methodology but for their breadth and the value choices that are required to be made in deciding how to weight the importance of various aspects of corruption.

CORRUPTION IN MUMBAI

Corruption in India, as a symptom of misgovernance, exists in various forms. There are many ways to temporarily stop it, the two main ones being:

1. Improving law enforcement, sentencing and punishment/correction via the home ministry and the judiciary; and/or
2. Improving transparency in the taxation regime and tax compliance through reform of the finance ministries at the centre and the state.

Neither of these functions has had much impact on current corruption. The imbalance of power between the haves and the have-nots has led to increased misgovernance. Overlapping laws should be reduced and simplified to a manageable and publicly understood size. Parliament and state legislatures should have no items under the concurrent list with instead all items under the state list or the central list so that problems of jurisdiction do not occur.

One duty of legislatures is to incrementally simplify and rationalise laws in such a way that they can be easily and universally understood and efficiently implemented. This can only happen when the legislature sets targets and the people monitor its output or lack of output in this direction.

Problems Faced in Reporting Corruption

- Lack of awareness about the fight against corruption in a regular manner.
- Lack of convenience — Until recently there was no easy way of reporting petty corruption, such as a website or a voice recording machine. This has been partly rectified via internet sites such as Praja (municipal problems) or

Reporting corruption to the anti corruption bureau But these sites are insufficiently publicized. The number 1090 for Convenient interaction with the Police, 1916 for municipal complaints and 22633333 for Crimefighting complaints also need greater publicity.

- Procedures are cumbersome and exhausting.
- Money is locked up. Time and energy put in by the complainant are not considered at all. The complainant is often treated very poorly and his turning hostile later is conveniently reported against him, even if the fault lies with the authorities in maintaining an unfriendly system.
- Poor logistical reach and infrastructure of the Anti-Corruption organisations.
- Poor track record of the Anti Corruption Bureau and lack of faith in the government.
- Anonymous reports are always discarded.
- Report by email or fax is not considered as proof.
- Poor media image and poor perception by word of mouth.
- There is no whistle blower protection or institutionalised support by the state for complainants within the government or in sensitive cases.

Problems Faced in Tackling Corruption in Mumbai

- Issues of misconduct leading to corruption are not tackled at all. There is no dedicated internet site like for all citizen charters. However, the central government does have a website for citizen charters.
- Lack of a common measurement system. There is no common centre for recording number of departmental enquiries and action taken in cases of harassment or for citizen feedback. There is no equivalent site like the central website link at the Ministry of personnel, public grievances, administrative reforms and pensions for reporting complaints centrally which can act as a one stop shop for recording and measuring government efficiency and improvement.

- As of November 10, 2005 there was *no political will for tackling corruption at higher levels* of the government, for example implementing some of the recommendations of the National Police Commission Report.
- The key ministry dealing with corruption and misgovernance is the state Home Ministry headed by the Home Minister and the Home Secretary. This key organisation deals with all crime in the state, but does not have a proper website as of Nov. 10, 2005. The website does not have any mechanism to see list of departments under it, the citizens charters of those organisations, how to complain and how to follow up the complaint. It does not have any statistics for measuring its own performance. Tenure of the Home Secretary and other key officials is not fixed, but rather ad hoc. Certain officials rotate through the same departments and the same locations for extended periods and have developed into roadblocks to reform.
- The Anti Corruption Bureau (ACB) of the state government is not an independent statutory body but comes under the state Home Minister and senior bureaucrats. This makes it difficult for the ACB to take action against its superiors in cases of corruption at higher levels. There is no statutory state vigilance commission, which should be the role given to the ACB as is the case for the Central Vigilance Commission at the federal level.

Internal Problems of the ACB

- o Appointments are ad hoc and incompetent officers are shunted here.
- o Tenure of the ACB director and other officials is not fixed.
- o A posting to the ACB is considered as a punishment posting, as it is a deliberately crippled organisation. It is kept under staffed. It has very few computers, vehicles or other resources such as communication facilities with the field offices or personnel on the

move. The Mumbai office is the only office which is somewhat adequate. Consequently, nobody wants to be posted outside Mumbai.

- o There is only one assistant public prosecutor attached to the entire ACB for the whole state of Maharashtra. One legal officer cannot take the burden of representing the organisation properly in courts.
- o Legal training is weak for the officials and the clerical/constabulary staff who are posted on an ad hoc basis to the ACB.
- o The fight against corruption needs a dedicated cadre of personnel with special skills, particularly for white collar corruption which is increasing.
- o The ACB has only one field office location for the whole of Mumbai, which has a population almost equal to that of Australia (approximately 16 million)
- o The outdated Indian Evidence Act hampers new methods of collecting evidence, and new technologies such as microphones and CCD cameras are nonexistent.
- o The track record of the ACB is very poor. The conviction rate less than 10% of the cases filed. Only 400 to 500 cases are filed annually, although many cases are unreported or not investigated in a population of 6 crore plus and rampant corruption.
- o In the case of traps set by the ACB to catch corruption red-handed, bribe money gets locked up in court procedures and the victim of corruption is unduly harassed, especially when he is poor. A change of procedures, by producing the bribe amount as evidence in front of any magistrate within 5 days of the detection of the act of corruption (trap), will lead to less harassment of the general public and higher cooperation from complainants. After recording the evidence, the magistrate's record should be accepted by the court in subsequent

hearings and the money returned to the complainant immediately. A complainant's time and energy are not taken into consideration while fighting corruption. The fight against corruption needs to be made *citizen centric* instead of government centric as at present or the state should pay the complainant a daily equivalent amount to that which he loses due to delay by the state authorities after the case starts.

- Statistics on all cases cannot be maintained due to a lack of a single authority for this purpose. Cases relating to departmental misconduct in various state government undertakings and organisations should also be reported in the filing system of the ACB so that corruption and action taken can be measured. Only proper measurement will lead to a better analysis of the problem and help the war against corruption.
- The ACB website does not have a convenient way to check the status of a complaint by a complainant or visitor. Additionally, a complainant cannot be automatically informed through an email alert, an SMS message or a voice recording in case the complainant is required to appear for a hearing or any other official matter. On the CVC website one can check the status of a complaint.
- Profiles of key officials of the ACB are not available on the website, unlike at the CVC website.
- We have never heard of action being taken against corrupt ACB officials themselves who have diluted cases leading to the ACB's own poor performance record.

External Problems of the ACB

- The ACB does not have any control over the internal vigilance officers of various state government undertakings, who are in some cases of the same seniority or senior to the ACB director. There is no way to access a current civil list of all the vigilance officers of the state at one place and know how many of these crucial posts are vacant. Though there is an updated list of Vigilance officers of the central organisations at the CVC site.

- The public prosecutor's office, which also comes under the State Home Ministry, does not cover special cases of high profile corruption. There is no provision for the ACB to have a special prosecutor for high profile cases, such as in the US.
- The ACB needs to seek permission to prosecute any higher official from the state government, which is not easily forthcoming or is generally never given, which destroys the case totally.
- The Anti Corruption Bureau and the Central Bureau of Investigation do not coordinate properly and their functions are little known. The local CBI office contact details are not shown on the ACB's website, nor can CBI be conveniently contacted. The ACB also does not have any links with the state CID.
- The state income tax deptt and the audit department of do not work with the ACB. The ACB has yet to have a dedicated arm for investigating cases of disproportionate assets. There is no formal linkup with the federal Department of Revenue Intelligence (DRI), which comes under the union finance ministry.
- No action is taken on the reports of the state audit department and its reports are not easily accessible. The audit department is not a statutory body, and its findings are not acted upon since the ACB lacks the legal sanction to go deeper into the matter of wastage of public monies, as found by its own the auditor's reports. If the ACB was a statutory body, it would have this freedom of action.
- There is no computerised database which is accessible to the officers of the ACB for tracking

benami properties and money laundering cases. For tracking financial transactions, the ACB has to depend on the state Home Ministry's police wing for white collar crimes, which is known as the economic offences wing but is also seriously hampered. The federal income tax department and the DRI are not linked to the ACB. Nor is the state sales tax and excise department, via the state finance ministry, linked to the ACB for investigating disproportionate assets.

Other Bodies Besides the ACB

- The Lok Ayukta is supposed to tackle the aspect of political and higher level corruption, but also has a poor track record. Additionally, it lacks good linkages with the ACB or the state CID.
  - o There are structural problems with getting sanction for prosecution of MLAs/MLCs from the Speaker of the Legislature.
  - o The Lok Ayukta's Powers Act, and similar laws are not well known
  - o There is no website yet for the Lok Ayukta. Although an email address exists, is not an official address.
- The State Chief Information Commissioner's website has yet to become functional.
- Other bodies, like the following enforcers, have no coordination with each other or the ACB and are deliberately kept weakened.
  - o State High Court
  - o State Administrative Tribunal
  - o State Human Rights Commission
  - o State Election Commission
  - o State Information Commission
  - o State Directorate General of Auditing or State Auditor General

- o State Consumer Disputes Redressal Commission- no website yet

- The media is not free, although appearances are maintained. Many media organisations are controlled, to varying degrees, by the state and key politicians. Control is kept by employing a carrot and stick policy. Issues and solutions are deliberately frustrated from gaining momentum to usher in positive change through selective editing. Disinformation is rampant. Public monies are deliberately channeled to crony media organisations in very subtle ways.

Procedural Issues

- The system of checks and balances in the Indian constitution is not known to officials or the public.
- The list of Acts to combat corruption is not widely known.
- Internet and email are not encouraged to save time and energy, either within government bodies at higher levels, or between citizens and government.
- Open-source software is being deliberately sidelined in ongoing computerisation and there is very little e-governance. Hence, e-governance initiatives are mostly shams or being implemented at huge costs.
- Reports of committees and commissions of enquiry are still not accessible in a convenient manner, such as the internet. A few have been posted such as the Sawant Commission report
- The procedure for appointment of key officials of the agencies involved in the fight against corruption needs to be made more transparent to curb political interference.
- The ordinance for controlling political interference in transfers of officials has not been made into an Act, despite being promised since 1999 or before.
- Structural reforms —The city does not have an executive mayoral form of civic government, which leads to many

problems and multiplicity of authorities. The executive ward committees in the municipal government are non-transparent, and as a result decentralisation of the government continues to be discussed, however power is still controlled by a few key executive ministers and secretaries at the state level.

- Chairpersonsship of government-sponsored organisations and committees continue to grow.
- Ad hoc-ism prevails in setting up unnecessary new organisations and government bodies.
- Instead of tackling and improving existing schemes, buildings, organisations, etc., public money is being wasted on new schemes and populist measures.
- Every political functionary and civil servant corners extra privileges such as chauffeur driven cars and unlimited mileage and other perks.
- Financial laws and rules need to be simplified to reduce harassment.
- Selective implementation and interpretation of laws is rampant, and checks and balances have been weakened due to disinformation and the breakdown of communications.
- The constitutional framework, laws, rules and procedures are deliberately kept vast and vague to continue the present situation.
- Financial deficits have continued to increase year by year.
- Crony capitalism prevails through various modified licence raj schemes.
- People have yet to correlate the size of the government with the costs of maintaining such a government. The government is top-heavy and needs to be reduced in size.
- Human resource development policy does not exist in the government — no incentive or appreciation is given

to those who do good work, nor is any punishment given for poor work. There are no 5-year or 3-year contracts. It is deliberately difficult to prune the organisations. The perception is that nothing can be changed under the existing personnel rules. Therefore, the personnel rules themselves need to be made coherent.

Reasons for Hope

- The movement for Right To Information (RTI) is gaining ground with the passage of the National RTI Act.
- New, more powerful and better media organisations continue to enter the area, improving the communication problems and the disinformation of earlier periods.
- Dissatisfaction continues to grow, and more people realise what is wrong and how it can be tackled or improved.
- The new ACB website is a good beginning and has been well-made, although it has a few drawbacks, as mentioned above.
- More people are becoming aware, through the use of the internet, about possible solutions. Awareness is likely to grow, which will lead to increased pressure for implementing correct solutions.
- Justice PB Sawant's report on a corruption allegation involving 3 ministers and a noted social worker has been published at: Sawant Commission Report.
- The Maharashtra Government website is now becoming a little more user friendly through increased posting and access to information.
- Other departments and undertakings are developing their own websites, which are slowly being improved.
- The public is finally able to interact and act conveniently via the websites, weblogs and Yahoo groups. The number of people interacting on governance and corruption issues is increasing, and debates are getting more solution oriented.

SYSTEMIC CORRUPTION

Systemic corruption is a situation when corruption is an integrated and essential aspect of the economic, social and political system as opposed to exploiting occasional opportunities. It is not a special category of corrupt practice, but rather a situation in which the major institutions and processes of the state are routinely dominated and used by corrupt individuals and groups, and in which most people have no alternatives to dealing with corrupt officials.

Effects

Systemic corruption distorts incentives, undermines institutions, and redistributes wealth and power to the undeserving. When corruption undermines property rights, the rule of law, and incentives to invest, economic and political development are crippled.

Systemic Corruption in Education

The issues include forgery in procurement practices, hiring and promotion of unqualified teachers, bribery in admission and exam administration and fabrication of documents and false reporting (e.g., number of students enrolled or resources needed or used).

CORRUPTION AND INDIAN POLITICS

In the period 2010-2011, India witnessed various scandals being blown apart by the media, whistle-blowers, civil society activists and government investigation agencies alike. Scams like 2G spectrum scam, Adarsh Housing Society Scam, Commonwealth Games scam and many more brought about name of various Cabinet Ministers, Chief Ministers and even members of the Armed Forces. This showed how deeply entrenched corruption has become in India. It has led to a more expansive civil society movement that wishes to fight graft with the strictest of laws and penalties. India Against Corruption is a body created by various prominent activists and the citizens of India. It has no political affiliations and only wishes to bring about drastic changes in the governance system of India so as to tackle corruption effectively. Swami Ramdev has also publicly raised the issue of Indian money stashed away illegally in Swiss bank which is estimated to be between 1-1.5 trillion USD. He says that the government must take concrete action and bring back the money as it belongs to the people of India and has been taken out of the country illegally.

Supreme Court's View

The Supreme Court has shown unusual interest in the subject and virtually forced the government to arrest Hasan Ali Khan, who is allegedly rolling in black money as the man charged with being the biggest tax evader in Indian history

Money use in Political Campaigns

The corrupt money lies hidden in the political system and at election time, can be seen on open display for those who care to look. In politics, a part of the money they spend on campaigns is black.

Government Contracts

There are chief ministers who have rate cards, that everyone knows about in business circles and these clearly state how much percentage of a government contract needs to be delivered upfront before a project can go ahead.

Indian Politicians Take

The Indian politicians of most of the parties admit the issue, but feel helpless due to systemic corruption in Indian politics. The present prime minister of India Manmohan Singh is considered honest by even opposition political parties, still he failed to stop corruption in his cabinet resulting in big scams like 2G spectrum scam, Adarsh Housing Society scam and Commonwealth Games Scandal.

CAPITAL PLIGHT

November has been a nightmare month for some Indian politicians, businessmen and bureaucrats. The cauldron of corruption, which in India is always bubbling quietly in the background, suddenly erupted — not once, but several times, in headline-hitting but unconnected instances. "It is a murky time," Tata Group chairman Ratan Tata told news channel NDTV. The biggest recent scam — and the largest in Indian history — involves the US$40 billion 2G (second generation) spectrum allotment. Union telecom minister A. Raja was forced to resign on November 14 as a result.

In the Western state of Maharashtra, Chief Minister Ashok Chavan was another casualty. The issue: a housing cooperative society called Adarsh which had set up an illegal multistoried building in downtown Mumbai. It was originally intended for war widows, but was eventually occupied by bureaucrats and the well-connected. The members included three of Chavan's relatives.

In another real estate related scam, on November 24 the Central Bureau of Investigation (CBI) arrested LIC Housing Finance chief executive Ramachandran Nair and seven others from the public sector insurance giant Life Insurance Corporation (LIC) and state-owned banks. Also rounded up were executives of non-banking finance company Money Matters. With Money Matters as middleman, Nair and the bank officials had been sanctioning large loans to builders in return for bribes.

The Securities & Exchange Board of India (SEBI) has started an investigation into the companies named by the CBI and the stock market has taken a tumble. Realty firms and banks have been the worst hit. "There will be repercussions in terms of increased caution by banks while lending to developers," says Anuj Puri, chairman and country head of real estate services firm Jones Lang LaSalle India. "Borrowing will become more expensive."

In Delhi, the continuing investigation into the Commonwealth Games (CWG) scam has seen three more arrests of members of the organizing committee. The net is spreading wider even as the CBI has been unearthing dozens of bank accounts and dubious deals. The chairman of the organizing committee, Suresh Kalmadi, has been forced to resign as secretary of the Congress Parliamentary Party.

In Bangalore, the rightist Bharatiya Janata Party (BJP) has been trying to rein in its chief minister, B.S. Yeddyurappa. Yeddyurappa stands accused of denotifying or changing the classification of land (in this case to commercially exploitable status) in favor of his family members. The US$100 million scam was unearthed through the Right to Information Act. No one has denied the facts; the chief minister's defense is that earlier chief ministers had done exactly the same thing. The case is now being actively followed by the Karnataka Lok Ayukta (ombudsman).

No Longer an Issue

"Corruption has ceased to be an issue in Indian politics since 1989," says M.R. Venkatesh, whose just-published book *Sense, Sensex and Sentiments: The Failure of India's Financial Sentinels* explores corruption in India in the financial arena. "The attitude today is: 'Your scam is bigger than mine.'" (In 1989, V.P. Singh defeated Rajiv Gandhi in the general elections over the Bofors scandal — one of the biggest defense kickbacks, involving Swedish armaments manufacturer Bofors. Large payments were made but the recipients have never been traced.)

If the November news was particularly eye-popping, it's not as though this has been an otherwise barren year. In April, union minister of state for external affairs Shashi Tharoor resigned after his alleged involvement in facilitating the entry of a new team in the lucrative Indian Premier League (IPL). The IPL commissioner, Lalit Modi, was accused of corruption and sacked by the country's cricketing authorities. And taking the action overseas, Swraj Paul and Amirali Alibhai Bhatia — both of Indian descent — were suspended from the House of Lords for falsifying expense statements. "Some things are in our blood," says Venkatesh.

While the most recent scandals were surfacing, Global Financial Integrity (GFI) in Washington published a report titled *The Drivers and Dynamics of Illicit Financial Flows from India: 1948-2008*. The report's findings are that during this period, India lost a total of US$213 billion dollars due to illicit flows, the present value of which is at least US$462 billion. "The total value of illicit assets held abroad represents about 72% of the size of India's underground economy which has been estimated at 50% of India's GDP (or about US$640 billion at end 2008)," says the report. Interestingly, the outflow of illicit funds has actually gone up in the post-liberalization period.

What Drives Illicit Flows

"There are three types of drivers of illicit flows — macroeconomic, structural and governance-related," says Dev Kar, lead economist at GFI. "The corrupt are much more concerned about hiding their ill-gotten wealth from the law, and macroeconomic considerations are hardly taken into consideration.

The drivers of illicit flows are primarily structural [such as higher rates of growth, skewed distribution of income, expansion of the traded sector] and governance-related [weak governance is captured by a growing underground economy]."

But why have illicit flows — a measure of corruption — gone up post liberalization? Fewer controls should mean fewer bribes. And fewer curbs on foreign exchange (coupled with a steady rupee) should be incentive to keep money at home. Kar says that liberalization has produced greater income inequality. The number of high net-worth individuals (HNIs) has gone up. Capital exodus is caused primarily by private companies and HNIs. "This may explain why faster economic growth in the post-reform period has spurred more capital flight rather than less," notes Kar.

Other data reflect Kar's view that corruption is on the rise. "India ranks poorly on the Transparency International (TI) Corruption Perceptions Index (CPI)," he says. "TI ranks India at 3.3 in 2010, lower than all developed countries and even some countries in Africa." India was ranked 16 in the Asia-Pacific region and 87 overall. China (3.5) is one rank ahead in Asia while the leaders are New Zealand (9.3), Singapore (8.3) and Australia (8.7). There has been a decline in India's showing over the years. Last year, it was ranked 84 (score 3.4); 85 (3.4) in 2008; and 72 (3.5) in 2007.

The fact of corruption is undeniable. The direction in which it is going also seems clear. "Corruption has social acceptance," says Pratyush Sinha, who recently retired as Central Vigilance Commissioner (CVC). Talking to daily newspaper *Mint*, he said: "There would be 20% of people in India even today who would be honest, regardless of the temptations, because this is how they are. They have a conscience, they would not be corrupt. There would be around 30% who would be utterly corrupt.

But the rest are the people who are on the borderline." The government has appointed P.J. Thomas as the new CVC. Ironically, at the end of November, the Supreme Court asked the government whether Thomas would be able to function in his new job as there were charges against him in the palm oil scam case in Kerala.

No Social Penalties

"After liberalization and the rise of adulation for the wealthy, regardless of how that wealth was acquired, there seems to be no social penalty attached to having illegal wealth, and it is rare for anyone — businessman or politician — to be caught and penalized for corruption," says M.V. Rajeev Gowda, professor of economics & social sciences & chairperson, Centre for Public Policy at the Indian Institute of Management Bangalore (IIMB).

In the West, law enforcement is regarded as one of the least corrupt professions. In India, policemen come one step below politicians in such rankings. According to another TI report, 87% of the people in India regard the police as corrupt.

What makes India and Indians so prone to corruption? Some give it a historical perspective. Corruption has been intrinsic to Indian society since the Mughal rule (1526-1757), particularly during its latter days. The word *baksheesh* was coined then and has passed into the English language now. *Baksheesh* (speed money) had to be paid to officials to get every small thing done. The concept — and acceptance — of a corrupt bureaucracy started from those days. Under British rule, the country was even more corrupt, experts point out: The man who is considered to have conquered India — Robert Clive — returned to England to face charges of corruption in Parliament. The first Governor General of India — Warren Hastings — had to face impeachment proceedings before the UK House of Commons. He was acquitted after seven years. Independent India inherited the same bureaucracy and has carried on in the same vein.

A "black money" culture also evolved over time. Taxation rates during both the Mughal and British periods were extortionate. There were taxes on land, on trees, on cattle, on marriage, etc. The Mughals had 40 different taxes. Both Mughal and British tax collectors (the *zamindars*) used to go to villages and impose tax on the appearance of prosperity. It was natural for people to hide their wealth. The combination of these factors and a shortage economy resulted in the phenomenon continuing.

Post Independence, there have been other factors such as the License Raj, the growing criminalization of politics and the absence of any hard measures or speedy action. "The British did not encourage Indian industry," says author Venkatesh. "So you had to take every advantage of the law to set up a company. But why go that far back? Post Independence it was the same thing. In a socialist economy, business was bad. The definitive Bollywood [Hindi cinema] image of those days was a poor villager taking on the big, evil monster — almost invariably a businessman. Corruption is part of our mental make-up."

There are many with little sympathy for such views. "This is true," says Kar. "But how does that help us? At some point, we need to unburden ourselves of the past. I don't think India's poor will find solace even if we could trace the current state of political corruption in India to how things were under the Mughal Empire or the British Raj." Adds Dipankar Gupta, former professor of sociology at the School of Social Sciences at Jawaharlal Nehru University: "I don't see any point in tracing our corruption to Mughal and even British times. The context is most important in all such matters. I would advise a more contemporary reading of issues or else we can very easily lose the plot. Black money, too, has little to do with Mughal times.

Similar instances can be found all over the world in the medieval and early modern period. Many European societies, Sweden included, were not the exemplars that they are now. Black money has to do with evasion of taxes, and taxes today are not the same as in the past when it was extortion and set around the whims of rulers and potentates."

One should learn from history, says Gowda of IIMB. "Corruption has certainly existed in India historically; Kautilya, in his *Arthashastra*, discusses how to combat it," he notes. "It arises because individuals realize that they have an opportunity to divert resources due to the government, and some choose to try and get away with diverting funds. But it has always been combated as the examples of Clive and Warren Hastings suggest.

Systems of oversight and professional values have also existed and these often induced people to stick to the straight and narrow, particularly in the bureaucracy before and after freedom. During the Gandhian era and for a generation after, simplicity and honesty were prized values. To succeed, the method of *Satyagraha* [non-violent resistance] required Indians to have superior moral standing compared to exploitative colonialists and this came in the way of corruption."

Drivers of Corruption

N. Balasubramanian, visiting professor at IIMB and IIM Ahmedabad, and former chair of the Centre for Corporate Governance and Citizenship, IIMB, also delves into the Indian ethos. "Both the *Mahabharata* and the *Arthashastra* among ancient Indian literature have admonished the King [or the State] to limit all kinds of taxation to no more than one sixth of an individual's earnings. The taxation structure now, taking into account all categories and not just income tax, is significantly higher than this golden mean.

"Corruption is universal in its origin and application. The word itself etymologically goes back to the French and the Latin. In essence, corruption connotes a deviation from socially accepted norms.

The propensity for corruption is generally determined by three contributing conditions: First, the pressures for amassing wealth (or status or recognition); second, the opportunities for achieving such objectives (such as discretionary powers to grant favors or inflict punishments); and third, the scope for rationalization (such as 'everyone does it', 'I deserve better but the establishment is not inclined to agree' and so on). Virtually every category of corruption in public life can be traced to the existence of these criteria. There should also be concomitant weaknesses in the system which will delay or even deny detection of such frauds."

4

Black Money

Black money is both an economic and a social problem. In the latter context, it is perceived as a problem with adverse sociological effects on society, like social inequalities, social deprivations, etc.; in the former context, it is perceived as a parallel economy, an underground economy or an unofficial economy that is the consequence of the economic policies of the government and has damaging effects on country's economy and nation's socialist planning development. When problem like poverty affects those people who are poor, unemployment affects those who are unemployed, alcoholism and drug abuse affect those who consume them, black money is a problem which does not affect those who have black money but it affects the common man in the society. No wonder, it has been described as a problem with a difference.

THE CONCEPT

Black money is tax-evaded income. It can be earned both through legal and illegal means. Its legitimate source is that the income-earners do not reveal their whole income for tax purposes. For example, government doctors earning money by private practice even when they get non-practising allowance, teachers earning money through examinations and book royalty and not including it in income-tax returns, advocates charging much higher fee than shown in their account books, and so forth. Its illegitimate source is bribe, smuggling, black-marketing, selling commodities at prices higher than the controlled prices, taking 'pugree' for house, shop, etc., selling house at a high price but showing it at a much lower price in the account books, and so forth.

It is possible to convert black money into white money and vice versa. For example, when a person manages to get the receipt from the shopkeeper by paying the sales-tax for a commodity but does not purchase it actually, his black money is converted into white money. In such case, the shopkeeper sells the same commodity to other person without giving him any receipt for it. On the other hand, if a person purchases something (say a scooter, or VCR, etc.) and pays Rs. 15,000 for it out of white money but gets a receipt of only Rs. 10,000, the balance of Rs. 5,000 becomes black money for the seller. In this case, the white money becomes the black money.

MAGNITUDE OF PREVALENCE

It is not easy to calculate the magnitude of black money in any society. The economists in the United States, United Kingdom, Norway, Sweden and Italy adopted different measures but could not estimate the amount involved in black money. Norway and Sweden used questionnaire method for eliciting answers from persons whether they had participated in illegal activities as buyers or sellers. Itlay attempted to estimate the underground economy by finding out the difference between the size of the labour-force officially reported and actually employed. This enabled to determine the productivity in the underground sector. The United Kingdom tried to assess parallel economy by comparing the official estimates of the Gross National Product (GNP) made from the consumption side with those made from the income side. In the United States, Guttman assumed that only cash is used in illegal transactions. He tried to find out the difference between currency required for economic transactions in a fixed period and actual currency held outside banks in the same period.

In spite of the varied methods used, it is not possible to estimate the magnitude of the black money in a society, even though it is described as a worldwide phenomenon. It is said to be in operation not only in the developing countries but also in the developed countries like United States, United Kingdom, USSR, Japan, Canada, France, Germany etc.

A study conducted by the IMF a few years back (Vito Tangani: *The Underground Economy,* December 1983: 13) showed that in regard to the size of the underground money, India holds the first rank followed by the United States and Canada having the second rank.

In India, the Hack money or the unaccounted wealth estimated by Prof. Kaldor in 1953-54 as Rs. 600 crore was estimated by Wanchoo Committee as Rs. 1,000 crore in 1965-66 and Rs. 1,400 crore in 1969-70. Rargrekar placed the figures of black money at Rs. 1,150 crore for 1961-62. Rs. 2350 crore for 1964-65, Rs. 2,833 crore for 1968-69, and Rs. 3,080 crore for 1969-70. Chopra's estimate (*Economic and Political Weekly.* Vol. XVII, Nos. 17 & 18, April, 24 and May 1,1982) showed that the black money in 1960-61 was Rs. 916 crore which increased to Rs. 8,098 crore in 1976-77. According to Gupta (*Economic and Political Weekly, Salivary* 16, 1982: 73),, the amount of black money in our country was Rs. 3,034 crore in 1967-68 and Rs. 40,867 crore in 1978-79. According to his estimate, the black money which constituted 9.5% of the GNP in 1967-68 swelled to nearly 49% in 1978-79. In 1981, black money was estimated by one source as Rs. 7,500 crore (6.8% of the national income at current prices) and by other source as Rs. 25,000 crore (22.7% of the national income ai current prices).

The National Institute of Public Finance and Policy estimated the quantum of black money in economy in 1985 al around Rs. 1,00,000 crore or about 20.0% of the national income. The Planning Commission study, however, has now estimated it to be in the range of Rs. 70,000 crore. Further, it is generated at the rate of Rs. 50,000 crore per year *(The Hindustan Times,* 2 August, 1991: 11). The flight of capital has resulted in an overseas stash which government officials conservatively place at $50 million (about Rs. 1,30,000 crore).

The scholars have also pointed out that of the total black money in the society, about one-fourth (26.0%) is from the tax-evaded income. In the United Slates, the black money in the society is expected to be about 8.0% of its Gross National Product (GNP). While in India, the black money is more from the illegal sources, in the United States it is more (about 75.0%) from the legal sources.

CAUSES OF GENERATING BLACK MONEY

Unrealistic Tax Laws

The increase in taxes and duties compel some people to evade them. The present rules (1991) prescribe the limit of Rs. 22,000 as free income for levying income tax. Can a person exist within this limit in this age of inflation ? A mason or a carpenter earns about Rs. 60 to Rs. 80 per day in a city and Rs. 80 to Rs. 100 per day in metropolitian areas. Even a good 'gol-gappa' seller or a 'pan' shopkeeper earns more than Rs. 100 a day. Assuming that these people work for 300 days in a year, their income will exceed the prescribed income tax limit. And how many of these workers pay income tax ?

A film actor getting Rs. 20 lakh per picture has to pay about throe-fourth of his income as income tax. Instead of piling such a huge tax, he maintains 'double' accounts and evades paying tax and possesses more black money. A doctor with a private practice of more than Rs. 500 per day, a surgeon charging a fee of Rs. 5,000 per operation and doing at least ten operations a month, an advocate charging Rs. 2,000 per hearing, a shopkeeper doing a business of more than Rs. 5,000 per day, a contractor with a turnover business of Rs. 1 crore per year, an industrialist with a profit of millions of rupees per year—all are bound to hide their real income to escape paying income tax between 50% to 70% of me total income. Indirect taxes, like excise duty, custom duty, sales tax and octroi, etc. also encourage evasion of taxes and increase in black money.

If income tax rate is reduced, there is more likelihood of hiding less and increasing revenue. This was demonstrated in 1985-86 when the maximum rate of income tax was lowered from 61.9% to 50.0%. As a result, incomes declared by the self-employed increased almost three times to Rs. 9,654 crore by 1988-89.

Different Rates of Excise Duty

Within similar products, there are different rates of excise duty. For instance, in textiles and cigarettes, this leads to tax evasion through mis-classification of output In textiles, separate rates of excise are charged for cloth of different varieties. Manufacturers regularly downgrade a product to pay tower rates of excise. This alone generates Rs. 1,000 crore a year in black money. For the entire manufacturing sector, including steel, evasion in excise, custom and sales taxes accounts for over Rs. 50,000 crore in black money every year.

Control Policy

Another cause of black money is the price-control policy of the government. In selecting commodities for control and in determining their prices, the government fails to take into account the elasticities involved in demand and supply. For example, according to the report of the National Council of Applied Economic Research (NCAER) for the year 1981, black money worth Rs. 840 crore was created in the Indian economy over the period of nine years from 1965-66 to 1974-75 as a result of the operation of price controls in six commodities, viz., cement, steel, paper, vanaspati, automobile tyres and fertilizers. Similarly, as a result of control on sugar, about Rs. 400 crore of black money were generated in the year 1979-80. Regulation of foreign exchange also leads to over-invoicing of imports and urder-invoicing of exports and black-marketing of currency. Thus, more stringent the measures of control and more regulated an economy, more will be the effort to violate it, which will increase hoarding, fraud, artificial scarcity and the resultant black money.

Quota System

Yet another source of black money is the quota system. The import quota, the export quota and the foreign exchange quota are generally misused by selling them at a premium.

Scarcity

Black money is also caused by scarcity and defective public

distribution system. When essential goods become scarce, people have to pay higher than the controlled prices, which generates black money. The scarcity of kerosene oil, sugar, refined oil etc. have always resulted in illegitimate transactions and black money.

Inflation

The increase in prices of commodities like petrol, etc. in international market, increase in prices of commodities due to high increase in duties and taxes imposed by the government, the conspicuous consumption created by the people with unaccountable money, diverting resources from production to speculation—all these cause inflation which in turn creates black money.

Elections in a Democratic System

Each election in the country involves thousands of crores of rupees. For contesting Lok Sabha election, a candidate normally spends more than one million rupees and for contesting Vidhan Sabha election, one spends more than Rs. 5 lakh in the present times. Since the expenditure allowed by law for a candidate is limited and the companies are not allowed to give donations to political parties for elections, the elections are generally financed by the black money holders. These people expect political patronage and economic concessions which are obtained with the consent and the connivance of political elites in power in the form of artificial controls on commodities, laxity in the means of distribution, etc. All these methods create black money.

Real Estate Transactions

Estate transaction is an important source of generating black money. In these days, purchasing a house and/or land is considered to be not only very profitable but too. There is a growing tendency of transforming the rural agricultural land to urban residential land due to the paucity of building sites in the urban areas. Establishing unapproved colonies on agricultural land is illegal. The transaction value shown by the colonisers in registration deeds is much less than the actual amount or the market value. This enables the seller of the land to evade capital gain tax. According to an estimate, the illegal transaction of property alone generates about Rs. 2,000 crore of black money in a year, assuming that there are about 50 lakh transactions in urban property every year. The high rates of stamp duty — ranging between 14.5% and 28.0% in different states — are a major cause for under-valuation of property and unreported deals, or both. The suggestion is that if duties are reduced to 2% to 3%, it will prevent evasion. Another hurdle is the Urban Land Ceiling Act, which reduces the supply of land and creates a black market. Roughly over Rs. 13,000 crore a year are generated through the real estate route.

SOCIAL EFFECTS

Besides the economic effects, there are many social consequences of black money also. In economic terms, black money robs the exchequer of its due share, increases economic inequality and hampers programmes of economic development. Socially, it increases social inequality, creates frustrations among honest people, increases crimes like smuggling, bribery, etc. and adversely affects social services programmes for the uplift of the poor and the weaker sections of society. It also distorts the measurement of true rates like growth rate, inflationary rate, unemployment rate, poverty, etc. which in turn affects the government policies for containing these problems.

MEASURES OF CONTROL

Over the past 40 years, the government has at various times announced seven schemes offering opportunities to bring black money overboard. Some of these schemes are : introducing the scheme of special Bearer Bonds, demonetising high denomination currency notes, stringent raids and scheme of voluntary disclosures. In July, 1991, the Union Finance Minister proposed a new scheme—National Housing Bank Scheme—to woo black money back into the legitimate operations of the national economy. The scheme offers possessors of unaccounted money an opportunity to deposit any amount of money (with a minimum limit of Rs. 10,000) with NHB without disclosing the source of funds. The offer remained open for seven months and closed on January 31, 1992. It permits the account holders facility to withdraw 60% of their deposits from the account while the remaining 40% are impounded to be used for projects such as slum clearance and housing for the poor. The withdrawals are to be made after stating the purpose for which the money is proposed to be used. These people are taxed at the rate of 40% while the balance amount is channeled back into the open economy.

The demonetisation of 1,000 rupee notes in 1978 brought out currency worth Rs. 29 crore. Voluntary Disclosure Scheme of 1951, 1955 and 1975 yielded Rs. 249 crore of disclosed account. The Disclosure Scheme launched in 1986 brought in just Rs. 67 crore. The 1991 scheme is open, till March 31, 1992. About 375 raids in 1978 yielded assets worth Rs. 217 lakh.

Some scholars have maintained that all these measures have touched only the tip of the iceberg. All the schemes have hardly fetched Rs. 5,000 crore over a period of fourty years. The main drawback in these schemes is that they touch the problem of black money already created but they do not go into the root cause of generation of black money and that why a person is prepared to take the risk of keeping black money despite so many problems. Unless this problem is tackled, the menace of black money will continue to increase.

It has been suggested that the problem of black money and parallel economy can be contained by reducing taxes in some areas, giving incentives for voluntary disclosure of income, overhauling the economic intelligence unit, curbing administrative corruption at various levels, exempting tax on money spent on house construction, doing away with control policies, and so forth. Isolated attempts may not yield much but a package of mutually reinforcing measures along with a strong political will and the commitment of political elites may prove to be successful to a large extent.

BLACK MONEY IN INDIAN POLITICS

Some reports have indicated that Indian politicians make use of black money. The *Times of India* argued that the rising cost of electoral expenses has made it necessary for many politicians to use black money to finance campaigns.

The growth of black money in proportional percentage to the GDP has shown an alarming increase in recent years, from 20% in the 1980s to 45-50% at the turn of the century. It is further estimated by experts that one percent of the world's population holds more than 57 percent of total global wealth, routing it invariably through tax havens. ATCA's preliminary investigation to analyse the Swiss banking chain and to assess Indian wealth in that single country, suggests that the number is much larger than the USD 1.4 trillion figure and is more likely to be near USD 3 trillion. The larger figure can be derived from the deposits in vaults of gold, diamonds and other precious gems alongside assets managed out of Switzerland in other tax havens.

"The recent scams involving unimaginably big amounts of money, such as the 2G spectrum scam, are well known. It is estimated that more than trillion dollars are stashed away in foreign havens, while 80% of Indians earn less than 2$ per day and every second child is malnourished. It seems as if only the honest people are poor in India and want to get rid of their poverty by education, emigration to cities, and immigration, whereas all the corrupt ones, like Hasan Ali Khan are getting rich through scams and crime. It seems as if India is a rich country filled with poor people, " the organisers of Dandi March II in the United States said.

INDIAN BLACK MONEY

Black money refers to funds earned on the black market, on which income and other taxes has not been paid. Black money deposited in various Swiss Banks by Indians is alleged to amount more than Rs 7,280,000 Crores (USD $1.4 trillion), but the exact figure is not yet known to the public. This amount is 13 times larger than the nation's foreign debt. In January 2011 the Supreme Court of India asked why the names of those who have stashed money in the Liechtenstein Bank have not been disclosed.

Black Money in Swiss Banks

Reports indicate that "huge" amounts of black money have

been deposited in foreign banks. India will have to wait until the 2011 year-end to get information on illicit funds in banks in Switzerland. The Supreme Court of India have expressed displeasure over the government's reluctance in coming forward with full information on the black money stashed by Indians in foreign banks, saying it is a theft of national wealth and amounts to "plunder" of the nation.

Indian black money is sometimes physically transferred abroad. The money is flown abroad out of Mumbai and Delhi airports to Zurich. Switzerland is the top destination for illegal funds because of its strict secrecy laws. Swiss banks sell additional masks to hide the identity of their rich clients, like trusts in the Cayman Islands, shell companies in Panama, or foundations in Liechtenstein, all run by nominees.

Efforts to Bring Back Black Money from Foreign Banks

There are efforts to bring back this black money from foreign banks. If all the funds were brought back, India would immediately be able to clear the country's foreign debt. Even if all taxes were abolished, the government could maintain the country easily for 30 years.

Black Money in Politics

Some reports have indicated that Indian politicians make use of black money. The *Times of India* argued that the rising cost of electoral expenses has made it necessary for many politicians to use black money to finance campaigns.

Black Money in Real Estate

The cash component of property transactions is widely believed to be as high as 50%. This helps tax evaders park untaxed money in property deals.

Black Money Holders List with Wikileaks

A former Swiss Bank executive Rudolf Elmer empowered whistleblower WikiLeaks by rendering two CDs containing details of more than 2,000 Swiss bank accounts. Assange confirmed that the website will expose the truth after verifying all data that the CDs contain.

Effects of Bringing Back Black Money

Swami Ramdev has publicly raised the issue of bringing back Indian money stashed away illegally in Swiss banks. He says that the government must take concrete action and bring back the money as it belongs to the people of India and has been taken out of the country illegally. He proposed that the exchange rate of the Indian rupee to the US dollar will raise from 50:1 ratio to 1:50 ratio if the black money is retrieved.

Solutions to Black Money Issue

Swami Ramdev propagates solutions based on economic science, by which use of black money can be iradicated. The six point solution are

1. Withdraw Rs.500 and Rs. 1000 notes
2. Agree and accept the UN convention against corruption– pending since 2006
3. Death penalty for the corrupt
4. Access, monitor, disrupt payment gateway servers enabling corrupt people to manage money in tax havens
5. Scrutinizing accounts of people having credit/debit cards of foreign banks without any foreign work/relation
6. Disabling operations of any bank from a tax haven country.

He declared at Bangalore that a people's movement to liberate the country from rampant corruption and build a strong spiritual 'Bharat' would be launched by him in June. The movement which is second phase of Bharath Swabhiman Yatra is named 'Satyagraha against Corruption'. He declared one of the main objectives of the movement was to bring about an end to corruption and bring back black money stashed away in various financial institutions in the country and abroad.

Other Banks Offering Privacy

Other states, such as Singapore, have attracted depositors

seeking privacy and protection. Having taken steps to make its banks more attractive, Singapore strengthened penalties for violators of bank secrecy (and now imposes steeper fines and longer jail sentences for offenders), and modified its laws on trusts and inheritance. Singapore is the location of Credit Suisse's international banking headquarters. Legal experts feel that action should be taken to track the flow of Indian black money to such banks from Swiss banks following recent changes in the Swiss bank privacy policy.

Methods to Track Black Money

Swiss banks recently modified their privacy rules to assist actions towards tax evaders in India and other states. Experts are of the view that the majority of black money that has flowed from India can be tracked by following bank-to-bank transactions that have happened from independence until the present day. Such a tracking mechanism is in the research stage.

MONITORING SUSPECIOUS BANKING ACTIVITY

A Reserve Bank of India (RBI) circular dated 2 December 2005 listed suspicious banking activity for banks to be alerted to with regards to black-money laundering. Banks are required to report to the RBI with recommendations by the end of March each year. But with banks themselves sometimes found to be willing partners in major stock-market scams, some of Asia's biggest black-money hoarders still have sufficient reason to feel secure.

Black Money & Indian Economy

As per various reports nearly 50% of the Indian economy is black money. If this is taken into consideration that the actual GDP and growth rate will be much better.

INDIAN BLACK MONEY IN SWISS BANKS

According to the data provided by the Swiss bank, India has more black money in foreign banks than rest of the world combined. There were also media reports which mentioned Wikileaks founder Julian Assange stating black money in Swiss banks mainly from India

Amount of Money

Though the exact amount of money is not known. There are reports in media that 500 Lakh crores of black money of Indian origin is in foreign banks. India tops the list for black money in the entire world with almost US$1456 billion in Swiss banks (USD 1.4 trillion approximately) in the form of black money. According to the data provided by the Swiss Banking Association Report (2006), India has more black money than the rest of the world combined. Indian Swiss bank account assets are worth 13 times the country's national debt. Indian black money is sometimes physically transferred abroad. The CEO of a Mumbai-based equity firm recently told journalists that the money is flown abroad in "special flights" out of Mumbai and Delhi airports to Zurich. Indeed Indians would be the largest depositors of illegal money in Swiss banks, according to sources in the banking industry. The estimated average amount stashed away annually from India during 2002–2006 is $27.3 billion US dollars.

Havens for Black Money

- Switzerland: Switzerland is the top destination for illegal funds because of its strict secrecy laws. Also, Swiss banks sell additional masks to hide the identity of their rich clients, like trusts in the Cayman islands, shell companies in Panama, or foundations in Liechtenstein, all run by nominees.
- Mauritius Route.

Supreme Court's Displeasure

The Supreme Court have chided the government for restricting names of those with black money stashed abroad in Liechtenstein Bank in Germany.

Government Response

The government is ready to share information with the Supreme Court but is not making it public. It says that it is in the process of getting more details of foreign accounts of Indians from other countries under the DTAA regime.

Names in Public

- Hasan Ali Khan: A Pune-based businessman is accused of stashing money in foreign banks..

Political Views

BJP: The party is of the view that the black money in foreign banks is 200 times bigger than the 2G scam.

Double Taxation Avoidance Agreement

The government is of the view that it is not possible to disclose information received from foreign governments under Double Taxation Avoidance Agreement (DTAT).

5

Black Economy

The black economy is a cash economy. It is liquid and fast. It increases the velocity of money. It injects much needed foreign exchange to the economy and inadvertently increases the effective money supply and the resulting money aggregates. In this sense, it defies the dictates of "we know better" institutions such as the IMF. It fosters economic activity and employs people. It encourages labour mobility and international trade. Black economy, in short, is very positive. With the exception of illegal activities, it does everything that the official economy does – and, usually, more efficiently.

So, what is morally wrong with the black economy? The answer, in brief: it is exploitative. Other parts of the economy, which are not hidden (though would have liked to be), are penalized for their visibility. They pay taxes. Workers in a factory owned by the state or in the government service cannot avoid paying taxes. The money that the state collects from them is invested, for instance, in infrastructure (roads, phones, electricity) or used to pay for public services (education, defence, policing). The operators of the black economy enjoy these services without paying for them, without bearing the costs and worse: while others bear the costs. These encourages them, in theory to use these resources less efficiently.

And all this might be true in a highly efficient, almost ideal market economy. The emphasis is on the word "market". Unfortunately, we all live in societies which are regulated by bureaucracies which are controlled (in theory, rarely in practice) by politicians. These elites have a tendency to misuse and to abuse resources and to allocate them in an inefficient manner. Even economic theory admits that any dollar left in the hands of the private sector is much more efficiently used than the same dollar in the hands of the most honest and well meaning and well planning civil servant. Governments all over the world distort economic decisions and misallocate scarce economic resources.

Thus, if the goals are to encourage employment and economic growth – the black economy should be welcomed. This is precisely what it does and, by definition, it does so more efficiently than the government. The less tax dollars a government has – the less damage it does. This is an opinion shares by most economists in the world today. Lower tax rates are an admission of this fact and a legalization of parts of the black economy.

The black economy is especially important in times of economic hardships. Countries in transition are a private case of emerging economies which are a private case of developing countries which used to be called (in less politically correct times) "Third World Countries". They suffer from all manner of acute economic illnesses. They lost their export markets, they are technologically backward, their unemployment skyrockets, their plant and machinery are dilapidated, their infrastructure decrepit and dysfunctional, they are lethally illiquid, they become immoral societies (obligations not honoured, crime flourishes), their trade deficits and budget deficits balloon and they are conditioned to be dependent on handouts and dictates from various international financial institutions and donor countries.

Read this list again: isn't the black economy a perfect solution until the dust settles?

It enhances exports (and competitiveness through imports), it encourages technology transfers, it employs people, it invests in legitimate businesses (or is practised by them), it adds to the wealth of the nation (black marketeers are big spenders, good consumers and build real estate), it injects liquidity to an otherwise dehydrated market. Mercifully, the black economy is out of the reach of zealous missionaries such as the IMF. It goes its own way, unnoticed, unreported, unbeknownst, untamed. It doesn't pay attention to money supply targets (it is much bigger than the official money supply figure), or to macroeconomic stability goals. It plods on: doing business and helping the country to survive the double scourges of transition and Western piousness and patronizing.

As long as it is there, Macedonia has a real safety net. The government is advised to turn a blind eye to it for it is a blessing in disguise.

There is one sure medicine: eliminate the population and both unemployment and inflation will be eliminated. Without the black economy, the population of Macedonia would not have survived. This lesson must be remembered as the government prepares to crack down on the only sector of the economy which is still alive and kicking.

Operational Recommendations

The implementation of these recommendations and reforms should be obliged to be GRADUAL. The informal economy is an important pressure valve for the release of social pressures, it ameliorates the social costs inherent to the period of transition and it constitutes an important part of the private sector.

As we said in the body of our report, these are the reasons for the existence of an informal economy and they should be obliged to all be tackled:

- High taxation level (in Macedonia, high payroll taxes);
- Onerous labour market regulations;
- Red tape and bureaucracy (which often leads to corruption);
- Complexity and unpredictability of the tax system.

Reporting Requirements and Transparency

- All banks should be obliged to report foreign exchange transactions of more than 10,000 DM (whether in one transaction or cumulatively by the same legal entity). The daily report should be submitted to the Central Bank. In extreme cases, the transactions should be investigated.

- All the ZPP account numbers of all the firms in Macedonia should be publicly available through the Internet and in printed form.
- Firms should be obliged by law to make a list of all their bank accounts available to the ZPP, to the courts and to plaintiffs in lawsuits.
- All citizens should be obliged to file annual, personal tax returns (universal tax returns, like in the USA). This way, discrepancies between personal tax returns and other information can lead to investigations and discoveries of tax evasion and criminal activities.
- All citizens should be obliged to file bi-annual declarations of personal wealth and assets (including real estate, vehicles, movables, inventory of business owned or controlled by the individual, financial assets, income from all sources, shares in companies, etc.).
- All retail outlets and places of business should be required to install – over a period of 3 years – cash registers with "fiscal brains". These are cash registers with an embedded chip. The chips are built to save a trail (detailed list) of all the transactions in the place of business. Tax inspectors can pick the chip at random, download its contents to the tax computers and use it to issue tax assessments. The information thus gathered can also be crossed with and compared to information from other sources. This can be done only after the full implementation of the recommendations in the section titled "Databases and Information Gathering". I do not regard it as an effective measure. While it increases business costs – it is not likely to prevent cash or otherwise unreported transactions.
- All taxis should be equipped with taximeters, which include a printer. This should be a licencing condition.

- Industrial norms (for instance, the amount of sugar needed to manufacture a weight unit of chocolate, or juice) should be revamped. Norms should NOT be determined according to statements provided by the factory-but by a panel of experts. Each norm should be signed by three people, of which at least one is an expert engineer or another expert in the relevant field. Thought should be dedicated to the possibility of employing independent laboratories to determine norms and supervise them.
- Payments in wholesale markets should be done through a ZPP counter or branch in the wholesale market itself. Release of the goods and exiting the physical location of the wholesale market should be allowed only against presentation of a ZPP payment slip.

Reduction of Cash Transactions

- Cash transactions are the lifeblood of the informal economy. Their reduction and minimization is absolutely essential in the effort to contain it. One way of doing it is by issuing ZPP payment (debit) cards to businesses, firm and professionals. Use of the payment cards should be mandatory in certain business-to-business transactions.
- All exchange offices should be obliged to issue receipt for every cash transaction above 100 DM and to report to the Central Bank all transactions above 1000 DM. Suspicious transactions (for instance, transactions which exceed the financial wherewithal of the client involved) should be duly investigated.
- The government can reduce payroll taxes if the salary is not paid in cash (for instance, by a transfer to the bank account of the employee). The difference between payroll taxes collected on cash salaries and lower payroll taxes collected on noncash salaries – should be recovered by imposing a levy on all cash withdrawals from banks. The banks can withhold the tax and transfer it to the state monthly.

- Currently, checks issued to account-holders by banks are virtually guaranteed by the issuing banks. This transforms checks into a kind of cash and checks are used as cash in the economy. To prevent this situation, it is recommended that all checks will be payable to the beneficiary only. The account-holder will be obliged to furnish the bank with a monthly list of checks he or she issued and their details (to whom, date, etc.). Checks should be valid for 5 working days only.
- An obligation can be imposed to oblige businesses to effect payments only through their accounts (from account to account) or using their debit cards. Cash withdrawals should be subject to a withholding tax deducted by the bank. The same withholding tax should be applied to credits given against cash balances or to savings houses (stedilnicas). Alternatively, stedilnicas should also be obliged to deduct, collect and transfer the cash withdrawal withholding tax.
- In the extreme and if all other measures fail after a reasonable period of time, all foreign trade related payments should be conducted through the Central Bank. But this is really a highly irregular, emergency measure, which I do not recommend at this stage.
- The interest paid on cash balances and savings accounts in the banks should be increased (starting with bank reserves and deposits in the central bank).
- The issuance of checkbook should be made easy and convenient. Every branch should issue checkbooks. All the banks and the post office should respect and accept each other's checks.
- A Real Time Gross Settlement System should be established to minimize float and facilitate interbank transfers.

Government Tenders

- Firms competing for government tenders should be obliged to acquire a certificate from the tax authorities that they owe no back-taxes. Otherwise, they should be barred from bidding in government tenders and RFPs (Requests for Proposals).

Databases and Information Gathering

- Estimating the informal economy should be a priority objective of the Bureau of Statistics, which should devote considerable resources to this effort. In doing so, the Bureau of Statistics should coordinate closely with a wide variety of relevant ministries and committees that oversee various sectors of the economy.
- All registrars should be computerized: land, real estate, motor vehicles, share ownership, companies registration, tax filings, import and export related documentation (customs), VAT, permits and licences, records of flights abroad, ownership of mobile phones and so on. The tax authorities and the Public Revenue Office (PRO) should have unrestricted access to ALL the registers of all the registrars. Thus, they should be able to find tax evasion easily (ask for sources of wealth-how did you build this house and buy a new car if you are earning 500 DM monthly according to your tax return?).
- The PRO should have complete access to the computers of the ZPP and to all its computerized and non-computerized records.
- The computer system should constantly compare VAT records and records and statements related to other taxes in order to find discrepancies between them.
- Gradually, submissions of financial statements, tax returns and wealth declarations should be computerized and done even on a monthly basis (for instance, VAT statements).
- A system of informants and informant rewards should be established, including anonymous phone calls. Up to 10% of the intake or seizure value related to the information provided by the informant should go to the informant.

Law Enforcement

- Tax inspectors and customs officials should receive police powers and much higher salaries (including a percentage of tax revenues). The salaries of all tax inspectors – regardless of their original place of employment – should be equalized (of course, taking into consideration tenure, education, rank, etc.).
- Judges should be trained and educated in matters pertaining to the informal economy. Special courts for taxes, for instance, are a good idea (see recommendation below). Judges have to be trained in tax laws and the state tax authorities should provide BINDING opinions to entrepreneurs, businessmen and investors regarding the tax implications of their decisions and actions.
- It is recommended to assign tax inspectors to the public prosecutors' office to work as teams on complex or big cases.
- To establish an independent Financial and Tax Police with representatives from all relevant ministries but under the exclusive jurisdiction of the PRO. The remit of this Police should include all matters financial (including foreign exchange transactions, property and real estate transactions, payroll issues, etc.).
- Hiring and firing procedures in all the branches of the tax administration should be simplified. The number of administrative posts should be reduced and the number of tax inspectors and field agents increased.
- Tax arrears and especially the interest accruing thereof should be the first priority of the ZPP, before all other payments.
- All manufacturers and sellers of food products (including soft drinks, sweetmeats and candy, meat products, snacks) should purchase a licence from the state and be subjected to periodic and rigorous inspections.
- All contracts between firms should be registered in the courts and stamped to become valid. Contracts thus

evidenced should be accompanied by the registration documents (registrar extract) of the contracting parties. Many "firms" doing business in Macedonia are not even legally registered.

Reforms and Amnesty

- A special inter-ministerial committee with MINISTER-MEMBERS and headed by the PM should be established. Its roles: to reduce bureaucracy, to suggest appropriate new legislation and to investigate corruption.
- Bureaucracy should be pared down drastically. The more permits, licences, tolls, fees and documents needed – the more corruption. Less power to state officials means less corruption. The One Stop Shop concept should be implemented everywhere.
- A general amnesty should be declared. Citizens declaring their illegal wealth should be pardoned BY LAW and either not taxed or taxed at a low rate once and forever on the hitherto undeclared wealth.

The Tax Code

- To impose a VAT system. VAT is one the best instruments against the informal economy because it tracks the production process throughout a chain of value added suppliers and manufacturers.
- The Tax code needs to be simplified. Emphasis should be placed on VAT, consumption taxes, customs and excise taxes, fees and duties. To restore progressivity, the government should directly compensate the poor for the excess relative burden.
- After revising the tax code in a major way, the government should declare a moratorium on any further changes for at least four years.
- The self-employed and people whose main employment is directorship in companies should be given the choice between paying a fixed % of the market value of their assets (including financial assets) or income tax.

- All property rental contracts should be registered with the courts. Lack of registration in the courts and payment of a stamp tax should render the contract invalid. The courts should be allowed to evidence and stamp a contract only after it carries the stamp of the Public Revenue Office (PRO). The PRO should register the contract and issue an immediate tax assessment. Contracts, which are for less than 75% of the market prices, should be subject to tax assessment at market prices. Market prices should be determined as the moving average of the last 100 rental contracts from the same region registered by the PRO.
- Filing of tax returns – including for the self-employed – should be only with the PRO and not with any other body (such as the ZPP).

Legal Issues

- The burden of proof in tax court cases should shift from the tax authorities to the person or firm assessed.
- Special tax courts should be established within the existing courts. They should be staffed by specifically trained judges. Their decisions should be appealed to the Supreme Court. They should render their decisions within 180 days. All other juridical and appeal instances should be cancelled – except for an appeal instance within the PRO. Thus, the process of tax collection should be greatly simplified. A tax assessment should be issued by the tax authorities, appealed internally (within the PRO), taken to a tax court session (by a plaintiff) and, finally, appealed to the Supreme Court (in very rare cases).
- The law should allow for greater fines, prison terms and for the speedier and longer closure of delinquent businesses.
- Seizure and sale procedures should be specified in all the tax laws and not merely by way of reference to the Income Tax Law. Enforcement provisions should be incorporated in all the tax laws.

- To amend the Law on Tax Administration, the Law on Personal Income Tax and the Law on Profits Tax as per the recommendations of the IRS experts (1997-9).

Customs and Duties

- Ideally, the customs service should be put under foreign contract managers. If this is politically too sensitive, the customs personnel should be entitled to receive a percentage of customs and duties revenues, on a departmental incentive basis. In any case, the customs should be subjected to outside inspection by expert inspectors who should be rewarded with a percentage of the corruption and lost revenues that they expose.
- In the case of imports or payments abroad, invoices, which include a price of more than 5% above the list price of a product, should be rejected and assessment for the purposes of paying customs duties and other taxes should be issued at the list price.
- In the case of exports or payments from abroad, invoices which include a discount of more than 25% on the list price of a product should be rejected and assessment for the purposes of paying customs duties and other taxes should be issued at the list price.
- The numbers of tax inspectors should be substantially increased and their pay considerably enhanced. A departmental incentive system should be instituted involving a percentage of the intake (monetary fines levied, goods confiscated, etc.).
- The computerized database system should be used to compare imports of raw materials for the purposes of re-export and actual exports (using invoices and customs declarations). Where there are disparities and discrepancies, severe and immediate penal actions should be taken. Anti-dumping levies and measures, fines and criminal charges should be adopted against exporters colluding with importers in hiding imported goods or reducing their value.

- Often final products are imported and declared to the customs as raw materials (to minimize customs duties paid). Later these raw materials are either sold outright in the domestic or international markets or bartered for finished products (for example: paints and lacquers against furniture or sugar against chocolate). This should be a major focus of the fight against the informal economy. I follow with an analysis of two products, which are often abused in this manner.
- I study two examples (white sugar and cooking oil) though virtually all raw materials and foods are subject to the aforementioned abuse.
- White Sugar is often imported as brown sugar. One way to prevent this is to place sugar on the list of LB (import licence required) list, to limit the effective period of each licence issued, to connect each transaction of imported brown sugar to a transaction of export, to apply the world price of sugar to customs duties, to demand payment of customs duties in the first customs terminal, to demand a forwarder's as well as an importer's guarantee and to require a certificate of origin. The same goes for Cooking Oil (which – when it is imported packaged – is often declared as some other goods).
- All payments to the customs should be made only through the ZPP. Customs and tax inspectors should inspect these receipts periodically.
- All goods should be kept in the customs terminal until full payment of the customs duties, as evidenced by a ZPP receipt, is effected.

Public Campaign

- The government should embark on a massive Public Relations and Information campaign. The citizens should be made to understand what is a budget, how the taxes are collected, how they are used. They should begin to view tax evaders as criminals. "He who does not pay his taxes – is stealing from you and from your children", "Why should YOU pay for HIM?" "If we all did not pay taxes-there would be no roads, bridges, schools, or hospitals" (using video to show disappearing roads, bridges, suffering patients and students without classes), "Our country is a partnership – and the tax-evader is stealing from the till (kasa)" and so on.

- The phrase "Gray Economy" should be replaced by the more accurate phrases "Black Economy" or "Criminal Economy".

6

Money Laundering in the Past, Present and Future

Cyberlaundering is a subset of money laundering and money laundering is a process of concealing crime and converting the proceeds of crime in to legitimate wealth. The bad guys are adopting this technique due to the reason that the modern technology is facilitating the financial institution in a very fast pace then the traditional way of money laundering. The processing speed of the technology is upgrading every six months while it take years to investigate and prosecute any case of money laundering. The legislation are their in every country except a few but the phenomena of investigation from jurisdiction to jurisdiction takes a lot of time and manpower. The online currency is still an open door for the criminals to take advantage of the fact that they can avoid human interaction and do their business online with out declaring the source of the money.

Governments

Governments all around the globe is required to monitor and report any suspicious activity with regards to money laundering both inside the government institutions and also in the public limited companies. Due to the fact that this phenomenon is of global scale, a well coordinated and combine effort is required to deal with this issue to control and prevent it. Seriously organized crime agency a UK based agency is also in the process of joining hands with all the other countries to cooperate and help to control this crime of money laundering.

Financial Institutions

The technological products such as prepaid cards, e-cash, swipe cards, e-gold and online banking has introduced a number of opportunities for the criminals to hide their identity or use some one else's identity to do a transaction and get away with it before being catch. Financial institution are required to submit suspicious activity report to the financial monitoring agencies and also required to know their customer through customer due diligence also called know your customer (KYC). Suspicious transaction means that a customer transaction that does not fit into his profile or a foreign transaction that is relatively unusual.

Department of Justice

Finally the department of justice is trying to encircle the issue of money laundering/Cyberlaundering through introducing several laws to deal with this issue and also imposing penalties and imprisonment over different offences related to money laundering/Cyberlaundering. The introduction of internet policing and e-crime unit is a good start to control the issue of Cyberlaundering along with other e-crime to bringing the criminals to justice.

DIFFERENT WAYS TO ACHIEVE CYBERLAUNDERING

Cyberlaundering can be achieved through directly interacting with the financial institution by presenting the identity in a way to hide the real intent (i.e. Cyberlaundering) through that financial institution. There are five classes of such dealings that are classified in relation to the issue of Cyberlaundering and are given as follows. "Concealment within Business Structures; Misuse of Legitimate Businesses; Use of False Identities, Documents, or Straw Men; Exploiting International Jurisdictional Issues; Use of Anonymous Asset Types;" However there is another way of achieving Cyberlaundering and is termed as indirect way or a way to avoid direct dealing with the financial institution to protect the transaction from being reported to financial agencies and that is the hawala system or alternate banking remittance. In addition to this system of remittance there are other products that can be used to achieve Cyberlaundering and they are listed as follows.

"E-Cash, Online Auctions, Bankruptcy frauds, Telemarketing fraud, Operation Cyber Sweep, Cyber terrorism, Online Banking, Iraqi internet scam, E-gold and Online Casinos"

Cyberlaundering is mostly all about the indirect way of dealing with the financial institution. Doing the job fast without drawing any unnecessary attention to the fact that the money is not linked to an authentic or legitimate source. In the words of Nick Kochan

"He describes about Cyberlaundering as the potential for easy and convenient laundering through e-auctions, online casinos, and telemarketing is all too real to ignore. The lack of a paper trail and government control makes this channel a tempting one for the goons to abuse, as they do".

A number of countries like USA, UK and Canada have advance level of check and balance but the majority of the countries still lack in infrastructure to monitor and control the Cyberlaundering and also the laws are not yet implemented to bring the criminals to justice.

Process of Cyberlaundering

The process of Cyberlaundering can be achieved by the three stages which is in contrast to its super set that is money laundering and the three stages such as placement, layering and integrity are explained below.

Placement

In the stage of placement electronic cash is used to buy goods to be resold which can be achieved by means of smart cards. Thus removing the need to involve any intermediary between the two parties require exchanging the money with the facility of anonymity. "Electronic money (or e-money) is money that is represented digitally and can be exchanged by means of smart card from one party to another without the need for an intermediary. It is anticipated that e-money will work just like paper money. One of its potential key features is anonymity. The proceeds of crime that are in the form of e-money could be used, to buy foreign currency and high value goods to be resold. E-money may therefore be used to place dirty money without having to smuggle cash or conduct face to face transactions".

The illegal money in the form of smart cards can be used in online casinos or to buy e-gold without even proving that the identity is authentic, this can be a source to convert dirty money in to legitimate in the form of refund from a casino in the same area or in a different area where the jurisdiction is less tolerant or have no check on the gambling activities.

Layering

In the stage of layering the criminal tries to separate the money from its origin by transferring the money through a number of accounts in different banks in the disguise of purchase of goods for re-sale or through off shore companies located in different jurisdictions. In this stage the criminals are more likely to be facilitated by the use of internet which if permits to open an account without linking to any authentic proof of identity and any traditional bank account. With this features the criminals can hide there identity or they can use a fake identity to open a bank account.

The transfer of funds from one jurisdiction to another leaves extensive audit trails. But the investigation in to a transaction to be legitimate requires a lot of man power and time compared to the instantaneous nature of the electronic transfer of money. Layering could be achieved much easier if the bank supports transfer of funds that deal with e-money. Then the source of income is virtually untraceable for some types of e-money transaction using the anonymity features that available with most of the plastic cards available in the market.

Integration

In the stage of integration the owner need to make sure

that the accumulation of illegal wealth should not appear to be so; rather it should appear legitimate. There are a number of ways to achieve that, the traditional way involves false invoices of goods while the other way is to open a shell company that render a service such as internet service provider. Open a bank account for this shell company and you don't even need to render service but rather use this shell company to make it appear that the services are being provided in return of payment of funds that have passed through layering process. This way the wealth of the owner looks legitimate which can be said as the profit of the service provider.

The later technique to provide a legitimate appearance to the funds has a greater scope then the traditional technique. As the traditional technique would require to be of limited use as the services can only be rendered in a limited geographical location while the internet service provider can be bared from this limitation and hence the profits can be far more then the traditional technique. One more benefit to opt for the later technique is the reduced suspicions if the funds are transferred from foreign banks.

Payment Systems in Cyberspace

While searching materials for the dissertation report I found this article on the website of World Bank it seem an important topic to add in this dissertation. Internet facilitates cyber-based payments and because of the anonymity feature it facilitates laundering of funds.

Other features to attract money laundering are the lack of regulation and movement of funds across jurisdiction to jurisdiction without interception. It is not difficult to rack the suspicious transaction but the fact that the investigation lags behind the trace of a transaction while the perpetuator is long gone or has hidden there identities or moved from one jurisdiction to another. This World Bank article described four models of cyber based payment systems the system that is growing exponentially and that facilitates the money laundering capabilities is the non-bank and peer-to-peer model. The four models are as follow:

- The Merchant Issuer Model: This model deals with the case of same entity that is both the issuer and the seller. E.g. Oyster card used by the Transport of London.
- The Bank Issuer Model: This model deals with the case that the issuers are separate entities from the merchant. This model is connected with the traditional financial system. E.g. Debit card used by account holders of any bank.
- Non-Bank Issuer Model: This model deals with issuer giving e-cash in exchange of traditional funds and spending this e-cash at participating merchants. E.g. Virgin pre-paid card and Freedom Eagle Cash Card.
- Peer-to-Peer Model: This model deals with e-cash that is transferable between users. Point of contact with the transitional financial system is when the e-cash is issued and when it is redeemed. E.g. PayPal funds transfer services.

Positive Factors

The benefits of using cyber based payments system is the increase of confidentiality between the parties of an agreed transaction while at the same time chances of identity theft also decreases. As we have analyzed that there are multiple methods of payments this gives the option of user friendliness and more control. The presence of a central server ensures the smooth running of the transaction.

Negative Factor

The drawback of this system is the infrastructure required with a constant need to be updated. This is the main reason of the high cost for the users in order to maintain the effectiveness of the cyber based payment system. Another factor that is important to bear in mind is that the company maintaining the cyber based payment system gathers too many records about the users due to the architecture of the system.

Techniques used in Cyberlaundering

Business Areas that are affected by Cyberlaundering or

under the threat of Cyberlaundering are Commercial banks, Credit unions, Post office, International business, Stock brokers/ mutual fund practitioners, Insurance companies and the industries that are vulnerable to Cyberlaundering are Online Banks and Internet Gambling. Let's review the techniques used in Cyberlaundering.

ONLINE BANKING

Online banks are under the threat of Cyberlaundering due to the introduction of internet banking. Cyberlaundering threats the online banks in two ways. One way is that the account holder can be assisting the process of Cyberlaundering in the phenomena called "smurfing" (explained below). Secondly internet as a means of opening an account without verifying the identities of their customer imposes a greater threat which criminals exploits to hide their identity. A recent report about the rise in the online banking fraud illustrated the vulnerability of on-line banking. The fraudster uses key logging viruses to record passwords and credit card numbers. This virus finds it way to users of online banking generally by clicking a link in junk mails. This way criminal took over other peoples account which is termed as card ID theft. This is precisely how online banking will be used by cyber launderers.

Online banking is regulated by the policies of the banking regulations that require knowing your customer and their business. Banks are required to report any suspicious transaction to the law enforcement agencies. The criminals can easily avoid such restrictions by opening online accounts with so many unregulated electronic banking companies that use electronic payment systems to provide online banking like functionalities with the added layer of hidden transaction. With the introduction of prepaid cards the criminals can be utilizing the anonymity feature of the card to help the layering and integrity stage of Cyberlaundering. The peer to peer model of the payment system enables the criminal to move the electronic cash from one card to another card without even getting any attention from the law enforcement agencies and without the need to report such transaction by the unregulated online banks. The problem with the regulation of the online banks accounts is that the jurisdiction of the website where it is registered does not require following any international standard of regulation to run an online bank. A lot of the countries are still not cooperating with the international treaty to share intelligence and suspicious transaction records with the member countries to monitor and control Cyberlaundering.

The technological advancement in the encryption of programs that are used to communicate and transfer electronic funds providing the confidentiality, integrity and accessibility to hide the information from law enforcement agencies and are immune to current Anti –Money laundering efforts made by the federal government of U.S. the result is that the transaction is both unlinkable and untraceable.

The electronic banking over the borderless environment of the World Wide Web provides the internet breath of reach and with the cost effectiveness of the medium it is the number one choice for the criminals to manipulate the technology to further their aims.

Due to the wide difference in the regulation, policies, standards and opinion about the Cyberlaundering it is still an undecided issue that under which jurisdiction a criminal will be prosecuted if the online banking account is based in China and you live in Pakistan and your main banking relationships are in the India, Iran and Malaysia.

Criminals buy cheaply available fake identities from hackers to use these identities to open accounts with electronic banking websites to accomplish the placement and layers stages of Cyberlaundering. Criminals can host scam website to spoof the users of this website and use the details of the users to hide their identities while requesting a prepaid card or a smart card and deposit the criminal gains to these cards to accomplish the layering and integrating stages of cyber laundering.

One important aspect of the electronic banking is that they are not the regulated banks like the once we have in the corner of the street. They only provide flowing of funds from one user to another regardless of the geographic location of the other user.

Hypothetical Case

The question of how, who, where and what requires that the criminal stay ahead of policies in place by the authorities to prevent Cyberlaundering the criminal proceeds. For hiring the services of legitimate people for Cyberlaundering task online job posting sites such as gumtree dot com and many other job sites can be used to attract the attention of people generally willing to earn extra cash. These people are called army of smurf.

There are two categories of smurf first category is people with criminal intent and second category is people with criminal background.

Criminal Background

These people can be hired from pubs, betting venues, through illegitimate access to public record of fraudulent personalities, people from foreign background, people with little or no moral standards for others, people seeking luxuries life style without much effort, dodge professionals such as solicitor/ ex-bankers that knows the system well and can advise an alternative to avoid attention from the authorities, people with creative mindset but destructive intent such as the criminals on the street corners and many of them can be found in online chat room.

Criminal Intent

These people are basically needy people who are not satisfied with whatever they have for example students that have no access to public fund but require to do retail jobs overtime any time all the time to make extra cash. Another type of people is those who are lazy workers that want to earn more with less effort. For example people living on benefit system they do not want to work hard jobs like night shifts or weekend shift. Others that come in this category are young people on low income scale; women with an appetite of shopping unnecessarily are always in need of extra cash and anti government party workers with an aim to destabilize the political government.

How: Both categories can be hired by cash-in-hand arrangement or registered charity organization with hidden agendas for example "common purpose" which is famous charity organization for its hidden agenda.

Who: The details of each person can be managed by managers willing to assist the business transaction of small amounts through online banks (electronic payment service) on account of cyber-launderer these managers will maintains the details of people willing to participate in return of some extra cash.

Where: The manager will meet these individuals personally to evaluate the risk associated with trust and after achieving a certain level of trust they will give them the instruction about the plan of task. These instructions will be given by anonymous emails with a preplanned code that is known to the individual beforehand

What: As it is mentioned in section 2.3 the individuals will be provided with details of charged cards that are preloaded with electronic cash through an encrypted software file and that will be used to deposit the instructed amount in an apparently unconnected transaction of paying monthly fee of an internet service provider

Internet Gambling

While researching for the online casinos or gambling sites the Google search engine returned almost 18 million links which show the growing popularity of online betting sites. Internet Gambling or online casino helps the layering and placement of illegal funds and is therefore ideal technique for Cyberlaundering. The traditional casino accepts cash and issues chips for the user to play games. There is a loss of funds while playing the games in the casino but the gain is the fact that the refund will be accepted as legitimate instrument to be deposited in any bank and the source is known to be the casino. The affect of Cyberlaundering on the depository service providers are in a legal sense because of the need for putting up a system to deter the transfer of illegal funds and reporting suspicious transaction in compliance of The Money Laundering Regulations 1993.

In conjunction to traditional casinos, online casino sites are also regulated within U.S since the introduction of Internet Gambling Prohibition Act. But the phenomena of borderless environment of the internet impose a hurdle to such regulations and the growing popularity of online casinos proves the fact that this channel of electronic movement of fund from one location to another is still a ripe to be abused by the goons. In addition it is hard to obtain the records that may be needed as evidence for any prosecution due to the reason that the online casino website is based offshore.

Having a physical address over the internet does not really mean that some thing exist their. Due to huge financial support from the criminals these online casinos some times operates anonymously with out the need to have a physical address (IP-address) and to register this anonymity on the internet the owners of the online casino pays huge monthly and annual fees to the government of that country. Due to the non-existent background checks by the jurisdiction of these online casinos website it is difficult to regulate this market to restrict Cyberlaundering.

Another fact is the use of corruption to further the cause of Cyberlaundering by the owners of the online casinos by hiring agents that help assist to achieve Cyberlaundering by the process called smurfing. In this process the owner can give the agents some cash to credit to his account with the online casino to play a few games and then cash out the total money minus commission money from the casino as agreed while the owner can have the rest of the money declared as business profit.

One important fact associate with these phenomena is that there is no need to provide information regarding the relevant technologies only a hand full of experts can accomplish the task of Cyberlaundering on behalf of criminals. One such example is the drumming up business scenario in the scenario the criminal is the owner of an online casino and hires an army of fifty smurf that can create fifty or more email addresses each. The criminal has e-cash which he has aggregated through the process of placement using smartcards and sends this e-cash to the server maintaining the list of each email created by his army of smurf's. Without coincidence the army receives this e-cash and uses it to play games on the online casino. With this activity the owner gathers all the money back to his account in the form of winnings revenue from unrelated several different parties.

Hypothetical Case

In section (internet gambling) it is shown that how drumming up business scenario can be used to achieve Cyberlaundering. Let us further examine how the funds are actually transferred from a country which has strict laws in place to prevent money laundering to a country that has no laws to prevent money laundering.

The products like PayPal prepay cards does not require to have a bank account and thus can be acquired on false identities. These prepay cards can then be loaded with unlimited cash. The technological solutions are already there for the criminals to further their aims.

Who: Sam is living in UK and he is a drug dealer. The proceeds of crime are required to be converted into legitimate wealth. So Sam hires an agent Jameel in Pakistan who runs an online casino website that has a merchant account in a local bank called bank alfalah. Sam asks Jameel to arrange 50 fake account using forged or fake identities which can be acquired from a hacker on the internet through anonymous email. Jameel hires an army of smurf to perform this business transaction. The hiring of the interested candidate can be achieved as previously shown in the army of smurf section.

Where: Sam arranges 500 charged cards from different shops loads these charged cards with 100 pounds each using ATM machines, post offices and paypoint facilities. He then securely sends the detail of all the cards to Jameel through encrypted software Jameel decrypt the details and distributed the card details to each one of the smurf with a ratio of 10:1.

What: The smurf's then creates false accounts in Jameel's online casino and play games there losing all the funds minus commission to Jameel casino which is then deemed as winnings of the online casino for Jameel. Jameel sends this money in monthly installments thought bank transfer to Sam for rendering services of promoting the online casino Website in UK. In the same way Sam can have more then one agents working for him in different countries to further his drug business and networking with other criminals.Chapter Three: What's being done to prevent Cyberlaundering?

What are the government, financial institution and department of justice doing to prevent Cyberlaundering? And how to combat the techniques used to electronically launder funds is the main theme of this chapter.

Electronic banking that provide ripe to abuse by the launders can be confronted by developing an encryption key recovery program. In this program all the public keys that are used by the electronic banks will be shared as per the regulation that will be set by the federal government and the private key required to view the transaction will be decrypted by the program that will be developed in collaboration of information security equipment vendors and professional of encryption science.

Each transaction should be required to have a digital signature that should hold the identification of the user, location of the teller machine where it was used with the amount of transaction it holds and the date/time stamp. This will be the minimum requirement to be embedded in the smart cards and the teller machine daily reporting system to counter the fraudulent use of the technology and the possibility of Cyberlaundering attempts.

The Neural Computing and Artificial Intelligence such as PRISM® Money Laundering Detection (MLD) can be used to form a pattern of similar transactions to one account or many accounts to form a universal group number (UGN) of that smart card which is used on one of the teller machine or a group of teller machine to transfer funds. When doing the same transaction over the internet the IP-Address should be used to locate the place where the electronic banking account creation is taking place. This will be helpful when law enforcement agencies are investigating any case of Cyberlaundering.

To implement any such solution to try to combat Cyberlaundering one of the problems that arises is the regulation of Domain Naming System. It is a known fact the service providers provide hidden address websites facilities to users in return of a very high value packages. An audit must be required to highlight any such discrepancies from the ISP's.

Preventive Measures

Let us review the improvements in the government agencies by comparing the yearly advancement to address the issue of Cyberlaundering. Although there are many organizations working in partnership with the government I have just mentions few of them here.

Federal Bureau of Investigation

According to the National Money Laundering Strategy 2007 FBI has set nine goals to control the issue of money laundering these goals are as follow.

Safeguard the Banking System, Enhance Financial Transparency in Money Services Businesses, Stem the flow of illicit bulk cash out of the United States, Attack Trade-based Money Laundering at home and abroad, Promote Transparency in the ownership of Legal Entities, Examine Anti-Money Laundering Regulatory oversight and enforcement at Casinos, Implement and Enforce Anti-Money Laundering Regulations for the Insurance Industry, Support Global Anti-Money Laundering Capacity Building and Enforcement Efforts and Improve how we measure our Progress.

In relation to Cyberlaundering the FBI is determent to cater the issue by supporting cooperation with other countries to achieve a global solution to cybercrimes. At the same time it is enforcing federal laws to control and prevent this issue inside U.S. They have identified banks, depository institution and traditional casino to be actively assisting money laundering. Gaming industry is on an increase in U.S driven by native Indian tribes. FBI Cybercrime investigation department is active against the national and transnational organized criminal enterprises involved in cybercrime.

National Accountability Bureau

National Accountability Bureau of Pakistan launched a project in February 2002 to fight against corruption which is the biggest problem of Pakistan. They have also highlighted the problems that are in the way to achieve a corruption less society. Criminals exploit this weakness of corruption and bribe the officials to avoid or to keep a close eye to act and report on any such information regarding money laundering.

Due to the complex stages of the process of money laundering and lack of control over financial institution and government officials it is easy to export and hide the fruits of criminal proceeds. The advance technological infrastructure used by the criminals to further their cause and the lack of such advancement in the law enforcement agencies infrastructure and non availability of any private sector industry to address this phenomena show a huge lack of concern to monitor and control Cyberlaundering.

According to Financial action task force on money laundering it is expected that a sum of $70 to 100 billion may be stashed away in foreign banks by Pakistanis in 1996. Money-changers are unregulated as they are using the alternate banking remittance. The need to achieve the foreign exchange requirements government is dealing with these money-changers and has turned a blind eye towards them in relation to money laundering.

The government has facilitated money laundering and made inward foreign remittances, tax free through financial institutions and without any kind of scrutiny by the auditors. The government is in the process of tightening regulation of money changers and formulating an Anti Money laundering law in collaboration with the FATF, World Bank, State Bank Federal investigation Agency and Asia Pacific Group.

In recent Past it is observed that cyber crime has increased dramatically and to counter their activities it was essential that there must be an organization to monitor, track and apprehend all such criminals. National response centre for cyber crime (NR3C) a Department of Federal Investigation Agency is dealing with all matters related to cyber crimes under the law of Pakistan electronic crime ordinance 2007-2008. It also provides training to different organization regarding cyber threat that can affect their information resources.

Drug Enforcement Administration

Money laundering is based on criminal proceeds mostly from trafficking of drugs. The mission of the Drug Enforcement Administration (DEA) is to control and prevent the trade of illegal drugs in U.S. and to assist the department of justice to enforce the controlled substances laws. The DEA's primary responsibility is to investigate and prepare a case for prosecution of major violators and drug gangs.

DEA helps in the management the national drug intelligence program by cooperation with government and law enforcement officials to collect, analyze, and disseminate strategic and operational drug intelligence information.

The traditional way of transporting the money from the buyer to the seller is changing dramatically due to availability of advance technological solution such as e-payment system. But the fact that drugs can only be transported using the same transportation channels and hence therefore DEA's role is important to control the drug trafficking.

Serious Organised Crime Agency

SOCA deals with suspicious activity reports (SARs) under the money laundering legislation POCA 2002 (Appendix A) that are provided by the financial institutions operating in UK. Its active life was widely critical of the banking and financial services sector and the financial institution for not reporting the suspicious activity reports.

SOCA is based in United Kingdom and operates in cooperation of law enforcement and department of justice to prevent money laundering through the banking channel and also coordination with FBI to detect and prosecute cyber criminals to prevent frauds and scams.

Financial Institution Preventive Measures

Let us review the improvements in the financial sector and the agencies deal with them to prevent crime.

Financial Crimes Enforcement Network

The U.S. Department of the Treasury established the Financial Crimes Enforcement Network FinCEN in 1990. In 1994 FinCEN operation was broadened to include regulatory responsibilities for administering the Bank Secrecy Act (Appendix A). The mission of FinCEN is to enhance and safeguard financial systems from criminals.

The Strategic Plan of FinCEN for Fiscal Years 2008-2012 outlines three outcomes that financial systems must be resistant to abuse by money launderers, Detection and deterrence of money laundering and efficient management of BSA information.

Financial Action Task Force

Financial Action Task force was established by G-7 summit in 1989 held at Paris and the main reason for its formation was the increasing concern about the money laundering issue. It has provided a standard policy that constitute forty recommendations to combat money laundering in 2005 the FATF comprises of 31 members and by 2007 this number increased to 170. The main task of FATF is to set standards for anti money laundering, monitor compliance of these standards and studying methods of money laundering. It was detected in 2007 that the new payments system is a growing method to accomplish money laundering. The use of prepaid cards, Internet payment systems, mobile payments, and digital precious metal currency show that the vulnerability of Cyberlaundering exists.

After reviewing the forty recommendations developed by FATF the central idea can be described as that the countries should criminalize money laundering and apply serious penalty to the criminals, that if the crime is intended by the criminal then the charges should be severe (criminal court equivalent) and if the intend is not there then the charges should be less sever (civil court equivalent), countries should adopt procedures to confiscate the criminal proceeds or property, the financial institution should not maintain anonymous account and know their customers by requiring KYC (know your customer) forms as mandatory, to be cautious about the politically exposed persons, to develop policy and procedure to address risk in non face to face business, and monitor transaction that have no apparent lawful and economic purpose.

Preventive Measures

Let us review the improvements that have taken place to address the Cyberlaundering issue by the Department of justice.

Legislation

The laws that can be used to prevent Cyberlaundering are Computer Misuse Act of 1990 (Appendix A) and EC Directives (Appendix A). As it is a known fact that for Online Banking or to play a game in online casino user is required to have a computer or an electronic device (3G Mobile) to make a transaction to assist the movement of funds (in this case illegal proceeds of crime) from one location to an other. This type of transaction in general goes through a server that is in between the sender and receiver of electronic cash. By using location of the server and the EC Directives that enable the government authorities to monitor sensitive information required to monitor suspicious activities can assist law enforcement authorities in investigation of a Cyberlaundering case.

Although the EC Directives excludes the information society services of gaming, betting and lotteries. The law that can be used to prevent Cyberlaundering through traditional Casinos and financial institutions is Bank Secrecy Act of 1970. This requires the financial institution to keep a record for five years of all the transaction and report any suspicious activity.

The UK Payments Association has reported that internet

card payments reached £34 billion in 2007. While the spending on charge cards was £133.2 billion. The electronic payment system operates with few restrictions and their value is limitless. Online casino lends itself to Cyberlaundering because these is no requirement to provide identity and authenticate parties; there is little or no record keeping or audit trailing; encryption services mean criminals can lock out law enforcement agencies and transactions can be conducted globally, therefore falling outside existing regulatory control.

According to KPMG's Fraud Barometer over £1.1 billion of fraud came to UK courts in 2008. This was the second highest level in 21 years. (KPMG, February 2009). The Chairman of the Cybercrime Working Party of the Fraud Advisory Panel Cyberlaundering is currently (2006) estimated to be running at $50 billion each year.

The Laws that are related to Cyberlaundering

After searching articles, books and internet sites the following list of laws that are related to Cyberlaundering in different ways is given these laws are defined in a concise way in the appendix A.

Federal Reserve Act of 1913, Bank Secrecy Act of 1970, The Solicitors Act 1974, The Privacy Act of 1974, Foreign Corrupt Practices Act 1977, The Right to Financial Privacy Act of 1982, Money Laundering Control Act of 1986, The Electronic Communications Privacy Act of 1986, Anti-Drug Abuse Act of 1988, The Crime Control Act of 1990, The FDIC Improvement Act of 1991, Criminal Justice Act of 1993, The Drug Trafficking Act of 1994, Human rights act 1998, Data protection act 1998, Proceeds of Crime Money Laundering Act of 2000, U.S.A. PATRIOT Act 2001, Sarbanes-Oxley Act 2002, Crime Act 2002, Serious Organised crime and Police Act 2005 etc.

The Money Laundering Offences

There are now five basic money laundering offences that in my view can be used in parallel to Cyberlaundering offenses as well.

- Assisting another to retain the benefit of crime;

- The offender can only be charged if it is proved that the intent to assist the criminal was there and the knowledge that the proceeds are directly or indirectly gains of an illegal act is there. The penalty for commission of an offence can range from six months to 14 years and a fine that is not exceeding the statutory maximum or both. This can also be used for Cyberlaundering offences.
- Acquiring, possession and use of criminal proceeds;
- The offender can be charged only if reasonable grounds are established that acquisition or possession of criminal proceeds has been acquired at less than full value. The penalty is same as assisting in retaining the benefit of criminal proceeds. With regards to Cyberlaundering technique that I have presented in second chapter the criminal can be using a charged card or making an internet payment system using funds that are criminal proceeds.
- Concealing or transferring,proceeds to avoid prosecution or a confiscation order (also called Own Funds money laundering).
- Disguising or transferring proceeds of crime for the purpose of avoiding prosecution. Disguising includes removing its nature, source, location, disposition, movement or ownership or any rights with respect to it. The use of encryption to hide the transaction of criminal proceeds can be an offence and the penalty is same as other offence mentioned above.
- Failure to disclose knowledge or suspicion of money laundering;
- The professional such as solicitors and banking experts that come to know any such suspicious transaction and do not report it then this will not get them any waiver of professional privilege. The penalty for this offence ranges from six month to five year and fine not exceeding the statutory maximum or both.
- Tipping off.

- If a criminal is tipped off that he is being investigated then the procedure of reporting a suspicious transaction is of no use. The penalty for this offence is the same as failure to disclose offence.

How Can We Prevent It?

In general all the crime are gain motivated and to have a luxuries life with less efforts. The problem associated with the gain is the identification of the source and to avoid any such problem criminals have to figure out a way to distance them from the crime scene. Hence there is a need to launder the criminal proceeds to reappear in their accounts as legitimate wealth earned from the revenue of there shell company.

The most popular source of illicit gains comes from the drugs trafficking and it was the initial catalyst for coordinated international efforts to prevent money laundering. This industry is a highly cash based and to avoid the burden of handling cash it is required to use the financial institutions and in particular online payment systems.

There are certain Choke points that (FATF) has identified in the money laundering process that is unavoidable by the criminals and is vulnerable to detection. The choke points identified are entry of cash into the financial institution (placement), transfers to and from the financial institution (layering) and cross-border flows of cash (integration).

The UK's system of reporting suspicious transactions through Suspicious Activity Report is an effective policy to deter Money laundering in the traditional financial institution However, cross-border flows of cash is one of the areas mentioned above where the launderer is vulnerable to detection. The police and customs service in UK are empowered by the legislation to seize cash they believe could be the proceeds of drug trafficking. The record keeping of transaction by financial organizations provides a useful audit trail and gives useful information on people and organizations involved in laundering of funds. Cyberlaundering is still an evolving issue and transfer of electronic cash is an unsolved mystery therefore government of Australia, Canada, UK, EU and U.S have implemented a likewise policy to log and monitor activity of internet users for five years before an internet service provider can use a clearing utility to clear the servers and loss the information that can assist to find the source of an electronic payment sender.

MONEY LAUNDERING

Strictly speaking, money laundering is the age-old process of disguising the illegal origin and criminal nature of funds (obtained in sanctions-busting arms sales, smuggling, trafficking in humans, organized crime, drug trafficking, prostitution rings, embezzlement, insider trading, bribery, and computer fraud) by moving them untraceably and investing them in legitimate businesses, securities, or bank deposits. But this narrow definition masks the fact that the bulk of money laundered is the result of tax evasion, tax avoidance, and outright tax fraud, such as the "VAT carousel scheme" in the EU (moving goods among businesses in various jurisdictions to capitalize on differences in VAT rates). Tax-related laundering nets between 10-20 billion US dollars annually from France and Russia alone. The confluence of criminal and tax averse funds in money laundering networks serves to obscure the sources of both.

THE SCALE OF THE PROBLEM

According to a 1996 IMF estimate, money laundered annually amounts to 2-5% of world GDP (between 800 billion and 2 trillion US dollars in today's terms). The lower figure is considerably larger than an average European economy, such as Spain's.

The System

It is important to realize that money laundering takes place within the banking system. Big amounts of cash are spread among numerous accounts (sometimes in free economic zones, financial off shore centers, and tax havens), converted to bearer financial instruments (money orders, bonds), or placed with trusts and charities. The money is then transferred to other locations, sometimes as bogus payments for "goods and services" against fake or inflated invoices issued by holding companies owned by lawyers or accountants on behalf of unnamed beneficiaries. The transferred funds are re-assembled in their destination and often "shipped" back to the point of origin under a new identity. The laundered funds are then invested in the legitimate economy. It is a simple procedure-yet an effective one. It results in either no paper trail-or too much of it. The accounts are invariably liquidated and all traces erased.

Why is It a Problem?

Criminal and tax evading funds are idle and non-productive. Their injection, however surreptitiously, into the economy transforms them into a productive (and cheap) source of capital. Why is this negative?

Because it corrupts government officials, banks and their officers, contaminates legal sectors of the economy, crowds out legitimate and foreign capital, makes money supply unpredictable and uncontrollable, and increases cross-border capital movements, thereby enhancing the volatility of exchange rates.

A multilateral, co-ordinated, effort (exchange of information, uniform laws, extra-territorial legal powers) is required to counter the international dimensions of money laundering. Many countries opt in because money laundering has also become a domestic political and economic concern. The United Nations, the Bank for International Settlements, the OECD's FATF (Financial Action Task Force), the EU, the Council of Europe, the Organisation of American States, all published anti-money laundering standards. Regional groupings were formed (or are being established) in the Caribbean, Asia, Europe, southern Africa, western Africa, and Latin America.

MONEY LAUNDERING IN THE WAKE OF THE SEPTEMBER 11 ATTACKS

Regulation

The least important trend is the tightening of financial regulations and the establishment or enhancement of compulsory (as opposed to industry or voluntary) regulatory and enforcement agencies.

New legislation in the US which amounts to extending the powers of the CIA domestically and of the DOJ extra-territorially, was rather xenophobically described by a DOJ official, Michael Chertoff, as intended to "make sure the American banking system does not become a haven for foreign corrupt leaders or other kinds of foreign organized criminals."

Privacy and bank secrecy laws have been watered down. Collaboration with off shore "shell" banks has been banned. Business with clients of correspondent banks was curtailed. Banks were effectively transformed into law enforcement agencies, responsible to verify both the identities of their (foreign) clients and the source and origin of their funds. Cash transactions were partly criminalized. And the securities and currency trading industry, insurance companies, and money transfer services are subjected to growing scrutiny as a conduit for "dirty cash".

Still, such legislation is highly ineffective. The American Bankers' Association puts the cost of compliance with the laxer anti-money-laundering laws in force in 1998 at 10 billion US dollars-or more than 10 million US dollars per obtained conviction. Even when the system does work, critical alerts drown in the torrent of reports mandated by the regulations. One bank actually reported a suspicious transaction in the account of one of the September 11 hijackers-only to be ignored.

The Treasury Department established Operation Green Quest, an investigative team charged with monitoring charities, NGO's, credit card fraud, cash smuggling, counterfeiting, and the Hawala networks. This is not without precedent. Previous teams tackled drug money, the biggest money laundering venue ever, BCCI (Bank of Credit and Commerce International), and... Al Capone. The more veteran, New-York based, El-Dorado anti money laundering Task Force (established in 1992) will lend a hand and share information.

More than 150 countries promised to co-operate with the US in its fight against the financing of terrorism-81 of which (including the Bahamas, Argentina, Kuwait, Indonesia, Pakistan, Switzerland, and the EU) actually froze assets of suspicious individuals, suspected charities, and dubious firms, or passed new anti money laundering laws and stricter regulations (the Philippines, the UK, Germany).

A EU directive now forces lawyers to disclose incriminating information about their clients' money laundering activities. Pakistan initiated a "loyalty scheme", awarding expatriates who prefer official bank channels to the much maligned (but cheaper and more efficient) Hawala, with extra baggage allowance and special treatment in airports. The magnitude of this international collaboration is unprecedented. But this burst of solidarity may yet fade. China, for instance, refuses to chime in. As a result, the statement issued by APEC in November 2001 on measures to stem the finances of terrorism was lukewarm at best. And, protestations of close collaboration to the contrary, Saudi Arabia has done nothing to combat money laundering "Islamic charities" (of which it is proud) on its territory. Still, a universal code is emerging, based on the work of the OECD's FATF (Financial Action Task Force) since 1989 (its famous "40 recommendations") and on the relevant UN conventions. All countries are expected by the West, on pain of possible sanctions, to adopt a uniform legal platform (including reporting on suspicious transactions and freezing assets) and to apply it to all types of financial intermediaries, not only to banks. This is likely to result in...

The Decline of off Shore Financial Centres and Tax Havens

By far the most important outcome of this new-fangled juridical homogeneity is the acceleration of the decline of off shore financial and banking centres and tax havens. The distinction between off-shore and on-shore will vanish. Of the FATF's "name and shame" blacklist of 19 "black holes" (poorly regulated territories, including Israel, Indonesia, and Russia)- 11 have substantially revamped their banking laws and financial regulators.

Coupled with the tightening of US, UK, and EU laws and the wider interpretation of money laundering to include political corruption, bribery, and embezzlement-this would make life a lot more difficult for venal politicians and major tax evaders. The likes of Sani Abacha (late President of Nigeria), Ferdinand Marcos (late President of the Philippines), Vladimiro Montesinos (former, now standing trial, chief of the intelligence services of Peru), or Raul Salinas (the brother of Mexico's President)-would have found it impossible to loot their countries to the same disgraceful extent in today's financial environment. And Osama bin Laden would not have been able to wire funds to US accounts from the Sudanese Al Shamal Bank, the "correspondent" of 33 American banks.

Quo Vadis, Money Laundering?

Crime is resilient and fast adapting to new realities. Organized crime is in the process of establishing an alternative banking system, only tangentially connected to the West's, in the fringes, and by proxy. This is done by purchasing defunct banks or banking licences in territories with lax regulation, cash economies, corrupt politicians, no tax collection, but reasonable infrastructure.

The countries of Eastern Europe-Yugoslavia (Montenegro and Serbia), Macedonia, Ukraine, Moldova, Belarus, Albania, to mention a few-are natural targets. In some cases, organized crime is so all-pervasive and local politicians so corrupt that the distinction between criminal and politician is spurious.

Gradually, money laundering rings move their operations to these new, accommodating territories. The laundered funds are used to purchase assets in intentionally botched privatizations, real estate, existing businesses, and to finance trading operations. The wasteland that is Eastern Europe craves private capital and no questions are asked by investor and recipient alike. The next frontier is cyberspace. Internet banking, Internet gambling, day trading, foreign exchange cyber transactions, e-cash, e-commerce, fictitious invoicing of the launderer's genuine credit cards-hold the promise of the future. Impossible to track and monitor, ex-territorial, totally digital, amenable to identity theft and fake identities-this is the ideal vehicle for money launderers. This nascent platform is way too small to accommodate the enormous amounts of cash laundered daily-but in ten years time, it may. The problem is likely to be exacerbated by the introduction of smart cards, electronic purses, and payment-enabled mobile phones.

In its "Report on Money Laundering Typologies" (February 2001) the FATF was able to document concrete and suspected abuses of online banking, Internet casinos, and web-based financial services. It is difficult to identify a customer and to get to know it in cyberspace, was the alarming conclusion. It is equally complicated to establish jurisdiction.

Many capable professionals-stockbrokers, lawyers, accountants, traders, insurance brokers, real estate agents, sellers of high value items such as gold, diamonds, and art-are employed or co-opted by money laundering operations. Money launderers are likely to make increased use of global, around the clock, trading in foreign currencies and derivatives. These provide instantaneous transfer of funds and no audit trail.

The underlying securities involved are susceptible to market manipulation and fraud. Complex insurance policies (with the "wrong" beneficiaries), and the securitization of receivables, leasing contracts, mortgages, and low grade bonds are already used in money laundering schemes. In general, money laundering goes well with risk arbitraging financial instruments.

Trust-based, globe-spanning, money transfer systems based on authentication codes and generations of commercial relationships cemented in honour and blood-are another wave of the future.

The Hawala and Chinese networks in Asia, the Black Market Peso Exchange (BMPE) in Latin America, other evolving courier systems in Eastern Europe (mainly in Russia, Ukraine, and Albania) and in Western Europe (mainly in France and Spain).

In conjunction with encrypted e-mail and web anonymizers, these networks are virtually impenetrable. As emigration increases, diasporas established, and transport and telecommunications become ubiquitous, "ethnic banking" along the tradition of the Lombards and the Jews in medieval Europe may become the the preferred venue of money laundering. September 11 may have retarded world civilization in more than one way.

HAWALA, OR THE BANK THAT NEVER WAS

In the wake of the September 11 terrorist attacks on the USA, attention was drawn to the age-old, secretive, and globe-spanning banking system developed in Asia and known as "Hawala" (to change, in Arabic). It is based on a short term, discountable, negotiable, promissory note (or bill of exchange) called "Hundi". While not limited to Moslems, it has come to be identified with "Islamic Banking".

Islamic Law (Sharia'a) regulates commerce and finance in the Fiqh Al Mua'malat, (transactions amongst people). Modern Islamic banks are overseen by the Shari'a Supervisory Board of Islamic Banks and Institutions ("The Shari'a Committee").

The Shi'a "Islamic Laws according to the Fatawa of Ayatullah al Uzama Syed Ali al-Husaini Seestani" has this to say about Hawala banking:

"2298. If a debtor directs his creditor to collect his debt from the third person, and the creditor accepts the arrangement, the third person will, on completion of all the conditions to be explained later, become the debtor. Thereafter, the creditor cannot demand his debt from the first debtor."

The prophet Muhammad (a cross border trader of goods and commodities by profession) encouraged the free movement of goods and the development of markets. Numerous Moslem scholars railed against hoarding and harmful speculation (market cornering and manipulation known as "Gharar"). Moslems were the first to use promissory notes and assignment, or transfer of debts via bills of exchange ("Hawala"). Among modern banking instruments, only floating and, therefore, uncertain, interest payments ("Riba" and "Jahala"), futures contracts, and forfeiting are frowned upon. But agile Moslem traders easily and often circumvent these religious restrictions by creating "synthetic Murabaha (contracts)" identical to Western forward and futures contracts. Actually, the only allowed transfer or trading of debts (as distinct from the underlying commodities or goods) is under the Hawala.

"Hawala" consists of transferring money (usually across borders and in order to avoid taxes or the need to bribe officials) without physical or electronic transfer of funds. Money changers ("Hawaladar") receive cash in one country, no questions asked. Correspondent hawaladars in another country dispense an identical amount (minus minimal fees and commissions) to a recipient or, less often, to a bank account. E-mail, or letter ("Hundi") carrying couriers are used to convey the necessary information (the amount of money, the date it has to be paid on) between Hawaladars. The sender provides the recipient with code words (or numbers, for instance the serial numbers of currency notes), a digital encrypted message, or agreed signals (like handshakes), to be used to retrieve the money. Big Hawaladars use a chain of middlemen in cities around the globe.

But most Hawaladars are small businesses. Their Hawala activity is a sideline or moonlighting operation. "Chits" (verbal agreements) substitute for certain written records. In bigger operations there are human "memorizers" who serve as arbiters in case of dispute. The Hawala system requires unbounded trust. Hawaladars are often members of the same family, village, clan, or ethnic group. It is a system older than the West. The ancient Chinese had their own "Hawala"-"fei qian" (or "flying money"). Arab traders used it to avoid being robbed on the Silk Road. Cheating is punished by effective ex-communication and "loss of honour"-the equivalent of an economic death sentence. Physical violence is rarer but not unheard of. Violence sometimes also erupts between money recipients and robbers who are after the huge quantities of physical cash sloshing about the system. But these, too, are rare events, as rare as bank robberies. One result of this effective social regulation is that commodity traders in Asia shift hundreds of millions of US dollars per trade based solely on trust and the verbal commitment of their counterparts.

Hawala arrangements are used to avoid customs duties, consumption taxes, and other trade-related levies. Suppliers provide importers with lower prices on their invoices, and get paid the difference via Hawala. Legitimate transactions and tax evasion constitute the bulk of Hawala operations. Modern Hawala networks emerged in the 1960's and 1970's to circumvent official bans on gold imports in Southeast Asia and to facilitate the transfer of hard earned wages of expatriates to their families ("home remittances") and their conversion at rates more favourable (often double) than the government's. Hawala provides a cheap (it costs c. 1% of the amount transferred), efficient, and frictionless alternative to morbid and corrupt domestic financial institutions. It is Western Union without the hi-tech gear and the exorbitant transfer fees.

Unfortunately, these networks have been hijacked and compromised by drug traffickers (mainly in Afganistan and Pakistan), corrupt officials, secret services, money launderers, organized crime, and terrorists. Pakistani Hawala networks alone move up to 5 billion US dollars annually according to estimates by Pakistan's Minister of Finance, Shaukut Aziz. In 1999, Institutional Investor Magazine identified 1100 money brokers in Pakistan and transactions that ran as high as 10 million US dollars apiece. As opposed to stereotypes, most Hawala networks are not controlled by Arabs, but by Indian and Pakistani expatriates and immigrants in the Gulf. The Hawala network in India has been brutally and ruthlessly demolished by Indira Ghandi (during the emergency regime imposed in 1975), but Indian nationals still play a big part in international Hawala networks. Similar networks in Sri Lanka, the Philippines, and Bangladesh have also been eradicated.

The OECD's Financial Action Task Force (FATF) says that:

"Hawala remains a significant method for large numbers of businesses of all sizes and individuals to repatriate funds and purchase gold.... It is favoured because it usually costs less than moving funds through the banking system, it operates 24 hours per day and every day of the year, it is virtually completely reliable, and there is minimal paperwork required."

Hawala networks closely feed into Islamic banks throughout the world and to commodity trading in South Asia. There are more than 200 Islamic banks in the USA alone and many thousands in Europe, North and South Africa, Saudi Arabia, the Gulf states (especially in the free zone of Dubai and in Bahrain), Pakistan, Malaysia, Indonesia, and other South East Asian countries. By the end of 1998, the overt liabilities of these financial institutions amounted to 148 billion US dollars. They dabbled in equipment leasing, real estate leasing and development, corporate equity, and trade/structured trade and commodities financing (usually in consortia called "Mudaraba").

While previously confined to the Arab peninsula and to south and east Asia, this mode of traditional banking became truly international in the 1970's, following the unprecedented flow of wealth to many Moslem nations due to the oil shocks and the emergence of the Asian tigers. Islamic banks joined forces with corporations, multinationals, and banks in the West to finance oil exploration and drilling, mining, and agribusiness. Many leading law firms in the West (such as Norton Rose, Freshfields, Clyde and Co. and Clifford Chance) have "Islamic Finance" teams which are familiar with Islam-compatible commercial contracts.

HAWALA AND TERRORISM

Recent anti-terrorist legislation in the US and the UK allows government agencies to regularly supervise and inspect businesses that are suspected of being a front for the "Hawala" banking system, makes it a crime to smuggle more than $10,000 in cash across USA borders, and empowers the Treasury secretary (and its Financial Crimes Enforcement Network-FinCEN) to tighten record-keeping and reporting rules for banks and financial institutions based in the USA. A new inter-agency Foreign Terrorist Asset Tracking Centre (FTAT) was set up. A 1993 moribund proposed law requiring US-based Halawadar to register and to report suspicious transactions may be revived. These relatively radical measures reflect the belief that the al-Qaida network of Osama bin Laden uses the Hawala system to raise and move funds across national borders. A Hawaladar in Pakistan (Dihab Shill) was identified as the financier in the attacks on the American embassies in Kenya and Tanzania in 1998. But the USA is not the only country to face terrorism financed by Hawala networks.

In mid-2001, the Delhi police, the Indian government's Enforcement Directorate (ED), and the Military Intelligence (MI) arrested six Jammu Kashmir Islamic Front (JKIF) terrorists. The arrests led to the exposure of an enormous web of Hawala institutions in Delhi, aided and abetted, some say, by the ISI (Inter Services Intelligence, Pakistan's security services). The Hawala network was used to funnel money to terrorist groups in the disputed Kashmir Valley.

Luckily, the common perception that Hawala financing is paperless is wrong. The transfer of information regarding the funds often leaves digital (though heavily encrypted) trails. Couriers and "contract memorizers", gold dealers, commodity merchants, transporters, and moneylenders can be apprehended and interrogated. Written, physical, letters are still the favourite mode of communication among small and medium Hawaladars, who also invariably resort to extremely detailed single entry bookkeeping.

And the sudden appearance and disappearance of funds in bank accounts still have to be explained. Moreover, the sheer scale of the amounts involved entails the collaboration of off shore banks and more established financial institutions in the West. Such flows of funds affect the local money markets in Asia and are instantaneously reflected in interest rates charged to frequent borrowers, such as wholesalers. Spending and consumption patterns change discernibly after such influxes. Most of the money ends up in prime world banks behind flimsy business facades. Hackers in Germany claimed (without providing proof) to have infiltrated Hawala-related bank accounts.

The problem is that banks and financial institutions-and not only in dodgy offshore havens ("black holes" in the lingo)-clam up and refuse to divulge information about their clients. Banking is largely a matter of fragile trust between bank and customer and tight secrecy. Bankers are reluctant to undermine either. Banks use mainframe computers which can rarely be hacked through cyberspace and can be compromised only physically in close co-operation with insiders. The shadier the bank-the more formidable its digital defenses. The use of numbered accounts (outlawed in Austria, for instance, only recently) and pseudonyms (still possible in Lichtenstein) complicates matters. Bin Laden's accounts are unlikely to bear his name. He has collaborators. Hawala networks are often used to launder money, or to evade taxes. Even when employed for legitimate purposes, to diversify the risk involved in the transfer of large sums, Hawaladars apply techniques borrowed from money laundering. Deposits are fragmented and wired to hundreds of banks the world over ("starburst"). Sometimes, the money ends up in the account of origin ("boomerang").

Hence the focus on payment clearing and settlement systems. Most countries have only one such system, the repository of data regarding all banking (and most non-banking) transactions in the country. Yet, even this is a partial solution. Most national systems maintain records for 6-12 months, private settlement and clearing systems for even less.

Yet, the crux of the problem is not the Hawala or the Hawaladars. The corrupt and inept governments of Asia are to blame for not regulating their banking systems, for over-regulating everything else, for not fostering competition, for throwing public money at bad debts and at worse borrowers, for over-taxing, for robbing people of their life savings through capital controls, for tearing at the delicate fabric of trust between customer and bank (Pakistan, for instance, froze all foreign exchange accounts two years ago). Perhaps if Asia had reasonably expedient, reasonably priced, reasonably regulated, user-friendly banks-Osama bin Laden would have found it impossible to finance his mischief so invisibly.

CASE STUDIES IN MONEY LAUNDERING

In recent years there have been several very successful cases in which law enforcement has uncovered money laundering schemes or in some cases facilitated money laundering for drug traffickers as a means of obtaining information that was subsequently used to disrupt the organization. A closer but brief look at these cases highlights the ingenuity with which money laundering schemes are devised-as well as the weaknesses of some of these schemes.

"Operation Dinero"

Operation Dinero was a joint law enforcement operation involving the Drug Enforcement Administration, the Internal Revenue Service, the Immigration and Naturalization Service and the Federal Bureau of Investigation as well law enforcement agencies in Italy, Spain, Canada and Britain. Directed against the Cali Cartel the operation resulted in 88 arrests, the seizure of about 9 tons of cocaine and over $50 million in cash and property.

The key to success was the DEA establishment and operation of an offshore bank in Anguilla that appeared willing to launder money for drug traffickers. Towards the end of 1994, the bank, which had increasingly been used by traffickers, was hired to sell a Reynolds, a Rubens and a Picasso for members of the Cali group-a development that revealed how drug trafficking organizations sometimes use acquisitions of art and antiques as a means of money laundering. In the event, the paintings were seized. Even more significant, however, the operation revealed a money laundering network that included Mexico, Southern California and Colombia; a scheme involving money movements between New York, Canada and Colombia; links between the Cali Cartel and the Pasquale Locatelli organization which was active in France, Romania, Spain, Greece, Italy and Canada; and the activities of the Severa organization in Italy which laundered money using three supermarkets and a car rental business.

"La Mina"

The "La Mina" operation involved 2 jewelry companies, Andonian Brothers and Ropex Corp. which successfully laundered hundreds of millions of dollars ostensibly obtained from gold and jewelry businesses in New York, Los Angeles and Houston. The cash was deposited in a variety of accounts and then wired to Latin America "under the guise of legitimate business transactions". The cover for the operation was provided by fictitious jewelry sales and also by what were presented as a series of gold purchases from Uruguay. In some instances lead bars painted gold were actually imported; in others the transactions were simply on paper.

The extent of the money laundering scheme was revealed in Department of Commerce statistics: "in 1985 the US Commerce Department had no records of any Uruguayan gold trade with the United States.... Yet by 1988, US Commerce department statistics indicted that Uruguay had become the second largest exporter of gold to the United States"-even though the country had no operating gold reserves. Although the scheme relied on the cover of apparently legitimate business, the Well Fargo Bank in Los Angeles reported to the FBI that the Andonian Brothers were making cash deposits on a much larger scale than most jwelry businesses. Around the same time an air shipment from New York to Ropex Corp in Los Angeles described as "gold scrap" broke open to reveal large bundles of cash. This too was reported to the authorities. The scheme, which was undertaken, for the Medellin Cartel, involved Banco de Occidente (which subsequently forfeited $5 Million) and extended to both Canada and Switzerland.

"Bausch and Lomb"

In October 1995 Business Week provided details of what appeared to be a money laundering scheme that had succeeded through the tacit acceptance by some officials at Bausch and Lomb, the large pharmaceutical company, of dubious payment practices. In the mid-1980s Bausch and Lomb established Lamex, a new Latin American export unit near the Miami airport. Reportedly, the division grew rapidly and by 1990 had sales of nearly $25 million. Yet some of the income that was generated was of suspicious origin.

"Latin American and Caribbean customers would arrive with up to $50,000 in cash to pay for Ray-Ban sunglasses; and in 1990 Lamex reportedly received $5.6 million-23% of its total sales-in cash, cash equivalents, and third-party checks. Although some questions were raised about the form of payments, "an urgency to meet the numbers" overrode all other considerations. This is not atypical. When money is flowing, expediency often overcomes both prudence and principle.

"The Bicycle Club"

Another example of an elaborate money laundering scheme involved a marijuana trafficker called Ben Kramer who transferred his drug proceeds through a bank in Liechtenstein to another offshore institution and eventually to something called the LCP Partnership (LCP) which, along with another California business established and ran a gambling club known as the Bicycle Club. This club was used for laundering and was eventually seized by the authorities, although not before over 10 million dollars of marijuana trafficking proceeds had been laundered through LCP.

THE SPENCE MONEY LAUNDERING NETWORK IN NEW YORK

A fascinating example of money laundering was uncovered in New York in 1994. It involved a network of 24 people including the honorary consul-general for Bulgaria, a New York city police officer, 2 lawyers, a stockbroker, an assistant bank manager in Citibank, 2 rabbis, a firefighter and 2 bankers in Zurich.

A law firm provided the overall guidance for the laundering effort while both a trucking business and a beer distributorship were used as cover. The Bulgarian diplomat, the firefighter and the rabbi acted as couriers picking up drug trafficking proceeds in hotel rooms and parking lots., while money was also transported by Federal Express to a New York trucking business.

The two lawyers subsequently placed the money into bank accounts with the assistance of a Citibank assistant manager. The money was then wired to banks in Europe including a private bank in Switzerland, at which two bankers ensured that it was remitted to accounts designated by drug traffickers. During 1993 and 1994 a sum of between $70M and $100M was laundered by the group.

In all these cases, the laundering process was uncovered, but not before significant amounts of money had been washed or put beyond the reach of United States law enforcement. Moreover, even though these schemes were ultimately unsuccessful, at least one or two of them displayed considerable ingenuity. They also reveal the kinds of techniques that are typically used to launder money.

Tchniques and Trends

Drug trafficking and other criminal organizations have developed a series of highly specialized techniques and methods designed to remove the taint from the money and to place it out of the reach of law enforcement. They are able to exploit the existence of a global financial system with multiple points of entry, the capacity for extremely rapid transmission of funds, major disparities among nations in the degree to which banking and other financial transactions are monitored and controlled, the susceptibility of members of the licit financial world to bribery and corruption, the existence in many countries of parallel or informal economies that are outside government control, and the vast mass of financial transactions that hampers discrimination and, therefore, the prevention and control of illicit activities.

The standard view of money laundering is that it involves three distinct stages: placement (putting it in the system), layering (actions to obscure the paper trail), and integration (where illicit money is mingled with licit finance). There is also broad agreement that, in some countries at least, the placement stage is the most risky for the criminal or money launderer. In the layering stage, an effort is made to ensure that the laundered money is difficult to differentiate from licit funds. This is done by exploiting the "frequency, volume or complexity" of transactions.

Layering is also accomplished by ensuring that the transactions cross several national borders. Following the money becomes much more difficult for law enforcement agencies when the money has moved beyond their jurisdiction. Indeed, what might be termed trans-jurisdictional money movement is a central component of most money laundering schemes. It ensures that illicit money is impossible to differentiate from money obtained through legitimate means, and that integration can, therefore, be achieved.

This framework is useful for understanding the dynamics of many money laundering schemes. Yet it should not be regarded as immutable. In many cases, for example, money has already been layered and even integrated before it goes into the financial system-it is already disguised as licit proceeds of legitimate business. This can be done through import-export schemes in which there is an over-invoicing for the goods, cash-based businesses such as restaurants, casinos, and card clubs. In the La Mina case discussed above, there was a major and initially very successful effort to provide what appeared to be a legitimate source for the money. To the extent that such efforts are successful then there is a short circuiting of what are widely regarded as the standard money laundering stages.

Another reason the three stage conceptualization of money laundering is not entirely adequate stems from the fact that some illicit money does not enter the formal banking system but is instead transmitted through underground or alternative banking systems such as the "hawala" in India and Pakistan. These "parallel banking systems are based on family or gang alliances and reinforced with an unspoken covenant of retributive violence". They work without a paper trail.

As Malhotra notes, a "Hawala banker issues neither written receipt for the sum received nor an order for payment of rupees in India. What he does make is a firm verbal commitment to the seller of dollars to make an equivalent rupee payment, at the agreed rate of exchange, through his agent in India; he then sends a coded message to his partner containing the designated recipient's name and the time, date, and address for the payment". For such services the dealer can charge up to 15 per cent of the sum exchanged.

In spite of the significant commission charges the hawala system handles large amounts of money. In 1992, for example, British authorities arrested a London-based Pakistani who had moved nearly $13 million a week, while in 1993 police in Delhi arrested a hawala banker who, over a two year period, had reportedly handled $1.45 billion in payments for his clients in Dubai. One of the reasons that these schemes work so effectively is that they are protected through bribery and corruption. As one hawala banker claimed: "It is very easy to purchase protection by bribing police, politicians, local governments".

The Chinese have a similar system that is known as "fie chien" or flying money. This is based on trust, family ties, local social structures, and the threat of ostracism for any breach of good faith. The result is that "a banker who breaks a trust effectively commits economic suicide". This system, which is also sometimes described as the chit system, generally involves depositing money in one country in exchange for a "chit" or a "chop" (ie. a seal) and the remittance of this money in another country on presentation of the chit. It is fast and convenient, does not involve the transportation of bulk cash, leaves little trail for investigators, has the virtue of anonymity, and the costs, apart from the commission to the banker, are fairly low.

Major Trends in Money Laundering

Money laundering involves a constant struggle between the launderers-who seek the paths of least resistance and lowest risk-and governments and law enforcement authorities who seek to detect, disrupt, and prevent the completion of the laundering cycle.

As a result, the money laundering industry is both innovative and highly dynamic. Launderers constantly seek new ways to circumvent regulation and minimize the likelihood that the funds from drug trafficking and other illicit enterprises will be subject to seizure. This does not mean that one method is necessarily superseded by another; simply that there are constant efforts to expand the repertoire of available and effective options. Methods that work tend to be replicated elsewhere-and even those schemes that are uncovered are sometimes used again in different locations or with slight modifications. Nevertheless, it is possible to discern a number of broad trends in money laundering:

The Employment of Specialists

As criminal activities have become more extensive and the profits from drug trafficking and other criminal enterprises have increased, there has been a recognition that laundering activities require specialists. Although some of these specialists can be found within the ranks of the criminal organizations themselves, there has been a growing recognition of the need to employ or co-opt specialists who operate in the licit financial and legal worlds, who can provide increasingly sophisticated methods of laundering and various other financial services, and who represent what Bosworh-Davies and Saltmarsh describe as an "emerging criminal class".

As the International Narcotics Control Strategy Report noted, an increasing number of drug trafficking organizations "do not directly manage the laundering or conversion of their proceeds, but rely predominantly on professional money brokers. Such brokers are increasingly crafting effective schemes to evade normal monitoring, detection and reporting devices". Although this means some loss of profits to the traffickers-who pay hefty commissions that can range from around 6 or 7 per cent of the money laundered to over 20 per cent-this is deemed worth it because it reduces the risks both to the money and to the criminals themselves. Specialists are able to obtain a relatively high fee for their services because they are an additional buffer between the criminal and law enforcement. In some cases, they also accept liability in the event that the money is seized.

Additionally, specialists provide good financial advice to the drug traffickers or other criminals. The 1996 State Department report noted that in treating money as a commodity, professional money launderers differ little from corporate money managers.

Movement of Bulk Cash

For all the use of specialists and highly sophisticated money laundering schemes, considerable amounts of money are still moved through bulk cash. The weight and size of large amounts of paper money poses problems but has not prevented the proceeds of drug deals being smuggled back to Mexico or Colombia in household goods such as washing machines or stereos or in general merchandise. On April 17, 1995, for example, police at Benito Juarez international airport discovered 6.2 million dollars in small bills stuffed inside air conditioners.

In some cases, traffickers develop elaborate schemes to facilitate the movement of cash. Reno International, a firm in Springfield, New Jersey was set up specifically to produce large fiber glass rolls with special compartments in which up to $700,000 in cash could be secreted. Indeed, according to The New York Times, drug traffickers have shipped cash to Colombia "in everything from used cars and dolls to television sets and refrigerated containers of bull semen". On occasion, concealment has been ignored in the hope of eluding the authorities. One such scheme which went awry occurred in October 1995 when Mexican soldiers seized over 12 million dollars brought in from the United States by plane.

In other cases, money has been intercepted when being sent through Federal Express or other delivery and postal services The increased emphasis on the physical transportation of the profits of drug trafficking and other crimes is highlighted by the increase in seizures, which in fiscal year 1994 totaled $314.4 million-up from $250.4 million in fiscal 1993.

EMERGING ANTI-MONEY LAUNDERING RISKS

The financial industry's responsibility to identify and stop money laundering affects its entire business process and failure to do so is loaded with risk. Such risks include operational, reputational, and financial risks as a result of regulatory penalties, forced operational and policy changes, lost revenue streams or frozen assets, and lost customer base because of negative publicity. A financial institution need only look to its FROs enforcement actions to understand its degree of risk, but money laundering in the post-9/11 world also makes big headlines outside of the industry. The risks we see emerging today are identified by bodies such as FATF and FFIEC, as well as the industry's observations, self-reported in SARs and

Currency Transaction Reports (CTRs) and compiled through the efforts of FinCEN. The most significant emerging money laundering risks are identified in funds transfers, including stored value cards, mobile payments and internet payments. Other money laundering risks are identified in shell corporations, and contractual transactions including real estate, exchange trades and insurance transactions.

FUNDS TRANSFERS

Stored Value Cards

Stored value cards, also known as prepaid cards, come in many forms and are available for various uses. They may be in the form of gift certificate alternatives for retail use in one store or multiple stores. They may be offered for specific purchases such as gasoline or auto services, phone services, or mass transit. Inasmuch as their use is widely diverse, stored value cards are typically categorized as either "open system" or "closed system" cards. Open system stored value cards are connected to the global funds networks such as Cirrus or Plus. They allow for access to worldwide ATM funds and purchases with nearly any merchant. They are often co-branded by financial institutions and may carry the VISA or MasterCard logo with their associated benefits. They may be geographically restricted, but are frequently available for use internationally and are marketed as a safer alternative to carrying cash. They may be used by anyone, including a non-purchaser and are typically reloadable6 with varying restrictions. The usual means of obtaining such a card begins with an individual registering for, prepaying funds into, and receiving a card.

This part of the process may occur at a financial institution, a retailer, the postal service, money service business, or similar companies. They may also be obtained over the Internet. Closed system cards are limited by the issuer and usually only available to purchase goods or services from the issuer. Their use may be as limited as to a single merchant, or as broad as to a family of businesses under the umbrella of a parent company, and they also may be reloadable, but usually only up to a certain dollar amount. Stored value cards are vulnerable to money laundering for a number of reasons. Unlike debit cards, stored value cards may be issued without the obligation of a depository account. Because the issuers and sellers of stored value cards are defined within the regulations under money services businesses, they currently are not required to register with FinCEN or to file Suspicious Activity Reports.

Frequently, a financial institution will have little direct contact with a purchaser and is not required to perform customer identification procedures on individual purchasers when a pooled account is utilized to process payments on the cards. There also appears to be some ambiguity of where the responsibility lies for AML and Customer Identification Program (CIP) provisions between banks, processors, and other entities involved in the issuance and redemption process. Moreover, although cards issued within the United States are subject to the Bank Secrecy Act, this is not true for cards issued outside the U.S., although they may still be used within its borders. For example transferring value across borders, as in a case where two $5,000 prepaid cards are used within the U.S. does not trigger the related currency reporting requirements.

Mobile Payments

The cellular phone industry is developing new technologies to facilitate funds transfers such as bill pay, cross border money transfers, and point-of-sale (POS) payments and is partnering with other service providers to achieve this in the U.S. Mobile payments are already widespread in many European and Asian countries. If not performed through a financial institution with an underlying account through an ACH debit or credit card transaction, payments are conducted with the wireless company acting as a financial intermediary that makes the payments and charges the user's service account (Bill to Phone). Such transactions may be made by charging a transaction to the account or by prepaying an account for future services or purchases. Money transmission may be made to or received from any mobile phone number or bank account.

Purchases can include travel tickets, and depending on the service provider, cash may be obtained at ATMs or over the counter at participating businesses. Mobile payments, or m-commerce, is not yet recognized as a potential money laundering threat by most Federal regulatory and oversight bodies. The 2007 National Money Laundering Strategy and Threat Assessment makes no mention of mcommerce. The FATF Report on New Payment Methods discusses mobile payments as mostly relying on the banking industry to facilitate transactions, but neglects to discuss money laundering risks associated with the growth of transactions that do not rely on financial institutions.

This field of commerce is largely unregulated directly and it is uncertain whether or how the regulations which apply to the financial institutions that facilitate these transactions would also affect mobile payments. Meanwhile, at least the same level of risk, and perhaps even greater risk, associated with transfer methods such as stored value cards, for example, would be found with m-commerce. This is in part, due to the fact that many emerging service providers do not fall within the definitions of institutions subject to the Bank Secrecy Act or USA PATRIOT Act.

Internet Payments

The rapidly growing number and variety of services and goods available through the Internet has created a proportional demand for methods of financing their purchase. Vendors and merchants are interested in payment methods that do not carry the same fee burdens as credit cards. Consumers, still wary of using credit cards over the Internet in spite of assurances of digital encryption security, or who do not have credit cards, prefer payment methods that do not require their use. In response, numerous service providers, such as well known PayPal, offer individuals the ability to make online purchases, funding accounts with wire transfers, money orders, and even cash.

These providers have tapped into a huge, still unsaturated market for Internet financial services. In 2004 Paypal did 339 million transactions totaling $18.9 billion dollars.9 In the last quarter of 2005 alone, it conducted 129.7 million transactions for a total of $8.1 billion dollars.

In most cases, the provider of this service will not have a face-to-face relationship with its customers and may even allow anonymous accounts. The ability to engage in transactions across international borders enhances the potential for money laundering as payments may be directed to off-shore Internet payment service providers that thereafter facilitate transactions unregulated by anti-money laundering laws of the United States. The potential for maneuvering around OFAC restrictions is also enhanced using similar means.

BUSINESS ENTITIES

Shell Corporations

Shell corporations are legal entities that are not publicly traded and have no assets, no employees, no operations, and no physical address. They are frequently created for the legitimate purposes of easing corporate mergers and the transfer of currency and assets between companies as well as to hold the stock or tangible assets of other businesses. They have also been used for less than legitimate purposes such as tax evasion and, more recently, money laundering. Because they are not publicly traded, they are not subject to many of the ownership disclosure requirements of other companies listed on the stock exchanges. Additionally, many states' incorporation laws do not require owners to be named at all and will allow other companies to own shell corporations, further clouding the ability to trace accountable parties. The formation of shell companies within the U.S. is often promoted abroad for the privacy protections they offer.

Shell companies create a risk for money laundering because they allow for access to the nation's financial institutions without the transparency required of the AML regulations. FinCEN notes there are 47 state jurisdictions within the U.S. that do not require the reporting of owners of an LLC. Aside from foreign shell banks, a subset of shell corporations, they are not defined within the Bank Secrecy Act so as to fall within the regulatory reporting provisions, and may be subject to the BSA's catch-all definitions only under certain conditions. Nevertheless, transactions with shell companies pose such a growing concern that, despite the need for substantially more rigorous due diligence to expose potential money laundering activity, it is well within a financial institution's best interests to develop policies and procedures to identify owners and monitor their business activities.

CONTRACTS

Real Estate

In November and December, 2006, FinCEN released two important assessments of the money laundering risks associated with real estate transactions, both commercial and consumer. In the 10 years through August 2006, of nearly 10,000 SARs filed involving commercial real estate transactions, more than 96 percent were filed by banks and other depository institutions. Of a sample analysis, 66 percent involved suspected money laundering, structuring, and related activities.

These activities included frequent transfers of funds between accounts for no apparent business purpose, multiple cash deposits and wire transfers, deposits of large numbers of traveler's checks, and withdrawals of cash to purchase monetary instruments that are later re-deposited.

By contrast, whereas suspicious activity reporting of mortgage loan fraud has nearly quadrupled since 2002, the percentage of reports that also indicated structuring or money laundering activity was less than one percent of the total. Nevertheless, the numbers represent a significant increase in such activity, roughly coinciding with the boom in the housing market. Mortgage lending activities that have been identified as increasing risk include automated loan processing and the use of document couriers and mortgage brokers. Automated loan processing, via the telephone or the Internet, as well as the use of couriers, diminish the ability of financial institutions to obtain positive, verifiable identification of the parties to a transaction.

Mortgage brokers are still largely unregulated in the current AML environment, face disparate licensing requirements state to state, and are frequently not subject to background checks.

"Persons Involved in Real Estate Closings and Settlements" are not required to have an AML program, file SARs or CTRs, or to have a CIP program in place.

Trade Based Money Laundering

Trade based money laundering is not the newest means of hiding the illicit sources of money. The Black Market Peso Exchange, recognized in the period surrounding the terrorist attacks of 2001, is one example of this method of laundering money. Additional means of trade based laundering are becoming more common, as terrorist financiers and launderers seek less obvious ways of infiltrating the financial industry. These methods frequently include the exchange of legitimate goods and even services.

The difference between trade based money laundering and legal business transactions, however, is in the price obtained or paid. An over-valuation of merchandise results in an importer paying a higher-than-market price which facilitates the transfer of additional funds offshore.

An under-valuation results in the opposite with funds moving into the country. Other methods of conducting trade based money laundering include double invoicing, misrepresenting the quantity of goods shipped, and misclassifying shipped merchandise as different products of higher or lower value. Trade based money laundering is often the most difficult to detect because of the potential complexity of the transactions and the number of individuals or merchants involved.

The financial services industry has little regulation when it comes to tradebased money laundering, but it should be noted that it is very involved in providing information to financial intelligence units. This is likely because financial institutions often already have in place the means by which they can evaluate the business practices and inventory of their customers. They may increase their ability to spot potential money launderers with the use of red flag indicators available through FATF.

Insurance

Insurance companies have gained the attention of money laundering observers as a result of the availability of certain products that lend themselves to greater risks. The penetration of traditional financial institutions into the insurance market makes it particularly important that these risks be understood. Financial institutions must be aware that the risks are apparent at every stage in the insurance cycle, from underwriting to termination and redemption.

Scenarios include third-party payment of premiums with illicitly obtained funds, borrowing against policies purchased with illegal money, one-off payments for policies that are subsequently terminated within the contract cancellation period, and fraudulent loss claims involving high value goods purchased with illegal funds.

One difficulty in tracking illegal activity through the insurance industry is the lack of anti-money laundering program and suspicious activity reporting requirements for one of the largest segments of the industry, agents and brokers. These obligations are left to the insurance companies and made more difficult to enforce in a competitive market when the agents and brokers are not their official employees.

MONEY LAUNDERING ENFORCEMENT

Money laundering is defined as an illicit money transfer. There are two main kinds of illicit money transfers. First, traditional money laundering entails transferring illegally obtained funds to conceal their origins and make them appear legal. For example, drug dealers deposit cash revenues in banks and later transfer them until the funds appear to originate from legitimate sources. Second, terrorism financing entails transferring mostly legal funds for illegal purposes. For instance, legal charity donations are transferred to fund terrorist attacks. In sum, both forms of money laundering are characterized by illicit and socially harmful fund transfers. Money laundering causes social harm because it facilitates crime and enables criminals to enjoy criminal revenues.

Money laundering can happen through various intermediaries. Bank transfers, both by wire and check, are the most common channels for illicit money transfers as described in Reuter and Truman (2004). Money transmitting businesses, such as Western Union, are also used for money laundering as detailed in The Wall Street Journal (2004b). These businesses are typically franchised or owned by individuals, who might have stronger incentives to turn a blind eye to money laundering than bank branch-managers. In the greyer area of finance, informal value transfer systems (IVTSs) provide money transmitting services usually without a proper paper trail. The hawala or hindi systems used by different ethnic communities are described, for instance, in El-Qorchi (2002).

Money laundering is an economically significant crime, though precise estimates are hard to obtain. According to Camdessus (1998), the consensus range of money laundering volume is between 2 and 5 percent of the global GDP. The FBI (2001) estimates the volume of globally laundered funds as falling between $600 billion and $1.5 trillion.

Laundering fees, i.e. what money launderers charge their criminal clients, are estimated at 5-15% of the laundered amount according to Lal (2003) and Reuter and Truman (2004). Thus, money laundering, including self-laundering, is estimated to be a $30 to $225 billion global 'industry'. Moreover, the harm caused for instance by terrorism financing shows that money laundering is potentially even more significant than what volumes and laundering revenues would suggest. Money laundering enforcement is particularly relevant for the United States. According to some lawmakers' estimates, half of the globally laundered funds are transferred through US Banks (FBI, 2001). Three known money laundering cases highlight the point. First, $7 billion of Russian funds were washed through the Bank of New York until 1999 (Reuter and Truman, 2004).

Responding to the threat of money laundering, the United States has developed one of the strongest anti-money laundering regulation. The Banking Secrecy Act (1970), which in fact curbed banking secrecy to fight money laundering, was followed by a series of laws, each one of them further strengthening money laundering enforcement: The Money Laundering Control Act (1986), the Annunzio-Wylie Money Laundering Act (1992), the Money Laundering Suppression Act (1994), The Money Laundering and Financial Crimes Strategy Act (1998) and finally the USA Patriot Act (2001).

Second, Stephen Saccoccia alone laundered up to $550 million of drug money for both the Calí and Medellin cartels until he was prosecuted in 1993 (Reuter and Truman, 2004). Third, terrorists transferred $0.5 million for the 9/11 attack (9/11 Commission Report, 2004). The examples also show that the volumes involved in laundering proceedings of tax evasion and drug trafficking are enormous compared to terrorism financing.

Money laundering enforcement relies on bank reporting to law enforcement and government agencies as reviewed in Reuter and Truman (2004). Banks provide two kinds of reports: rule-based and discretionary reports. For instance, banks file the rule-based currency transaction report (CTR) for any cash transactions exceeding $10,000. Enforcing rule-based reporting is a standard disclosure problem as bank actions are ex-post verifiable. They are, however, insufficient, because money launderers are aware of the rules and can circumvent them.

For instance, money launderers usually 'smurf', i.e. break down large cash deposits over $10,000 into smaller deposits below the reporting threshold. Nevertheless, rule-based reporting makes money laundering more cumbersome.

The weaknesses of rule-based reports led to the introduction of a discretionary report, the suspicious activity report (SAR), in 1996. The suspicious activity report is filed for any activity that the bank considers to be 'suspicious'. For instance, if the bank spots several transactions just below $10,000, it can identify them as suspicious because they hint at smurfing.

The notion of suspicion is intentionally left vague so as to leave both money launderers and banks uncertain. Thus, money launderers cannot rely on simple rules to avoid being reported. Furthermore, banks are forced to constantly improve their understanding of how money laundering is done.

This intentional vagueness can be understood as another form of constructive ambiguity. The SARs are filed to the Financial Crime Enforcement Network (FinCEN), which might forward them to law enforcement agencies for further investigation.

Banks incur costly screening, monitoring and reporting because of the threat of sanctions.

Failing to file SARs led to fines of $25 million for Riggs Bank (FinCEN, 2004a), $24 million for Arab Bank (FinCEN, 2005f), $50 million for AmSouth Bank (FinCEN, 2004b) and $80 million for ABN-AMRO Bank (FinCEN, 2005g). Most importantly, sanctions or fines are levied for false negatives, i.e. for not reporting transactions which are later prosecuted as money laundering or judged to be suspicious ex-post.

Banks are not fined for false positives, i.e. for reporting legal transactions as money laundering. This 'safe harbor' provision strengthens banks incentive to report.

7

Anti-corruption Efforts in India

India has seen a lot of corruption in the last 60 years since independence. The economy of India was under socialist-inspired policies for an entire generation from the 1950s until the late 1980s. The economy was subject to extensive regulation, protectionism, and public ownership, leading to slow growth. There was also pervasive corruption in a system of bureaucratic controls (License Raj), which was often at the core of corruption.

1993

The Vohra Report was submitted by the former Indian Union Home Secretary, N.N. Vohra, in October 1993. It studied the problem of the criminalisation of politics and of the nexus among criminals, politicians and bureaucrats in India.

2010-2011

In the period 2010-2011, India witnessed various scandals being blown apart by the media, whistle-blowers, civil society activists and government investigation agencies alike. Scams like 2G spectrum scam, Adarsh Housing Society Scam, Commonwealth Games scam and many more brought about name of various Cabinet Ministers, Chief Ministers and even members of the Armed Forces. This showed how deeply entrenched corruption has become in India. It has led to a more expansive civil society movement that wishes to fight graft with the strictest of laws and penalties. India Against Corruption is a body created by various prominent activists and the citizens of India. It has no political affiliations and only wishes to bring about drastic changes in the governance system of India so as to tackle corruption effectively.

ANTI-CORRUPTION INITIATIVES BY CIVIL SOCIETY IN INDIA

A variety of public *anti-corruption initiatives* have been created by in India.

India Against Corruption

India Against Corruption is a movement created by a citizens from a variety of professions and statuses to work against corruption in India. It is currently headed by Anna Hazare.

Jaago Re

Jaago Re! One Billion Votes from Tata Tea has now changed its focus from voter registration to fighting corruption.

Zero Rupee Notes

5th Pillar is an organization that is promoting the use of Zero Rupee notes as a symbolic gesture when asked to pay bribes by government officials. to fight corruption by shaming the officials who ask for bribe.

Nobribe.org

Another popular initiative nobribe.org is another platform for corruption free India and advocates the use of direct and regular measurement of corruption to force the hands of the leadership into dealing with corruption related issues.

Ekakizunj.com

This site is attempting to create a database of the corruption in India. It includes names and details of many scams and scamsters since independence. It is inspired by G. R. Khairnar, the previous Mumbai Municipal Deputy Commissioner who is known for his fight against corruption.

2011 INDIAN ANTI-CORRUPTION MOVEMENT

The 2011 Indian anti-corruption movement consists of a series of protests for the Jan Lokpal Bill (Citizen Ombudsman Bill) that sprang up across India especially after April 5, 2011. The protesters want the Government of India to draft a strong anti-graft Lokpal bill which follows the originally drafted bill and not the changes the government plans to bring in, which will make the Lokayukta just another advisory body with no actual power in the vast Indian bureaucracy. Following continuous calls in vain to the government to work effectively towards passing the bill, a civil society activist and Gandhian, Anna Hazare, went on an indefinite hunger strike until death until his demands in support of the bill were met. Anna demanded for a joint committee of civil society members and government representatives to draft a strong anti-graft bill.

The protests led to the creation of an unprecedented movement that saw protests being organised in various cities and towns of India. Protests included fasts, candlelight vigils and rallies. The protests are especially one of their kind in India as they have no political affiliation and the protesters have been very hostile to any political party trying to grab the initiative to meet its own political goals from the activists. The protests to some extent have similarities in methodologies to Jayaprakash Narayan's Bihar Movement (commonly called the JP Movement) of 1974. There were also similarities to the methods and philosophies used in the 2011 Egyptian revolution and the Tunisian revolution, that have rocked the very foundations of governments in the Arab world.

The Right to Information Act (RTI Act) that came into force in 2005 has helped civilians work effectivley towards tackling corruption. The RTI Act allows all Indian citizens (except those living in Jammu and Kashmir) to request information from a "public authority" (a body of Government or "instrumentality of State") which is required to reply expeditiously or within thirty days, all for a meagre sum of 10 (US$ 0.22). It has also helped activists uncover graft cases against various politicians and bureaucrats. To quell the findings made by RTI activists, there have been instances where RTI activists have been attacked and even killed in some cases.

In the period 2010-2011, India witnessed various scandals being blown apart by the media, whistle-blowers, civil society activists and government investigation agencies alike. Scams like 2G spectrum scam, Adarsh Housing Society Scam, Commonwealth Games scam and many more brought about name of various Cabinet Ministers, Chief Ministers and even members of the Armed Forces. This showed how deeply entrenched corruption has become in India. It has led to a more expansive civil society movement that wishes to fight graft with the strictest of laws and penalties. India Against Corruption is a body created by various prominent activists and the citizens of India. It has no political affiliations and only wishes to bring about drastic changes in the governance system of India so as to tackle corruption effectively.

The original idea behind the Jan Lokpal Bill is to have the independent body which would investigate cases of corruption within a year and ensure speedy trial within the next year. India Against Corruption has made it its prime objective to bring about the passing in parliament and subsequent effective enforcement of the Jan Lokpal Bill. It has also become a force organizing protests in support of the bill.

Protest Timeline

13 March 2011 (2011-03-13)

A group of Delhi residents dressed in white shirts and t-shirts took a four-hour drive around the city to drum up campaign against corruption and rally support for the Jan Lokpal Bill.

28 March 2011 (2011-03-28)

According to the organisers of the protests held globally on that day-"As many as 45 cities in USA, 40 cities in India and 8 other countries globally joined in an anti-corruption movement. Indians across the globe, as far as from Nagpur to New Jersey and Sydney to Seattle shouted in one voice to enact 'Jan Lokpal Bill' and ratify the UN Convention against Corruption." Many of the marchers were planning to continue the movement by joining Anna Hazare's fast in Delhi on 5 April for the same cause.

4 April 2011 (2011-04-04)

Anna Hazare, the anti corruption activist leader announced his fast unto death till Jan Lokpal Bill is enacted

5 April 2011 (2011-04-05)

- Anna Hazare, initiated his fast unto death at Jantar Mantar in Delhi
- Around 6,000 Mumbai residents joined Anna Hazare for a one-day fast to support the demand for implementation of the Jan Lokpal Bill.
- In Pune over 6,000 residents joined the campaign.
- The Freedom Park in Banglore was the cynosure of all eyes on Thursday as Bangaloreans from all walks of life thronged the place to support Anna Hazare.

7 April 2011 (2011-04-07)

- 2 rounds of talks with the government failed.
- Anna Hazare continued on with his fast.
- Narendra Modi, the chief Minister of Gujarat lashes out at Manmohan Singh for resisting the passage of the Jan Lokpal Bill
- Sonia Gandhi, the president of the Indian National Congress party and the head of the National Advisory Council appealed to Anna Hazare to end his indefinite fast.

8 April 2011 (2011-04-08)

- Protests spreaded to Mumbai, Kolkata, Hyderabad, Bangalore, Chennai, Patna, Bhopal, Ahmedabad, Ranchi, Pune, Nashik and Kochi.
- Protests were organised at Jammu University in Jammu, Thiruvananthapuram, Guwahati and Jaipur too.
- The government continued to squabble with the activists stating that the bill drafting committee will be headed

by a government appointed minister and not a civil society member as the protesters demanded to avoid allowing the government to make the bill less powerful.

- The Prime Minister Dr. Manmohan Singh met with the President of India to outline to her how the government was going ahead with the demands of the population.
- 15 supporters of Anna Hazare on fast were hospitalized.
- Bollywood came out completely in support of the protests-with famed actors, musicians and directors speaking in support of the movement and Anna Hazare. Director Farah Khan, actor Anupam Kher, music director Vishal Dadlani, poet-filmmaker Pritish Nandy and actor Tom Alter all visited Jantar Mantar. Meanwhile famed Indian actors Aamir Khan, Hrithik Roshan and Amitabh Bachchan all stated their support for the movement via social networking websites or the media. Oscar winning Indian composer A. R. Rahman also declared his support for the anti-graft movement. Kareena Kapoor, Shabana Azmi, Shekhar Kapur, Sushmita Sen, Bipasha Basu, Shahid Kapoor, Riteish Deshmukh, Vivek Oberoi, Neha Dhupia, Jackky Bhagnani, Shirish Kunder, Kailash Kher, Punit Malhotra all tweeted their support for Anna Hazare further feulling the masses to join the movement.
- Famed Qatari artist M. F. Hussain showed his support by drawing a cartoon of Anna Hazare.
- Indian students at Cambridge University, the former alma-mater of the Indian prime minister also addressed their support for the movement.
- Many prominent people from the government agencies as well as from various corporate houses came out in support of the movement. Some of them were-Delhi Metro chief E. Sreedharan (also called the Metro Man of India), Punj Lloyd chairman Atul Punj, Maruti Suzuki chairman RC Bhargava, Hero group's Sunil Munjal, Tata Steel vice-chairman B Muthuraman, Bajaj Auto Chairman Rahul Bajaj, Godrej Group head Adi Godrej, Biocon Chairman and Managing Director Kiran

Mazumdar-Shaw and Kotak Mahindra Bank vice-chairman & managing director Uday Kotak. They all declared their support for Anna Hazare and the movement.

- ASSOCHAM President Dilip Modi and FICCI Director General Rajiv Kumar, both came out in support of the movement too.
- The Government of India accepted the compromise formula that there be a politician chairman and an activist, non-politician Co-Chairman. It was reported that Pranab Mukherjee will be the Chairman of the draft committee while Shanti Bhushan will be the co-chairman. Shanti Bhushan was one of the original drafters of the Lokpal Bill along with Anna Hazare, Justice N. Santosh Hegde, advocate Prashant Bhushan, and RTI activist Arvind Kejriwal.

9 April 2011 (2011-04-09)

- After accepting all the demands of Anna Hazare, the Government of India issued a Official Gazette saying that the draft of lokpal would be made and presented in the coming monsoon session of Lok Sabha.
- Victory celebrations were held all over India from Jantar Mantar-the centre of the protests to Hyderabad, Jammu, Mumbai, Nagpur, Chennai, Kolkatta, Allahabad and even Anna Hazare's village.
- Bollywood lauded the victory of Anna Hazare, once again echoing their support for the movement and the support of the Indian citizenry.
- Anti-Corruption protestors at India Gate booed and drove away controversial journalist Barkha Dutt.
- Protesters and leaders of the movement alike stated that the path to attaining complete passing of the bill is still a difficult one, and the movement has to see more harsher days ahead.
- The movement has become a symbol of civil society's power in India. After being widely televised by the

Indian media, and widely supported by almost every Indian citizen (as the issue of corruption has been an issue every Indian holds very negative views about), the movement has attained a certain level of credibility in the eyes of the Indian masses. Its uniqueness in the fact that it was completely apolitical; was a movement solely of the people; did not wish to put in disarray the country as in the case of total shutdowns organised by politcal parties (Commonly called a Bandh) ; and was able to bend the government-is something new for India. Many commentators have called the movement the 'wake-up' call for India. Meanwhile social networking chatter has been filled with fears that Indians will once again go back to 'sleep' with time.

Drafting Committee of the Bill

The 10 member Drafting Committee of the Jan Lokpal Bill will have an equal representation of both politicians and civil society members. On 8 April 2011, the Ministry of Law and Justice issued an official notification, The Gazette of India, regarding the Joint Drafting Committee of the bill. A copy of the notification can be found here

Chairmen

The Government of India accepted that there be a politician Chairman and an activist, non-politician Co-Chairman. It is reported that Pranab Mukherjee, from the political arena, and Shanti Bhushan, from the civil society, will be the Chairmen of the Drafting Committee.

Government Representation

Five Cabinet ministers will be a part of the Drafting Committee. They are:

1. Pranab Mukherjee, Finance Minister, *Co-Chairman*
2. P. Chidambaram, Minister of Home Affairs, *Panel Member*
3. Veerappa Moily, Minister of Law and Justice, *Panel Member*

4. Kapil Sibal, Minister for Communications and Information Technology, *Panel Member*
5. Salman Khursid, Minister of Water Resources, *Panel Member*

Civil Society Representation

Five leading socialists will be a part of the Drafting Committee. They are:

1. Shanti Bhushan, Former Minister of Law and Justice, *Co-Chairman*
2. Anna Hazare, Social Activist, *Panel Member*
3. Prashant Bhushan, Lawyer, *Panel Member*
4. N. Santosh Hegde, Lokayukta (Karnataka), *Panel Member*
5. Arvind Kejriwal, RTI activist, *Panel Member*

Allegations against Panel Members

Adding a new chapter in Lokpal Bill issue, the candidature of Shanti Bhushan, veteran lawyer, former union law minister and co-chairman of the new committee formed as a result of Anna Hazare's recent hunger strike to draft a law on corruption, has come under scanner after a new CD controversy.

Shanti Bhushan said that "it certainly appears to be a motivated, mallicious campaign to derail the draft of the Lokpal bill.". Some pro-corruption supporters or those who would benefit from the status quo are drumming up support against this anti corruption movement by using the usual old tactics of attempting to cast doubt on Anna Hazare, the committee members, the who movement and how it was handled in the media and the press etc.

First Lokpal Bill Draft Meeting

First Lokpal Bill draft meeting was held on 16 April 2011, Eight days after Gandhian Anna Hazare called off his fast demanding a stronger Lokpal law. The government has agreed to audio-recording of all meetings of the Lokpal Bill panel and to holding public consultations before a final draft of the anti-graft law is prepared. Next meeting will be held on 2 May 2011. Anna Hazare insisted to telecast the live proceedings video, but government denied stating certain "drawbacks" of doing so and so the first meeting was held recording the audio for future references.

Use of Social Networks

Within a day of the beginning of the agitation, more than 30,000 people pledged their support to the Lokpal Bill. Organisers of the India Against Corruption said 30,000 people from Maharashtra expressed their support on their website. With an active Facebook page comprising of over 60,000 fans and a Twitter profile with more than 3300 followers, the "India Against Corruption" movement has already been a big success.

The website has 20,000 members in Mumbai alone. Within a few days the Facebook page for India Against Corruption had more than 150,000 likes. There was heightened political activity on social networking websites like Twitter and Facebook. Various support group pages and events were created on the websites to show support and rally the masses.

Nonpartisan Nature

Hazare and the protesters have tried to keep the protests non-political. No politicians were welcome at the site of the fast. Former Haryana Chief Minister Om Prakash Chautala, former Madhya Pradesh Chief Minister Uma Bharti and pro Sonia Gandhi journalist Barkha Dutt were forced by civilians to leave, after the protesters objected against their presence which they believed was harming the integrity of their movement.

Government Response

Hazare's protest has led to the resignation of Agriculture Minister Sharad Pawar from the Group of Ministers on corruption after Anna took potshots at him. On 8 April, the government started seriously considering the demands of the protesters. The government has stated that it will table the bill in the parliament in the upcoming Monsoon session. On 9 April, the government finally agreed to have a 50:50 distribution of the Government appointed officials and the members of the civil society.

Political Response

Bhartiya Janata Party

Bhartiya Janata Party supported Anna Hazare. Senior Bharatiya Janata Party (BJP) leader Arun Jaitley urged the Congress-led UPA Government to take veteran social activist Anna's indefinite fast very seriously.

Senior BJP leader, L.K. Advani suggested that a meeting of political parties should be convened to discuss this issue "particularly in the context of black money and curbing money-power in elections".

BJP leader and Chief Minister of Gujarat Narendra Modi posted on his Facebook account that he was diligently praying for Anna Hazare's health.

He also published an open letter to Anna Hazare thanking him for the latter's support for the development work in Gujarat (being spearheaded by Narendra Modi himself as the chief minister of the state). Narendra Modi also cautioned Anna Hazare of possible vilification by a certain 'powerful-group' that wishes to defame Narendra Modi and Gujarat. He reiterated his support for the Jan Lokpal Bill, stating that he was also just another common man.

Communist Party of India (Marxist)

The Communist Party of India (Marxist) came out in support of Anna Hazare. Prakash Karat pledged support to Hazare over the Jan Lokpal Bill.

Indian Black Money in Swiss Banks

Swami Ramdev has also publicly raised the issue of Indian money stashed away illegally in Swiss bank which is estimated to be between 1-1.5 trillion USD. He says that the government must take concrete action and bring back the money as it belongs to the people of India and has been taken out of the country illegally.

The bill is a first step towards anti-corruption measures and will not be complete without addressing certain major reformations like bringing back black money. He wanted the government to make it mandatory for those who have deposited money in foreign banks to declare them and also to close the Mauritius route, which is a haven for tax evaders

Satyagraha against Corruption (SAC)

Swami Ramdev declared that a people's movement to liberate the country from rampant corruption and build a strong spiritual 'Bharat' would be launched by him in June. The movement which is second phase of Bharath Swabhiman Yatra is named 'Satyagraha against Corruption'.

He declared one of the main objectives of the movement was to bring about an end to corruption and bring back black money stashed away in various financial institutions in the country and abroad.

INDIA AGAINST CORRUPTION

India Against Corruption (IAC) is a people's movement to demand comprehensive reforms of anti-corruption systems in India. Several eminent citizens have come together to force the Government of India to enact the Jan Lokpal Bill. This initiative is supported by several eminent citizens of India including religious leaders, Right To Information Activists, social reformers and bureaucrats.

Strategy

Inspired with Hong Kong's Independent Commission Against Corruption the leaders of the IAC initiative have prepared a draft Jan Lokpal Bill. The Jan Lokpal Bill provides for a strong, efficient and politically independent institutions, the Lokpal and the Lokayuktas for investigation of corruption charges against public officials and politicians. The bill also provides for time bound grievance redressal and speedy investigation.

In March 2011, the organization sent an open letter to PM Manmohan Singh and Haryana chief minister Bhupinder Singh Hooda for a CBI probe as recommended by Central government committee into "irregularities in the forest department", and into the harassment of IFS officer Sanjiv Chaturvedi.

In April 2011, Anna Hazare gave a call to the nation to press the government for the enactment of Jan LokPal bill. In hundreds of cities, towns and villages across the length and breadth of the country, people took initiative and formed teams for supporting Annaji's indefinite fast. Hundreds of people joined Annaji in his fast at home/office/event venues on the 5 April 2011.

This event has turned out to be the single largest people's movement since India's independence. The movement ended the indefinite fast on 9 April 2011 with the assurance by the government to constitute a committee to enact Jan LokPal bill. This people's mass movement has vowed to carry on staging fight against corruption.

Anna Hazare's Role

Social worker Anna Hazare has declared to go on an indefinite fast starting 5 April 2011 to persuade Government of India to introduce and enact the Jan Lokpal Bill in place of the government proposed Lokpal Bill.

"I solemnly pledge that I would not vote for that party which does not pass Jan Lokpal or Lokayukta Bill drafted by Citizens wherever it is in power-either at centre or at state level."

VOTE FOR INDIA PLEDGE

Vote Bank Against Corruption

The India Against Corruption initiative is creating a Vote Bank (Vote For India). They encourage Indian citizens to register on this website and take a pledge that they will not vote for a party which does not pass the Jan Lokpal bill.

Political Support

Several political parties have come to support the movement

for Jan Lokpal Bill. Political leaders from different parties – Sudhakar Reddy, A B Bardhan, Abani Roy (Left front), H D Devegowda (JDS) Mysora Reddy (TDP) and Jayant Chowdhry (RLD) signed a joint statement indicating their support to the movement.

Jan Lokpal Bill

The Jan Lokpal Bill was drafted in consultation with the India Against Corruption movement to counter the dilutions in the government sponsored Lokpal Bill.

THE CORRUPTION IN INDIA

Corruption slows down economic growth. It foils attempts of social welfare within the country. India is considered to be one of the most corrupted countries in the world. The global corruption index for India is a badge. Is the situation really that shocking? A quick peek into the situation in India.

Let's first define corruption. What is corruption? Is it some kind of anti social activity? Well, it is, unless you are in a country like India. We, Indians are proud to have topped so many things and corruption is one of them.

When a criminal is involved in anti-social activities he will be called antisocial and when a government official is involved in similar thing we will call him corrupt. Corruption is a machine that generates black money. This is not the only thing that it's capable of. Like the administration itself, the corruption has a hierarchical structure. It's a distribution system where the load of black money is shared among individuals.

A personnel who introduced himself as one from Intelligence Bureau arrives for the verification of documents, which is a necessary step for having an international passport. Now since this man arrived he has been looking for contradictions, flaws in these documents.

He asks for documents that are not even mentioned as necessary in the guidelines. He is provided with everything. Surprisingly, the very fact that every thing is okay makes him upset. He then says, "We are supposed to be paid for the processing" and then declares the sum. The good citizen who doesn't want trouble gives in to his demand. That almost immediately stops further questioning and verification. The official has got what he was looking for, thus is quite satisfied. He leaves with the money and documents.

Another official, who is the Officer in Charge of the local police station, starts frequenting the locality as he was informed that some construction work is going on in the area. This is quite odd. In the time of crisis these officials take hours to reach to the place even after repeatedly calling them. What aroused them so unexpectedly? We will soon see. The official and his colleague identify the construction site and its owner. They immediately meet him and ask for bribe.

There is no need to be surprised at these incidents. The cops are not the only ones. Nor are they the only benefactors. The total amount of black money thus gathered will have its upward flow. Corruption doesn't start from bottom of this hierarchy.

It starts from the very top and goes all the way to the bottom, just opposite to the direction of money. If I take bribe to do my job, will I be able to take actions against my subordinates who do the same? Probably, not. My sinister mind, instead, will device a system where if there is any such transaction, a share is sent immediately at my desk.

There are many people who, in spite of having a house, don't have any postal address. This is because most of them have refused to pay bribe to the officials of local Municipal Corporation.

They all come up with the same excuse that the salary they are being paid is not enough whereas the truth is that their greed knows no bound. If your file is stuck in one of those offices there is a high possibility that the job will take years to complete. It will take years for your file to get passed from one desk to the next desk located in the same room.

Will these officials never be convicted? Well, it is really difficult to accuse a government official of corruption. The primary reason is that it is hard to trace the money under undocumented transactions. The peaceful citizens don't want to get into trouble so they are encouraging corruption by giving away bribes.

Who will arrest these officials? It's another official from the same department or someone sharing similar vile principles? Unfortunately, we the Indians have only the extreme preference for criminals. Either we totally ignore them, or, shoot them in fake encounters.

All this proves our lack of respect in democracy. A huge part of the funds that are being sanctioned for different social welfare policies are absorbed in the system before even reaching the targeted beneficiaries. Do we call this underutilization or overutilization of money?

A new mayor, who seems totally obsessed with 'water', has been elected. On the very first day he declared that he will make sure that the inhabitants will not face any problems regarding water. He addressed several germane issues. But aren't we forgetting something here? How is he to do all this with all those corrupt officials, especially when they are working in the same building as his? The mayor has honest purpose and we do appreciate that. Not all officials are corrupt, but such workers are indeed, outnumbered.

The money we earn through illegitimate channels often becomes the cause of our peril. There is certainly a limit beyond which a healthy human being fails to consume. A corrupt police officer, who was also a renowned drunkard is counting the last days of his life, bed ridden, half paralyzed. He doesn't have the job, but the amount of money he had earned by several means was enough to provide for his family. The unfortunate and shocking piece of information is that his only daughter earns her living by prostitution and is a drunkard herself.

Here I present a few legitimate questions that these officials might have overlooked.

- Does your family know that you are being corrupt? Do your children know it? How will they feel if some of their peers call them the children of a dishonest person?

- Why don't you try to drink less, be less frequent in expensive parties and buy less furniture? Will buying one television instead of two decrease your reputation to nothing? You will save enough money not to take bribes.
- Do you know that there is a maximum limit you can consume in your entire life? The rest, which could actually benefit others, are entirely wasted. You are earning way above what you can consume. Are you doing it considering the future of your children? Let me tell you this, the future you are giving them through this is rather shameful and disintegrated.

8

Cyberpayment System

The discussion of Cyberpayment systems examined the question of whether this type of payment instrument was a generalized problem for law enforcement and payment system regulators, or whether particular types of Cyberpayment products constituted unique risks of abuse and misuse. Participants did not articulate a consensus on this subject, other than a general observation that *for their own reasons Cyberpayment system operators would tend to invest heavily in designing systems that minimized their degree of exposure to fraudulent use.* This position was extended to argue for a collaborative standards-based approach to regulatory action in the area of system soundness and safety.

Many participants argued strongly that Cyberpayment system operators should be free to select any system architecture (network-based or stored value-card in character, or some fusion of the two types) and payment instrument feature set (i.e., Peer-to-Peer functionality and high denomination limits), so long as they were able to meet governmental standards of regulator and law enforcement transparency and issuer safety and soundness. From this perspective, the determination of product type is best set by the free market, with overall Cyberpayment oversight issues addressed in a fashion which reflects societal concerns with safety and security. This approach was questioned by some participants who asserted that in seeking to pursue a "hands off" policy on product type, the government would "back into" intrusive oversight because of concerns with potential abuse deriving from particular Cyberpayment instrument characteristics (i.e., the relative anonymity of Cyberpayment value transfers conducted on a Peerto-Peer basis). From this perspective the government's hands-off posture would need to be changed to develop measures of effectiveness for both traditional and computer-based payment system investigative techniques.

Some participants observed that computer-based techniques would hold a potentially important advantage in investigations due to the quantifiable and reproducible nature of much of the data. Others argued, however, that such information would only be useful if used in a complementary fashion with traditional investigative techniques. This issue arose in the exercise scenario when a decision on whether to use purely computer-based techniques or such investigative tools alongside traditional means arose. Most participants favored the use of both sets of investigative tools with considerable skepticism expressed regarding sustaining the value of traditional law enforcement anti-money laundering techniques. Another argument consistent with this position was that the government would need to articulate *in the near term* a policy on the encryption schemes acceptable for deployment within the Cyberpayment industry. Participants expressed strong differences on the issue of whether government legal requirements on encryption had any place within the Cyberpayments domain. One perspective argued for governmental encouragement of the highest possible encryption protection for the Cyberpayments industry. Preserving the safety and soundness of Cyberpayment value issuers was the principal rationale for supporters of this position. It was also argued that as long as the government enjoyed assured access to Cyberpayment records *under established legal procedures* the deployment of strong encryption products within Cyberpayment applications could be positively encouraged. Those favoring this position differed on the extent to which government legal requirements would be useful in achieving the undoubtedly positive end of high levels of security in Cyberpayment networks.

The alternate view was that a governmental position on encryption standards for Cyberpayment products was premature, and that in any case the overall societal debate on such issues was nowhere near closure. Adopting an overt position in the short-run would unduly influence the market-driven selection of encryption and other technical features of Cyberpayment products. It was argued that the market should decide these issues in the short-term and that only following a potentially lengthy "shake-out" process would such decisions be appropriate for public sector authorities. The international elements of this issue were also the subject of considerable debate, with a general consensus emerging that any standards reached within the United States should be mirrored in the international community for them to have any enduring validity or relevance.

DEFINITIONAL ISSUES

The issue of how Cyberpayment value is to be defined was vigorously discussed. The debate was framed by the concern with establishing an appropriate regulatory oversight regime for Cyberpayment systems, while at the same time not imposing onerous (and costly) requirements on a maturing industry.

Within the context of anti-money laundering policy, some participants favored the inclusion of emergent Cyberpayment systems under the current Bank Secrecy Act with Cyberpayment value to be defined as equivalent to traditional circulating paper currency (i.e., cash). It was observed that the existing regulatory environment was already establishing customary rules — on an incremental basis — that would establish the setting for different Cyberpayment system models. In this area, draft regulations promulgated under the Bank Secrecy Act already affect entities involved in Cyberpayment product tests, as well as those likely to consider the deployment of such products in the future. It was generally felt that related regulatory decisions should be made with an eye to not disadvantaging (or advantaging) any particular Cyberpayment system type, but rather that the marketplace should be allowed to make the determination.

In terms of short and long run decision-making necessities on this subject, differences emerged as to the degree to which current decisions could be isolated from a longer-term determination of regulatory style in the Cyberpayment domain. Some argued that as an entirely new form of value transfer vehicle, Cyberpayment value necessitated an entirely new treatment from the regulatory and law enforcement standpoints. Others argued that even if this were true, short-run decisions would be made in the context of existing laws and perceived problems.

These participants sought to reframe the debate in the following terms: What is the appropriate oversight model for Cyberpayment value viewed as an analog to cash? This was contrasted to the question of what the correct model might be if Cyberpayment value were viewed as some other type of consumer-level electronic payment products or services. Finally, some participants argued that decisions made prematurely in the short-run could actually impede longer-term policymaking on the unique characteristics of Cyberpayment systems and counseled caution in the design of "interim" solutions to difficult law enforcement or regulatory questions.

Discussions also extended to those features of Cyberpayment products, (i.e., the high theoretical velocity of electronic value circulation, the relative anonymity of transactions, low or zero levels of transactions costs, and unprecedented transaction volume) of potential utility for money launderers and others seeking to conceal financial activities from governmental authorities. In this contract, consistent with the concern with not imposing additional costs on industry, or disadvantaging any particular Cyberpayment models, some argued that *product types* should be the basic unit of concern (i.e., products offering peer-to-peer functionality, or those offering a relatively high degree of payer anonymity), with only a small number of general regulations applying to all Cyberpayment instruments.

If the features of the Cyberpayment instrument were the most important new facts, it was argued, these features should be targeted as narrowly as possible in order to mitigate any potential fraud or abuse. Alternately, others held that the novel features of Cyberpayment instruments posed highly unique regulatory and law enforcement challenges. In this sense, traditional regulatory and law enforcement methods were found particularly wanting. Disagreements were present on estimates of the rapidity with which these challenges would become real, but few doubted that a potentially very important change in the consumer-level payments system could be about to occur.

Differences in perspective on the precise definition of what constitutes Cyberpayment value were thus correlated with different estimates as to the timing of the Cyberpayment challenge to existing regulatory and law enforcement frameworks and according to the extent of anticipated uniformity of different Cyberpayment products. It was argued by some that a fuller appreciation of the electronic nature of the new payment products would allow for much more objective and technically advanced system oversight procedures. An analogy was made with the New York Stock Exchange and NASDAQ with respect to the potentially large contribution that computer-based investigative techniques might make to Cyberpayment system oversight. Defined as a cash equivalent, Cyberpayment systems hold considerable uncertainty with respect to both regulatory and law enforcement impact. At the same time the definition — or legal and regulatory status — of Cyberpayment value relative to other electronic and traditional payment products, remains a critical issue for the ultimate determination of the appropriate Cyberpayment oversight regime.

CONVERGENT PERSPECTIVES ON CYBERPAYMENT SYSTEM OVERSIGHT

Discussions during the exercise yielded a wide-ranging set of perspectives on the scale and significance of the Cyberpayment challenge to law enforcement anti-money laundering policies. These perspectives almost of necessity also articulated positions on the appropriate governmental regime for conducting oversight of the emerging Cyberpayment industry. Discussions of appropriate public and private sector roles both converged and diverged on the issue of whether Cyberpayment value was to be treated as an equivalent to traditional currency (i.e. Cash). Positions on this issue were an excellent predictor of subsequent positions on governmental roles in standards setting, international coordination of legal rules, and provisions governing law enforcement's access to transactional information. While a wide-range of debate occurred, three discernible schools— or approaches — to Cyberpayment systems were evident.

Schools of Thought in Cyberpayment System Oversight

RAND's analysis of exercise deliberations identified three schools of thought with respect to Cyberpayment system oversight. The following labels refer to these schools below:

Model 1: "Government Lead"

Model 2: "Collaborative"

Model 3: "Self-Regulatory"

The three approaches to Cyberpayment system anti-money laundering oversight differ in many ways, but the central differences stem from the perceived appropriateness of independent governmental action in setting mandates for Cyberpayment systems. Indeed, the overwhelming consensus among exercise participants was in favor of collaborative regulation of Cyberpayment systems — with industry and government sharing the central roles of defining standards and policing fraud and abuse. One interesting omission in most of the discussions was the absence of a significant perceived role for public interest advocates in the construction of the oversight regime. The highly negative perspective on government mandates broke down somewhat when the question of whether a necessary identity of interests could be assumed between business and government. In this area many argued that an irreducible minimum *societal interest* existed that may conflict with the commercial preferences of Cyberpayment issuers.

From this position grew a further debate on the appropriate *timing* of government action. Because the Cyberpayment industry was seen to be maturing, there was a general consensus that whatever regulations that were drafted should not be put in place until the market had more fully developed. More directly, the process through which regulations were designed and made subject to public comment and criticism was identified as a critical issue. The central point of debate seemed to be on the degree of collaboration between business and government in the drafting of regulations governing the Cyberpayment industry. Those arguing for Model 1 viewed it as important that government maintain an entirely "arms length" relationship with the industry. Central features of the Model 1 control perspective are:

- Highly structured and rule-governed contacts between industry and government;
- Direct government-to-government negotiation of harmonized rules for international Cyberpayment anti-money laundering oversight, which would then be drafted into regulations governing national firms;
- Government mandates for procedural and technical standards to be used within Cyberpayment systems, with law enforcement and payment system regulatory requirements for information and transparency the principal drivers of regulatory design;
- Mandates governing the features of particular Cyberpayment products would be imposed reflecting the concerns of law enforcement regarding potential misuse of Cyberpayment systems for criminal purposes;
- All Cyberpayment systems would operate under close government supervision because they are perceived to be issuing Cyberpayment value — which some hold is fully analogous to traditional currency;

Those arguing this perspective are decidedly unconvinced by calls for increased deregulation of the financial industry, and instead perceive a need to prevent a potentially catastrophic degradation in the utility of traditional regulatory and law enforcement tools for fighting payment system abuse.

Model 2 offers a similar but slightly different approach to Cyberpayment system oversight. The central difference between this approach and the one outlined above is that most of the government mandates would derive from a structured process of public consultation where Cyberpayment industry representatives and the broader public would have the right to argue their positions before an administrative board or committee.

To summarize this approach:

- A moderately loose process for consultations between industry and government on prospective regulatory action affecting Cyberpayment systems;
- Direct government-to-government negotiation of harmonized rules for international Cyberpayment oversight would be paralleled by a process of industry consultations on prospective rule changes;
- Government mandates for procedural and technical standards to be used within Cyberpayment systems would be weak, perhaps only involving those systems used by government agencies for payments. Law enforcement and payment system regulators would remain the most significant articulators of the governments concerns with Cyberpayment system oversight;
- Cyberpayment systems would operate under a fixed set of rules administered by an independent oversight agency; Model 3 represents something of a middle ground between the weak and strong variants of traditional governmental oversight. Rather than seeking to impose regulations (deriving from either domestic rule making or international negotiation) on the Cyberpayment industry, this model is based on close collaboration with the private sector on both technical standards and rule making.. The principal features of this approach are:
- Close government-industry collaboration on setting rules governing entities permitted to operate as issuers of Cyberpayment value. An industry-level body might well become the principal partner of government in constructing a flexible and coherent regulatory framework for Cyberpayment systems;

- Oversight is inherently international in scope. This would mean that industry would be represented within governmental fora where international negotiating positions on Cyberpayment standards and oversight were crafted. The government might also elect to allow industry to set its own standards within internationally constituted standards organizations. In this case only broad governmental requirements for safety and soundness concerns would need to be mandated.
- Emphasis is placed on appropriate procedural and technical standards in the underlying infrastructure of Cyberpayment systems. Because these are determined principally by economic and technological factors, government would refrain from setting explicit technical or procedural requirements, instead focusing on overall information access mandates and broad operating standards;
- Qualitative differentiation of applications within the Cyberpayment environment is critical, with different regulatory treatment appropriate for each. This approach argues that a single regulatory regime for all Cyberpayment products is not advisable, and that more qualitatively sensitive decisions must be made regarding the perceived vulnerabilities of particular products to fraud and abuse;
- Government mandates are the last resort for regulation of Cyberpayment products.

Model One is the perspective most "friendly" to an expanded regulatory role for government in supervising Cyberpayment systems, with Models 2 and 3 representing the most deregulated forms of Cyberpayment system oversight. Without prejudice to the issue of which model is the most suitable to emerging Cyberpayment systems, it appears clear that Model 1 conflicts the most with contemporary trends favoring the deregulation of the financial services industry.

Model 2 could be interpreted as a transitional stage, where models of industry-government collaboration could provide a "proof of principle" for concepts of industry self-regulation and governmental "arms length" supervision. This interpretation would leave Model 3 as an oversight framework perhaps best suited for a mature and well-understood Cyberpayments industry.

With established frameworks of industry-government and inter-governmental information and knowledge sharing, it is possible that this sort of oversight model could allow for the reconciliation of market efficiency and competitiveness concerns with public issues regarding the safety and soundness of an emerging payments industry.

CYBERPAYMENT TECHNOLOGY

Progress toward technical and commercial standards in the Cyberpayment industry has been steady and the emergence of Cyberpayment systems is gathering momentum. At present, a small number of stored-value type smart card and network-based products are undergoing pilot testing. These tests are taking place on a global basis, thus underscoring the international nature of the emerging Cyberpayments infrastructure.

Some Cyberpayment instrument features such as peer-to-peer value transfer and payer anonymity offer to the consumer an instrument with much of the flexibility and convenience of cash together with an enhanced ability to conduct purchases on an almost global basis. This technology suggests that law enforcement must begin to consider the potential implications of an environment where the wide availability of Cyberpayment instruments could substantially reduce the use of physical currency in consumer-level transactions.

In considering the potential Cyberpayments-money laundering nexus, it should be noted that the same technologies underlying Cyberpayment products could also be used as new information gathering tools by law enforcement and payment system regulators. The privacy implications of enhanced government surveillance of information networks is an issue that was addressed at considerable length during the exercise. Any policies in this area would have to be carefully crafted so as to meet constitutional protections of individual privacy and governmental concerns with critical infrastructure protection.

CYBERPAYMENT SYSTEMS FOR MONEY LAUNDERING

The RAND exercise focused on identifying potential characteristics in Cyberpayment systems that could be exploited by money launderers. By their nature, Cyberpayment systems have the potential to eliminate the money launderer's biggest problem, the physical movement of large amounts of cash. The globalization of many proposed Cyberpayment systems may also offer money launderers opportunities to exploit national differences in security standards and oversight rules to conceal the movement of illicit funds. Previous forums such as the Financial Action Task Force (FATF) have identified a number of features that law enforcement must consider with respect to Cyberpayment transactions. Among them are (1) Disintermediation; (2) A Potential Wide Variety of Cyberpayment Service Providers; (3) Peer-to-Peer Transfers; (4) Transaction Anonymity and; (5) Denomination Limits and Expiration Dates.

Each of these basic features is described in more detail below. While these basic features make Cyberpayments attractive as a potential means to reduce transaction costs in commerce and contribute to the increased efficiency of payment methods, these features are also consistent with existing vulnerabilities that have been exploited by criminals conducting financial transactions using traditional means.

Disintermediation

Historically, law enforcement and regulatory officials have relied on the intermediation of banks and other regulated financial institutions to provide "choke points" through which funds must generally pass and where records would be maintained. Disintermediation involves the transfer of financial value between entities without the intermediate involvement of an identifiable third party subject to governmental oversight (e.g., record-keeping requirements via a bank). Should

Cyberpayment systems permit disintermediated value transfers in unlimited amounts, money launderers could use this as an opportunity to avoid traditional law enforcement money tracing methods.

Cyberpayment Service Providers

Bank and non-bank entities may be subject to different rules regarding their operation of Cyberpayment systems. This difference is already the case in several nations where non-bank Cyberpayment issuers are currently subject to a different set of rules from banks.

A simple extension of traditional payment system oversight to new non-bank Cyberpayment issuers may address some of the concerns regarding potential system abuse by money launderers. However, the new systems are configured differently and constantly mutating, so a "one size fits all" regulatory approach is not necessarily appropriate or even possible.

Peer-To-Peer Transfers of Value

Some Cyberpayment systems allow consumers to transfer value peer-to-peer (and thus, disintermediated) using an electronic "wallet," a telephone, or via the Internet. Such value transfers pose perhaps the most direct challenge to governmental oversight of Cyberpayment systems. In the absence of intelligence information or evidence from non-Cyberpayment system sources (e.g., physical surveillance) triggering an investigation into specific suspect stored value instrument activity, clearly illicit or suspicious peer-to-peer transfers of value are unlikely to be detected.

Transaction Anonymity

In some emerging Cyberpayment products, the origins of funds are relatively opaque and the identity of the individual or entity transferring them difficult to determine. In fact, payer anonymity (the identity of the party initiating a Cyberpayment value transfer) is a central characteristic of some proposed systems. For Cyberpayment value transfers (e.g., via the Internet or the basic telephone system), transaction anonymity could be an almost insuperable barrier to law enforcement detection. While candidate solutions for this problem have been put forward, they raise issues concerning individual privacy.

Denomination Limits and Expiration Dates

Cyberpayment product issuers are likely to limit the maximum amounts that can be stored on smart cards or other devices, to reduce the risks of fraud or other losses. As with credit cards, Cyberpayment issuers will also likely establish needs-based denomination limits that would be determined by commercial and market factors. (Recent consumer tests of Cyberpayment systems indicate likely consumer limits of approximately $1,000-$3,000). Cyberpayment products held by retailers are likely to have a much larger value limit than those for most individuals and differ widely between retailers. Cyberpayment value could also be programmed to expire after a certain number of transfers. As early technology adopters, money launderers could be expected to exploit whatever limits are established, just as they do now by structuring transactions under currency reporting limits, obtaining multiple cards (credit or debit), using multiple names, or employing multiple issuers.

THE EXERCISES

The time frame for the exercise was intended to be far enough in the future so that Cyberpayment systems would have progressed substantially. The third step returned to the present or, more precisely, the very near future. The basic steps of the exercise were:

Step One

First phase of the crisis. Competing Mexican and Colombian drug traffickers increasingly exploit Cyberpayment technologies for money laundering. U.S. decisionmakers face a series of difficult tactical and strategic issues in the areas of law enforcement, international financial institution collaboration, and bilateral initiatives to improve U.S.-Mexican Cyberpayment system oversight. The participants were asked to consider, debate and select appropriate tactical responses to the emerging crisis.

Step Two

Second phase of the crisis. Escalation in the "Mexican Drug War" and further exploitation of Cyberpayment systems for money laundering by the drug cartels, in spite of more aggressive law enforcement efforts. Cartel efforts threaten the financial and perhaps political stability of Mexico.

The participants discovered that Mexico was in the middle of a financial crisis, that the new Cyberpayment system had a flawed encryption scheme and that Mexican drug cartels were taking advantage of the situation. By laundering money, the cartels were causing major economic and price destabilization through manipulating Cyberpayment systems. As the Mexican crisis escalated to the point where money was flowing out of the country in massive amounts, the participants were again asked to prepare a memorandum with the objectives of protecting the U.S. Cyberpayment industry from spillover damage caused by the Mexican Crisis. The participants were to recommend short term measures to respond to security problems in the systems and attempt to stimulate broader international measures to improve the industry.

Step Three

Return to the present/near future; lessons learned/ implications stage of the exercise. Participants were asked to address the challenge of formulating a strategy and policy "Action Plan" that would make the hypothetical events portrayed in the foregoing scenario impossible, less likely, and/or more manageable. Specific focus was placed on the development of ideas for:

(1) government-industry cooperation and

(2) regulatory, law enforcement, and legislative recommendations to prevent the potential abuse of Cyberpayment systems for money laundering.

Cyberpayment Network Targeting Order

The exercise used a hypothetical analogue to a law enforcement technique used currently, the Geographic Targeting

Order (GTO). A GTO gives the Treasury Department the authority to require a financial institution or a group of financial institutions in a geographic area to file special reports or maintain records beyond the ordinary requirements imposed by BSA regulations.

A recent GTO in New York in 1996-97 required 3,200 money transmitter agents to report identifying information on all cash remittances of $750 or more to Colombia. This led to a dramatic reduction in the volume of suspected drug-related funds flowing through money transmitters to Colombia, and triggered a number of large seizures of cash at air and sea ports along the eastern seaboard as traffickers shifted to more vulnerable means of moving their money.

The physical movement of cash remains a critical weak point in drug trafficker attempts to launder illicit funds. Therefore, GTOs are especially effective because of their ability to target a particular area of cash movement. The RAND exercise employed a hypothetical Cyberpayment Network Targeting Order (CNTO). The CNTO enabled law enforcement authorities to trace transfers of value within Cyberpayment networks. A combination of traditional investigative methods and the hypothetical CNTO was seen by some as a means of more effective detection of illicit activity within cyberspace. Others, however, saw it as beyond the bounds of existing law and technology.

The exercise illuminated potential problems flowing from the possible use of Cyberpayment systems by money launderers working for international narcotics cartels. Participants in the exercise discussed law enforcement and Cyberpayment oversight problems that flowed from the perceived abuse of these systems and evaluated potential remedial measures, such as the CNTO, for safeguarding Cyberpayment network security.

POTENTIAL POLICY IMPLICATIONS

Five general policy issues were identified in the exercise as areas of money launderingrelated concern:

(1) law enforcement issues;

(2) regulatory issues;

(3) international policy coordination;

(4) Cyberpayment system architecture and design issues; and

(5) traditional definitions of currency.

Each of these issue areas carries important implications for the future of government and industry roles in managing these new payment system technologies so as to prevent their abuse. Because the exercise participants represented the entire spectrum of interests in this evolving technology, the responses to the exercises varied dramatically. Participants considered these hypothetical policy issues within a decision-making process linked to the events of the scenario. Their responses were collected by exercise designers and reported to all participants during a discussion session led by the group chairpersons. This information was in turn analyzed by using the participants' annotated briefing books which contained individual responses to the questions presented during the exercises and operational notes taken by conference designers during exercise deliberations. While no clear consensus on any overall approach to the potential concerns in the Cyberpayment-money laundering nexus was identified during the exercise, an important structuring and focusing of the debate in the five areas did occur. The findings listed below reflect RAND's evaluation of the focused discussion of the participants as well as RAND's independent research.

Due to the breadth of the subject, other larger issues concerning monetary policy and regulatory oversight emerged that were outside the direct scope of the exercise. Additional consideration of these issues, over time, will be needed to evaluate Cyberpayment systems and to ensure an effective and consistent process for governmental oversight.

Law Enforcement

The discussion of law enforcement issues focused predominantly on the perceived potential value of Cyberpayment instruments to money launderers and others attempting to conceal financial activities from government oversight. The second focus of these deliberations was on potential regulatory and law enforcement responses to perceived Cyberpayments abuse, and the place of computer-based investigative techniques alongside more traditional investigative techniques, in countering patterns of abuse.

Without proper precautions, Cyberpayment systems could have the potential to undermine traditional law enforcement investigative tools and techniques Current antimoney laundering law enforcement strategies and techniques rely on extensive use of manpower and paper trails left by traditional monetary transactions. Since Cyberpayments are not personnel-intensive and could potentially leave little or no paper trail, they could facilitate a means for circumventing current techniques.

Law enforcement authorities may require new tools and techniques in order to conduct effective surveillance and analysis of Cyberpayment network information flows Some international sharing of these information resources may also be required Computer-based investigative techniques may allow Cyberpayment system regulators and law enforcement authorities to trace questionable electronic fund flows. Law enforcement authorities may employ computer investigative techniques to evaluate information regarding suspected Cyberpayment system abuse.

This evaluation depends, however, on some sort of infrastructure being developed for identifying value flows within networks that meet certain suspicious criteria, or more pointedly on differentiating Cyberpayment value from broader traffic flows within the Internet. International information sharing in pursuit of coordinated Cyberpayment system oversight and protection may involve risk.

Jurisdictional issues involving federal, state, and local government law enforcement activities pertaining to potential Cyberpayment system abuse will need to be addressed if effective counters to potential abuse are to be implemented. Individual privacy concerns are a significant issue in the design of oversight procedures for Cyberpayment systems As noted, government concerns with the potential abuse of Cyberpayment systems create calls from some for extensive surveillance capabilities to be developed for Cyberpayment networks. However, this suggestion raises privacy concerns for individuals and potential constitutional issues for society. Consumer privacy advocates, in particular, have warned of possible abuses of surveillance techniques. Reconciling divergent perspectives on this issue will likely require continuous dialogue between and among the many stakeholders in the Cyberpayments arena.

Regulatory Issues

During the exercise, regulatory questions were perhaps the most vigorously discussed of any of the defining concerns involved with Cyberpayment systems. As an overlapping area of interest, regulatory concerns are themselves dependent on more general decisions on the importance of international policy coordination on the oversight of Cyberpayment systems, and on decisions regarding the legal character of Cyberpayment value as a payment instrument. Beginning with the issue of which institutions or entities would have the legal authority to provide Cyberpayment services, participants voiced a number of differing perspectives on the topic.

A majority of participants argued that whichever regulatory approach was adopted, it should be based on the ongoing collaborative public-private partnership. Under this rubric, however, differences of opinion were voiced on the character and intrusiveness of governmental *mandates* with respect to both Cyberpayment system operators and the electronic payment instruments themselves. Public-private collaboration will be key to crafting and implementing a coherent and sustainable Cyberpayment system infrastructure protection process The expanding dialogue between government and private industry on Cyberpayment network standards and product features in the U.S. and elsewhere is a major positive step towards coming to grips with potential abuses of Cyberpayment systems. Many participants voiced concern that, at least initially, cyberpayment system providers that operate with or through banks should be subject to laundering controls analogous to those that apply to banks and other financial institutions.

Policy, regulation, and enforcement in the Cyberpayment area will consistently be challenged to keep up with the rapidly evolving technology. For the foreseeable future, law enforcement and financial payment system regulators will not experience a stable technical environment in the Cyberpayment arena. National regulations imposed in the absence of mature international technical and market standards will need to be inherently flexible in responding to this evolutionary environment.

This situation could also inhibit the development of reliable technical means for tracing transactions within Cyberpayment networks when investigating illicit financial activity. One suggestion for addressing this concern was developing minimum standards for appropriate government access to Cyberpayment data as a condition of licensing – without prejudice to the particular encryption and product protection technologies implemented in a particular application.

Domestically, the US government may need to play a facilitating role for both industry and consumers to accelerate the achievement of effective standards for Cyberpayment systems Because of the centrality of financial payment systems to the U.S. economy and the potential impact of a commercially mature and successful Cyberpayment industry on our economy, a Cyberpayment system failure could negatively affect the credibility of the entire Cyberpayment industry. It was also suggested that the public perception that these systems are more (or less) prone to fraud or financial abuse than traditional payment methods may significantly affect consumer acceptance of Cyberpayment transactions. Any regulatory and law enforcement actions designed to monitor consumer behavior within the Cyberpayment environment will need to be closely integrated into a broader infrastructure assurance policy in order to protect the industry's acceptance in the financial marketplace.

International Policy Coordination

The discussion on international policy issues raised by the Cyberpayment systems focused on the degree to which national guidelines and regulations on system characteristics could be rendered ineffective and/or circumvented by international variation in oversight and regulations. Participants agreed that Cyberpayment products were inherently international in nature, and that any longer-term governmental actions would need to be international in scope.

International strategy and policy coordination will be central to effective Cyberpayment system oversight. The global nature of the Cyberpayment infrastructure suggests that some harmonization of guidelines and standards for Cyberpayment system operators will be imperative for effective oversight of the Cyberpayment industry. Because the Cyberpayment industry is evolving, a comprehensive and thorough regulatory regime is unlikely to be achieved prior to the stabilization of commercial and technical conditions. The recent discussions within a number of relatively recently established international bodies such as the G-7 Financial Action Task Force (FATF) have been an especially effective means for sharing insights on international Cyberpayment system oversight.

9

The Functions of Money

We have seen that three inconveniences attach to the practice of simple barter, namely, the improbability, of coincidence between persons wanting and persons possessing; the complexity of exchanges, which are not made in terms of one single substance; and the need of some means of dividing and distributing valuable articles. Money remedies these inconveniences, and thereby performs two distinct functions of high importance, acting as—

(1) A medium of exchange.

(2) A common measure of value.

In its first form money is simply any commodity esteemed by all persons, any article of food, clothing, or ornament which any person will readily receive, and which, therefore, every person desires to have by him in greater or less quantity, in order that he may have the means of procuring necessaries of life at any time. Although many commodities may be capable of performing this function of a medium more or less perfectly, some one article will usually be selected, as money *par excellence,* by custom or the force of circumstances.

This article will then begin to be used as a measure of value. Being accustomed to exchange things frequently for sums of money, people learn the value of other articles in terms of money, so that all exchanges will most readily be calculated and adjusted by comparison of the money values of the things exchanged.

A Standard of Value

A third function of money soon develops itself. Commerce cannot advance far before people begin to borrow and lend, and debts of various origin are contracted. It is in some cases usual, indeed, to restore the very same article which was borrowed, and in almost every case it would be possible to pay back in the same kind of commodity. If corn be borrowed, corn might be paid back, with interest in corn; but the lender will often not wish to have things returned to him at an uncertain time, when he does not much need them, or when their value is unusually low. A borrower, too, may need several different kinds of articles, which he is not likely to obtain from one person; hence arises the convenience of borrowing and lending in one generally recognized commodity, of which the value varies little. Every person making a contract by which he will receive something at a future day, will prefer to secure the receipt of a commodity likely to be as valuable then as now. This commodity will usually be the current money, and it will thus come to perform the function of a *standard of value.* We must not suppose that the substance serving as a standard of value is really invariable in value, but merely that it is chosen as that measure by which the value of future payments is to be regulated. Bearing in mind that value is only the ratio of quantities exchanged, it is certain that no substance permanently bears exactly the same value relatively to another commodity; but it will, of course, be desirable to select as the standard of value that which appears likely to continue to exchange for many other commodities in nearly unchanged ratios.

A Store of Value

It is worthy of inquiry whether money does not also serve a fourth distinct purpose—that of embodying value in a convenient form for conveyance to distant places. Money, when acting as a medium of exchange, circulates backwards and forwards near the same spot, and may sometimes return to the same hands again and again. It subdivides and distributes property, and *lubricates* the action of exchange.

But at times a person needs to condense his property into the smallest compass, so that he may hoard it away for a time, or carry it with him on a long journey, or transmit it to a friend in a distant country. Something which is very valuable, although of little bulk and weight, and which will be recognised as very valuable in every part of the world, is necessary for this purpose. The current money of a country is perhaps more likely to fulfil these conditions than anything else, although diamonds and other precious stones, and articles of exceptional beauty and rarity, might occasionally be employed. The use of esteemed articles as a store or medium for conveying value may in some cases precede their employment as currency. Mr. Gladstone states that in the Homeric poems gold is mentioned as being hoarded and treasured up, and as being occasionally used in the payment of services, before it became the common measure of value, oxen being then used for the latter purpose. Historically speaking, such a generally esteemed substance as gold seems to have served, firstly, as a commodity valuable for ornamental purposes; secondly, as stored wealth; thirdly, as a medium of exchange; and, lastly, as a measure of value.

Separation of Functions

It is in the highest degree important that the reader should discriminate carefully and constantly between the four functions which money fulfils, at least in modern societies. We are so accustomed to use the one same substance in all the four different ways, that they tend to become confused together in thought. We come to regard as almost necessary that union of functions which is, at the most, a matter of convenience, and may not always be desirable. We might certainly employ one substance as a medium of exchange, a second as a measure of value, a third as a standard of value, and a fourth as a store of value. In buying and selling we might transfer portions of gold; in expressing and calculating prices we might speak in terms of silver; when we wanted to make long leases we might define the rent in terms of wheat, and when we wished to carry our riches away we might condense it into the form of precious stones. This use ot different commodities for each of the functions of money has in fact been partially carried out. In Queen

Elizabeth's reign silver was the common measure of value; gold was employed in large payments in quantities depending upon its current value in silver, while corn was required by the Act 18th Elizabeth, c. VI. (1576), to be the standard of value in drawing the leases of certain college lands.

There is evident convenience in selecting, if possible, one single substance which can serve all the functions of money. It will save trouble if we can pay in the same money in which the prices of things are calculated. As few people have the time or patience to investigate closely the history of prices, they will probably assume that the money in which they make all minor and temporary bargains, is also the best standard in which to register debts and contracts extending over many years. A great mass of payments too are invariably fixed by law, such as tolls, fees, and tariffs of charges: many other payments are fixed by custom. Accordingly, even if the medium of exchange varied considerably in value, people would go on making their payments in terms of it, as if there had been no variation, some gaining at the expense of others.

One of our chief tasks in this book will be to consider the various materials which have been employed as money, or have been, or may be, suggested for the purpose. It must be our endeavour, if possible, to discover some substance which will in the highest degree combine the characters requisite for all the different functions of money, but we must bear in mind that a partition of these functions amongst different substances is practicable. We will first proceed to a brief review of the very various ways in which the need of currency has been supplied from the earliest ages, and we will afterwards analyse the physical qualities and circumstances which render the substances employed more or less suited to the purpose to which they were applied. We may thus arrive at some decision as to the exact nature of the commodity which is best adapted to meet our needs in the present day.

EARLY HISTORY OF MONEY

Living in civilized communities, and accustomed to the use of coined metallic money, we learn to identify money with gold and silver; hence spring hurtful and insidious fallacies. It is always useful, therefore, to be reminded of the truth, so well stated by Turgot, that every kind of merchandise has the two properties of measuring value and transferring value. It is entirely a question of degree what commodities will in any given state of society form the most convenient currency, and this truth will be best impressed upon us by a brief consideration of the very numerous things which have at one time or other been employed as money. Though there are many numismatists and many political economists, the natural history of money is almost a virgin subject, upon which I should like to dilate; but the narrow limits of my space forbid me from attempting more than a brief sketch of the many interesting facts which may be collected.

Currency in the Hunting State

Perhaps the most rudimentary state of industry is that in which subsistence is gained by hunting wild animals. The proceeds of the chase would, in such a state, be the property of most generally recognised value. The meat of the animals captured would, indeed, be too perishable in nature to be hoarded or often exchanged; but it is otherwise with the skins, which, being preserved and valued for clothing, became one of the earliest materials of currency. Accordingly, there is abundant evidence that furs or skins were employed as money in many ancient nations. They serve this purpose to the present day in some parts of the world.

In the book of Job (ii. 4) we read, "Skin for skin, yea, all that a man hath will he give for his life;" a statement clearly implying that skins were taken as the representative of value among the ancient Oriental nations. Etymological research shows that the same may be said of the northern nations from the earliest times. In the Esthonian language the word *râha* generally signifies money, but its equivalent in the kindred Lappish tongue has not yet altogether lost the original meaning of skin or fur. Leather money is said to have circulated in Russia as late as the reign of Peter the Great, and it is worthy of notice, that classical writers have recorded traditions to the effect that the earliest currency used at Rome, Lacedæmon, and Carthage, was formed of leather.

We need not go back, however, to such early times to study the use of rude currencies. In the traffic of the Hudson's Bay Company with the North American Indians, furs, in spite of their differences of quality and size, long formed the medium of exchange. It is very instructive, and corroborative of the previous evidence to find that, even after the use of coin had become common among the Indians the skin was still commonly used as the money of account. Thus Whymper says, "a gun, nominally worth about forty shillings, bought twenty 'skins.' This term is the old one employed by the company. One skin (beaver) is supposed to be worth two shillings, and it represents two marten, and so on. You heard a great deal about 'skins' at Fort Yukon, as the workmen were also charged for clothing, etc., in this way."

Currency in the Pastoral State

In the next higher stage of civilization, the pastoral state, sheep and cattle naturally form the most valuable and negotiable kind of property. They are easily transferable, convey themselves about, and can be kept for many years, so that they readily perform some of the functions of money.

We have abundance of evidence, traditional, written, and etymological, to show this. In the Homeric poems oxen are distinctly and repeatedly mentioned as the commodity in terms of which other objects are valued. The arms of Diomed are stated to be worth nine oxen, and are compared with those of Glaucos, worth one hundred.

The tripod, the first prize for wrestlers in the 23rd Iliad, was valued at twelve oxen, and a woman captive, skilled in industry, at four. It is peculiarly interesting to find oxen thus used as the common measure of value, because from other passages it is probable, as already mentioned, that the precious metals, though as yet uncoined, were used as a store of value, and occasionally as a medium of exchange. The several functions of money were thus clearly performed by different commodities at this early period.

In several languages the name for money is identical with that of some kind of cattle or domesticated animal. It is generally allowed that *pecunia,* the Latin word for money, is derived from *pecus,* cattle. From the Agamemnon of Æschylus we learn that the figure of an ox was the sign first impressed upon coins, and the same is said to have been the case with the earliest issues of the Roman *As.* Numismatic researches fail to bear out these traditions, which were probably invented to explain the connection between the name of the coin and the animal. A corresponding connection between these notions may be detected in much more modern languages. Our common expression for the payment of a sum of money is *fee,* which is nothing but the Anglo-Saxon *feoh,* meaning alike money and cattle, a word cognate with the German *vieh,* which still bears only the original meaning of cattle. It is even supposed by Grimm that the same root reappears in the Teutonic and Scandinavian languages, in the Gothic, *skatts,* the modern High German *schatz,* the Anglo-Saxon, *scät* or *sceat,* the ancient Norsk *skat,* all meaning wealth, property, treasure, tax, or tribute, especially in the shape of cattle. This theory is confirmed by the fact that the Frisian equivalent, *sket,* has retained the original meaning of cattle to the present day. In the Norsk, Anglo-Saxon, and English, *scat* or *scot* has been specialized to denote tax or tribute.

In the ancient German codes of law, fines and penalties are actually defined in terms of live-stock. In the Zend Avesta, as Professor Theodores further informs me, the scale of rewards to be paid to physicians is carefully stated, and in every case the fee consists in some sort of cattle. The fifth and sixth lectures in Sir H. S. Maine's most interesting work on "The Early History of Institutions," which has just been published, are full of curious information showing the importance of live-stock in a primitive state of society. Being counted *by the head,* the kine was called *capitale,* whence the economical term *capital,* the law term *chattel,* and our common name *cattle.*

In countries where slaves form one of the most common and valuable possessions, it is quite natural that they should serve as the medium of exchange like cattle. Pausanias mentions their use in this way, and in Central Africa and some other places where slavery still flourishes, they are the medium of exchange along with cattle and ivory tusks. According to Earl's account of New Guinea, there is in that island a large traffic in slaves, and a slave forms the unit of value. Even in England slaves are believed to have been exchanged at one time in the manner of money.

Articles of Ornament as Currency

A passion for personal adornment is one of the most primitive and powerful instincts of the human race, and as articles used for such purposes would be durable, universally esteemed, and easily transferable, it is natural that they should be circulated as money. The wampumpeag of the North American Indians is a case in point, as it certainly served as jewellery. It consisted of beads made of the ends of black and white shells, rubbed down and polished, and then strung into belts or necklaces, which were valued according to their length, and also according to their colour and lustre, a foot of black peag being worth two feet of white peag. It was so well established as currency among the natives that the Court of Massachusetts ordered, in 1649, that it should be received in the payment of debts among settlers to the amount of forty shillings. It is curious to learn, too, that just as European misers hoard up gold and silver coins, the richer Indian chiefs secrete piles of wampum beads, having no better means of investing their superfluous wealth.

Exactly analogous to this North American currency, is that of the cowry shells, which, under one name or another—chamgos, zimbis, bouges, porcelanes, etc.—have long been used in the East Indies as small money. In British India, Siam, the West Coast of Africa, and elsewhere on the tropical coasts, they are still used as small change, being collected on the shores of the Maldive and Laccadive Islands, and exported for the purpose. Their value varies somewhat, according to the abundance of the yield, but in India the current rate used to be about 5000 shells for one rupee, at which rate each shell is worth about the two-hundredth part of a penny. Among our interesting fellow-subjects, the Fijians, whale's teeth served in the place of cowries, and white teeth were exchanged for red teeth somewhat in the ratio of shillings to sovereigns.

Among other articles of ornament or of special value used as currency, may be mentioned yellow amber, engraved stones, such as the Egyptian scarabæi, and tusks of ivory.

Currency in the Agricultural State

Many vegetable productions are at least as well suited for circulation as some of the articles which have been mentioned. It is not surprising to find, then, that among a people supporting themselves by agriculture, the more durable products were thus used. Corn has been the medium of exchange in remote parts of Europe from the time of the ancient Greeks to the present day. In Norway corn is even deposited in banks, and lent and borrowed. What wheat, barley, and oats are to Europe, such is maize in parts of Central America, especially Mexico, where it formerly circulated. In many of the countries surrounding the Mediterranean, olive oil is one of the commonest articles of produce and consumption; being, moreover, pretty uniform in quality, durable, and easily divisible, it has long served as currency in the Ionian Islands, Mytilene, some towns of Asia Minor, and elsewhere in the Levant.

Just as cowries circulate in the East Indies, so cacao nuts, in Central America and Yucatan, form a perfectly recognised and probably an ancient fractional money. Travellers have published many distinct statements as to their value, but it is impossible to reconcile these statements without supposing great changes of value either in the nuts or in the coins with which they are compared. In 1521, at Caracas, about thirty cacao nuts were worth one penny English, whereas recently ten beans would go to a penny, according to Squier's statements. In the European countries, where almonds are commonly grown, they have circulated to some extent like the cacao nuts, but are variable in value, according to the success of the harvest.

It is not only, however, as a minor currency that vegetable products have been used in modern times. In the American settlements and the West India Islands, in former days, specie used to become inconveniently scarce, and the legislators fell back upon the device of obliging creditors to receive payment in produce at stated rates. In 1618, the Governor of the Plantations of Virginia ordered that tobacco should be received at the rate of three shillings for the pound weight, under the penalty of three years' hard labour. We are told that, when the Virginia Company imported young women as wives for the settlers, the price per head was one hundred pounds of tobacco, subsequently raised to one hundred and fifty. As late as 1732, the legislature of Maryland made tobacco and Indian corn legal tenders; and in 1641 there were similar laws concerning corn in Massachussets. The governments of some of the West India Islands seem to have made attempts to imitate these peculiar currency laws, and it was provided that the successful plaintiff in a lawsuit should be obliged to accept various kinds of raw produce, such as sugar, rum, molasses, ginger, indigo, or tobacco. Such endeavours to establish a kind of multiple currency will be found to possess considerable interest.

The perishable nature of most kinds of animal food prevents them from being much used as money; but eggs are said to have circulated in the Alpine villages of Switzerland, and dried codfish have certainly acted as currency in the colony of Newfoundland.

Manufactured and Miscellaneous Articles as Currency

The enumeration of articles which have served as money may already seem long enough for the purposes in view. I will, therefore, only add briefly that a great number of manufactured commodities have been used as a medium of exchange in various times and places. Such are the pieces of cotton cloth, called *Guinea pieces,* used for traffic upon the banks of the Senegal, or the somewhat similar pieces circulated in Abyssinia, the Soulou Archipelago, Sumatra, Mexico, Peru, Siberia, and among the Veddahs. It is less easy to understand the origin of the curious straw money which circulated until 1694 in the Portuguese possessions in Angola, and which consisted of small mats, called libongos, woven out of rice straw, and worth about

1½*d.* each. These mats must have had, at least originally, some purpose apart from their use as currency, and were perhaps analogous to the fine woven mats so much valued by the Samoans, and also treated by them as a medium of exchange.

Salt has been circulated not only in Abyssinia, but in Sumatra, Mexico, and elsewhere. Cubes of benzoin gum or beeswax in Sumatra, red feathers in the Islands of the Pacific Ocean, cubes of tea in Tartary, iron shovels or hoes among the Malagasy, are other peculiar forms of currency. The remarks of Adam Smith concerning the use of handmade nails as money in some Scotch villages will be remembered by many readers, and need not be repeated. M. Chevalier has adduced an exactly corresponding case from one of the French coalfields.

Were space available it would be interesting to discuss the not improbable suggestion of Boucher de Perthes, that, perhaps, after all, the finely worked stone implements now so frequently discovered were among the earliest mediums of exchange. Some of them are certainly made of jade, nephrite, or other hard stones, only found in distant countries, so that an active traffic in such implements must have existed in times of which we have no records whatever.

There are some obscure allusions in classical authors to a wooden money circulating among the Byzantines, and to a wooden talent used at Antioch and Alexandria, but in the absence of fuller information as to their nature, it is impossible to do more than mention them.

Qualities of the Material of Money

Many recent writers, such as Huskisson, MacCulloch, James Mill, Garnier, Chevalier, and Walras, have satisfactorily described the qualities which should be possessed by the material of money. Earlier writers seem, however, to have understood the subject almost as well. Harris explained these qualities with remarkable clearness in his "Essay upon Money and Coins," published in 1757, a work which appeared before the "Wealth of Nations," yet gave an exposition of the principles of money which can hardly be improved at the present day.

Eighty years before, however, Rice Vaughan, in his excellent little "Treatise of Money," had written a brief but satisfactory statement of the qualities requisite in money. We even find that William Stafford, the author of that remarkable dialogue of the Elizabethan age (1581), called "A Brief Conceipte of English Policy," showed perfect insight into the subject. Of all writers, M. Chevalier, however, probably gives the most accurate and full account of the properties which money should possess, and I shall in many points follow his views.

The prevailing defect in the treatment of the subject is the failure to observe that money requires different properties as regards different functions. To decide upon the best material for money is thus a problem of great complexity, because we must take into account at once the relative importance of the several functions of money, the degree in which money is employed for each function, and the importance of each of the physical qualities of the substance with respect to each function. In a simple state of industry money is chiefly required to pass about between buyers and sellers. It should, then, be conveniently portable, divisible into pieces of various size, so that any sum may readily be made up, and easily distinguishable by its appearance, or by the design impressed upon it. When money, however, comes to serve, as it will at some future time, almost exclusively as a measure and standard of value, the system of exchange, being one of perfected barter, such properties become a matter of comparative indifference, and stability of value, joined perhaps to portability, is the most important quality. Before venturing, however, to discuss such complex questions, we must proceed to a preliminary discussion of the properties in question, which may thus perhaps be enumerated in the order of their importance:—

1. Utility and value.
2. Portability.
3. Indestructibility.
4. Homogeneity.
5. Divisibility.

6. Stability of value.

7. Cognizability.

Utility and Value

Since money has to be exchanged for valuable goods, it should itself possess value, and it must therefore have utility as the basis of value. Money, when once in full currency, is only received in order to be passed on, so that if all people could be induced to take worthless bits of material at a fixed rate of valuation, it might seem that money does not really require to have substantial value.

Something like this does frequently happen in the history of currencies, and apparently valueless shells, bits of leather, or scraps of paper, are actually received in exchange for costly commodities.

This strange phenomenon is, however, in most cases capable of easy explanation, and if we were acquainted with the history of every kind of money the like explanation would no doubt be possible in other cases. The essential point is that people should be induced to receive money, and pass it on freely at steady ratios of exchange for other objects; but there must always be some sufficient reason first inducing people to accept the money.

The force of habit, convention, or legal enactment may do much to maintain money in circulation when once it is afloat, but it is doubtful whether the most powerful government could oblige its subjects to accept and circulate as money a worthless substance which they had no other motive for receiving.

Certainly, in the early stages of society, the use of money was not based on legal regulations, so that the utility of the substance for other purposes must have been the prior condition of its employment as money.

Thus the singular *peag* currency, or *wampumpeag,* which was found in circulation among the North American Indians by the early explorers, was esteemed for the purpose of adornment, as already mentioned, (p. 24). The cowry shells, so widely used as a small currency in the East, are valued for ornamental purposes on the West Coast of Africa, and were in all probability employed as ornaments before they were employed as money. All the other articles mentioned in Chapter IV., such as oxen, corn, skins, tobacco, salt, cacao nuts, etc., which have performed the functions of money in one place or other, possessed independent utility and value.

If there are any apparent exceptions at all to this rule, they would doubtless admit of explanation by fuller knowledge. We may, therefore, agree with Storch when he says:—"It is impossible that a substance which has no direct value should be introduced as money, however suitable it may be in other respects for this use."

When once a substance is widely employed as money, it is conceivable that its utility will come to depend mainly upon the services which it thus confers upon the community. Gold, for instance, is far more important as the material of money than in the production of plate, jewellery, watches, gold-leaf, etc. A substance originally used for many purposes may eventually serve only as money, and yet, by the demand for currency and the force of habit, may maintain its value. The cowry circulation of the Indian coasts is probably a case in point. The importance of habit, personal or hereditary, is at least as great in monetary science as it is, according to Mr. Herbert Spencer, in morals and sociological phenomena generally.

There is, however, no reason to suppose that the value of gold and silver is at present due solely to their conventional use as money. These metals are endowed with such singularly useful properties that, if we could only get them in sufficient abundance, they would supplant all the other metals in the manufacture of household utensils, ornaments, fittings of all kinds, and an infinite multitude of small articles, which are now made of brass, copper, bronze, pewter, German silver, or, other inferior metals and alloys.

In order that money may perform some of its functions efficiently, especially those of a medium of exchange and a store of value, to be carried about, it is important that it should be made of a substance valued highly in all parts of the world, and, if possible, almost equally esteemed by all peoples. There is reason to think that gold and silver have been admired and valued by all tribes which have been lucky enough to procure them. The beautiful lustre of these metals must have drawn attention and excited admiration as much in the earliest as in the present times.

Portability

The material of money must not only be valuable, but the value must be so related to the weight and bulk of the material, that the money shall not be inconveniently heavy on the one hand, nor inconveniently minute on the other. There was a tradition in Greece that Lycurgus obliged the Lacedæmonians to use iron money, in order that its weight might deter them from overmuch trading.

However this may be, it is certain that iron money could not be used in cash payments at the present day, since a penny would weigh about a pound, and instead of a five-pound note, we should have to deliver a ton of iron. During the last century copper was actually used as the chief medium of exchange in Sweden; and merchants had to take a wheelbarrow with them when they went to receive payments in copper dalers. Many of the substances used as currency in former times must have been sadly wanting in portability. Oxen and sheep, indeed, would transport themselves on their own legs; but corn, skins, oil, nuts, almonds, etc., though in several respects forming fair currency, would be intolerably bulky and troublesome to transfer.

The portability of money is an important quality not merely because it enables the owner to carry small sums in the pocket without trouble, but because large sums can be transferred from place to place, or from continent to continent, at little cost. The result is to secure an approximate uniformity in the value of money in all parts of the world. A substance which is very heavy and bulky in proportion to value, like corn or coal, may be very scarce in one place and over abundant in another; yet the supply and demand cannot be equalized without great expense in carriage. The cost of conveying gold or silver from

London to Paris, including insurance, is only about four-tenths of one per cent.; and between the most distant parts of the world it does not exceed from two to three per cent.

Substances may be too valuable as well as too cheap, so that for ordinary transactions it would be necessary to call in the aid of the microscope and the chemical balance. Diamonds, apart from other objections, would be far too valuable for small transactions.

The value of such stones is said to vary as the square of the weight, so that we cannot institute any exact comparison with metals of which the value is simply proportional to the weight. But taking a one-carat diamond (four grains) as worth £15, we find it is, weight for weight, 460 times as valuable as gold. There are several rare metals, such as iridium and osmium, which would likewise be far too valuable to circulate. Even gold and silver are too costly for small currency. A silver penny now weighs 7¼ grains, and a gold penny would weigh only half a grain. The pretty octagonal quarter-dollar tokens circulated in California are the smallest gold coins I have seen, weighing less than four grains each, and are so thin that they can almost be blown away.

Indestructibility

If it is to be passed about in trade, and kept in reserve, money must not be subject to easy deterioration or loss. It must not evaporate like alcohol, nor putrefy like animal substances, nor decay like wood, nor rust like iron. Destructible articles, such as eggs, dried codfish, cattle, or oil, have certainly been used as currency; but what is treated as money one day must soon afterwards be eaten up. Thus a large stock of such perishable commodities cannot be kept on hand, and their value must be very variable. The several kinds of corn are less subject to this objection, since, when well dried at first, they suffer no appreciable deterioration for several years.

Homogeneity

All portions of specimens of the substance used as money should be *homogeneous,* that is, of the same quality, so that equal weights will have exactly the same value. In order that we may correctly count in terms of any unit, the units must be equal and similar, so that twice two will always make four. If we were to count in precious stones, it would seldom happen that four stones would be just twice as valuable as two stones. Even the precious metals, as found in the native state, are not perfectly homogeneous, being mixed together in almost all proportions; but this produces little inconvenience, because the assayer readily determines the quantity of each pure metal present in any ingot.

In the processes of refining and coining, the metals are afterwards reduced to almost exactly uniform degrees of fineness, so that equal weights are then of exactly equal value.

Divisibility

Closely connected with the last property is that of divisibility. Every material is, indeed, mechanically divisible, almost without limit. The hardest gems can be broken, and steel can be cut by harder steel. But the material of money should be not merely capable of division, but the aggregate value of the mass after division should be almost exactly the same as before division.

If we cut up a skin or fur the pieces will, as a general rule, be far less valuable than the whole skin or fur, except for a special intended purpose; and the same is the case with timber, stone, and most other materials in which reunion is impossible. But portions of metal can be melted together again whenever it is desirable, and the cost of doing this, including the metal lost, is in the case of precious metals very inconsiderable, varying from ¼*d.* to ½*d.* per ounce. Thus, approximately speaking, the value of any piece of gold or silver is simply proportional to the weight of fine metal which it contains.

Stability of Value

It is evidently desirable that the currency should not be subject to fluctuations of value. The ratios in which money exchanges for other commodities should be maintained as nearly as possible invariable on the average. This would be a matter of comparatively minor importance were money used only as a measure of values at any one moment, and as a medium of exchange. If all prices were altered in like proportion as soon as money varied in value, no one would lose or gain, except as regards the coin which he happened to have in his pocket, safe, or bank balance.

But, practically speaking, as we have seen, people do employ money as a standard of value for long contracts, and they often maintain payments at the same invariable rate, by custom or law, even when the real value of the payment is much altered. Hence every change in the value of money does some injury to society.

It might be plausibly said, indeed, that the debtor gains as much as the creditor loses, or *vice versâ,* so that on the whole the community is as rich as before; but this is not really true. A mathematical analysis of the subject shows that to take any sum of money from one and give it to another will, on the average of cases, injure the loser more than it benefits the receiver. A person with an income of one hundred pounds a year would suffer more by losing ten pounds than he would gain by an addition of ten pounds, because the degree of utility of money to him is considerably higher at ninety pounds than it is at one hundred and ten.

On the same principle, all gaming, betting, pure speculation, or other accidental modes of transferring property involve, on the average, a dead loss of utility. The whole incitement to industry and commerce and the accumulation of capital depends upon the expectation of enjoyment thence arising, and every variation of the currency tends in some degree to frustrate such expectation and to lessen the motive; for exertion.

Cognizability

By this name we may denote the capability of a substance for being easily recognized and distinguished from all other substances. As a medium of exchange, money has to be continually handed about, and it will occasion great trouble if every person receiving currency has to scrutinize, weigh, and test it. If it requires any skill to discriminate good money from bad, poor ignorant people are sure to be imposed upon. Hence the medium of exchange should have certain distinct marks which nobody can mistake. Precious stones, even if in other respects good as money, could not be so used, because only a skilled lapidary can surely distinguish between true and imitation gems.

Under cognizability we may properly include what has been aptly called *impressibility,* namely, the capability of a substance to receive such an impression, seal, or design, as shall establish its character as current money of certain value. We might more simply say, that the material of money should be *coinable,* so that a portion, being once issued according to proper regulations with the impress of the state, may be known to all as good and legal currency, equal in weight, size, and value to all similarly marked currency. We shall afterwards consider more minutely what is involved in the manufacture of a good coin.

10

Return of Fiduciary Money to the Issuer

The view has sometimes been expressed that if an issuing body wishes to secure equivalence between its fiduciary media and the money to which they refer, it should take precautions so as to be able to redeem those fiduciary media that are returned to it through lack of confidence on the part of the holders.

It is impossible to subscribe to this view; for it completely fails to recognize the significance and object of a conversion fund. It cannot be the function of a conversion fund to enable the issuing body to redeem its fiduciary media when its counters are besieged by holders who have lost confidence in them. Confidence in the capacity of circulation of fiduciary media is not an individual phenomenon; either it is shared by everybody or it does not exist at all.

Fiduciary media can fulfill their function only on the condition that they are fully equivalent to the sums of money to which they refer. They cease to be equivalent to these sums of money as soon as confidence in the issuer is shaken even if only among a part of the community.

The yokel who presents his note for redemption in order to convince himself of the bank's capacity to pay, which nobody else doubts, is only a comic figure that the bank has no need to fear It need not make any special arrangements or take any special precautions on his account. But any bank that issues fiduciary media is forced to suspend payments if everybody begins to present notes for redemption or to withdraw deposits. Any such bank is powerless against a panic; no system and no policy can help it then. This follows necessarily from the very nature of fiduciary media, which imposes upon those who issue them the obligation to pay a sum of money which they cannot command.

The history of the last two centuries contains more than one example of such catastrophes. Those banks that have succumbed to the onslaughts of noteholders and depositors have been reproached with bringing about the collapse by granting credit imprudently, by tying up their capital, or by advancing loans to the state; extremely serious charges have been brought against their directors.

Where the state itself has been the issuer of the fiduciary media, the impossibility of maintaining their redeemability has usually been ascribed to their having been issued in defiance of precepts based on banking experience. It is obvious that this attitude is due to a misunderstanding.

Even if the banks had put all their assets in short investments, that is, in investments that could have been realized in a relatively short time, they would not have been able to meet the demands of their creditors. This follows merely from the fact that the banks' claims fall due only after notice has been given, while those of their creditors are payable on demand. Thus there lies an irresolvable contradiction in the nature of fiduciary media. Their equivalence to money depends on the promise that they will at any time be converted into money at the demand of the person entitled to them and on the fact that proper precautions are taken to make this promise effective. But-and this is likewise involved in the nature of fiduciary media-what is promised is an impossibility insofar as the bank is never able to keep its loans perfectly liquid. Whether the fiduciary media are issued in the course of banking operations or not, immediate redemption is always impracticable if the confidence of the holders has been lost.

CASE AGAINST THE ISSUE OF FIDUCIARY MONEY

Recognition of the fact, which had been pointed out before the time of Ricardo, that there is no way in which an issuer of fiduciary media can protect itself against the consequences of a panic or avoid succumbing to any serious run, may lead, if one likes, to a demand that the creation of fiduciary media should be prohibited.

Many writers have adopted this attitude. Some have demanded the prohibition of the issue of such notes as have no metal backing; others, the prohibition of all clearing transactions except with full metallic cover; others again, and this is the only logical position, have combined both demands.

Such demands as these have not been fulfilled. The progressive extension of the money economy would have led to an enormous extension in the demand for money if its efficiency had not been extraordinarily increased by the creation of fiduciary media. The issue of fiduciary media has made it possible to avoid the convulsions that would be involved in an increase in the objective exchange value of money, and reduced the cost of the monetary apparatus. Fiduciary media tap a lucrative source of revenue for their issuer; they enrich both the person that issues them and the community that employs them. In the early days of the modern banking system they played a further part still by strengthening the credit-negotiating activities of the banks (which in those times could hardly have proved profitable if carried on for their own sake alone) and so brought the system safely past those obstacles which obstructed its beginnings.

Prohibition of the issue of all notes except those with a full backing and of the lending of the deposits which serve as the basis of the check-and-clearing business would mean almost completely suppressing the note issue and almost strangling the check-and-clearing system. If notes are still to be issued and accounts opened in spite of such a prohibition, then somebody must be found who is prepared to bear unrecompensed the costs involved. Only very rarely will this be the issuer, although occasionally such a thing happens.

The United States created silver certificates in order to relieve the business world of the inconveniences of the clumsy silver coinage and to remove one of the obstacles in the way of an extended use of the silver dollar, which it was thought desirable to encourage for reasons of currency policy. Similarly for reasons of currency policy, gold certificates were created, so as to bring gold money into use despite the public preference for paper.

Sometimes the public may be willing to use notes, checks, or giro transfers for technical reasons, even if it has to make a certain payment to the bank for the facility. There are sometimes objections to the physical use of coins, which are not involved in the transfer of claims to deposited sums of money.

The storage of considerable sums of money and their insurance against risk from fire and flood and from robbery and theft are not always a small matter even for the individual merchant, and still less so for the private person. Warrants payable to order and checkbooks whose folios have no significance until they have been signed by an authorized person are less liable to dishonest handling than are coins, whose smooth faces tell no tales of the methods by which they have been acquired.

But even banknotes, which retain no relationships to individuals, are yet easier to preserve against destruction and to secure against depredation than are bulky pieces of metal. It is true that the large accumulations of money deposited in the banks constitute all the more profitable and therefore attractive an objective for criminal enterprise; but in their case it is possible to take such precautionary measures as will afford almost complete safety, and it is similarly easier to safeguard such large deposits against the risk of accidental damage by the elements.

It has proved a more difficult matter to withdraw the coffers of the banks from the grasp of those in political power; but even this has eventually been achieved, and such coups de main as those of the Stuarts or Davousts have not been repeated in modern times.

A further motive for the introduction of payment through the mediation of the banks has been provided by the difficulty of determining the weight and fineness of coins in the ordinary course of daily business. In this way debasement of the coinage led to the establishment of the famous banks of Amsterdam and Hamburg.

The commission of one-fortieth percent which the customers of the Bank of Amsterdam had to pay on each deposit or withdrawal was far outweighed by the advantages offered by the trustworthiness of the bank currency. Finally; the saving of costs of transport and the greater handiness are other advantages of banking methods of payment that have similarly entered into consideration, especially in countries with a silver, or even a copper, standard. Thus in Japan as early as the middle of the fourteenth century, certain notes issued by rich merchants were in great demand because they offered a means of avoiding the costs and inconveniences involved in the transport of the heavy copper coinage. The premium at which banknotes sometimes stood as against metallic currency before the development of the interlocal check-and-clearing business and the post-office-order service can most easily be explained along these lines.

It is clear that prohibition of fiduciary media would by no means imply a death sentence for the banking system, as is sometimes asserted. The banks would still retain the business of negotiating credit, of borrowing for the purpose of lending. Not consideration for the banks, but appreciation of the influence of fiduciary media on the objective exchange value of money; is the reason why they have not been suppressed.

REDEMPTION FUND

A person who holds money substitutes and wishes to transact business with persons to whom these money substitutes are unfamiliar and therefore unacceptable in lieu of money is obliged to change the money substitutes into money. He goes to the body that is responsible for maintaining equivalence between the money substitutes and money and proceeds to enforce the claim that the money substitutes embody. He presents the notes (or token coins or similar form of currency) for conversion or withdraws his deposits. It follows from this that whoever issues money substitutes is never able to put more of them into circulation than will meet the needs of his customers for business among themselves.

All issues in excess of this will return to the issuer, who will have to accept them in exchange for money if he does not wish to destroy the confidence on which his whole business is built up. (In view of what has been said in the preceding chapter and remains to be said in the following chapter, it should not be necessary to state expressly in this place also that this is true only when several coexisting banks issue money substitutes which have a limited capacity of circulation. If there is only a single bank issuing money substitutes, and if these money substitutes have an unlimited capacity of circulation, then there are no limits to the extension of the issue of fiduciary media. The case would be the same if all the banks had a common understanding as to the issue of their money substitutes and extended the circulation of them according to uniform principles.)

Thus, in the circumstances assumed, it is not possible for a bank to issue more money substitutes than its customers can use; everything in excess of this must flow back to it. There is no danger in this so long as the excess issue is one of money certificates; but an excess issue of fiduciary media is catastrophic. Consequently the chief rule to be observed in the business of a credit-issuing bank is quite clear and simple: it must never issue more fiduciary media than will meet the requirements of its customers for their business with each other. But it must be admitted that there are unusually big difficulties in the practical application of this maxim for there is no way of determining the extent of these requirements on the part of customers. In the absence of any exact knowledge on this point the bank has to rely upon an uncertain empirical procedure which may easily lead to mistakes. Nevertheless, prudent and experienced bank directors-and most bank directors are prudent and experienced-usually manage pretty well with it.

It is only exceptionally that the clienteles of the credit-issuing banks as such extend beyond political boundaries. Even those banks that have branches in different countries give complete independence to their individual branches in the issue of money substitutes. Under present political conditions, uniform administration of banking firms domiciled in different countries would hardly be possible; and difficulties of banking technique and legislation, and finally difficulties of currency technique, stand in the way also.

Furthermore, within individual countries it is usually possible to distinguish two categories of credit banks. On the one hand there is a privileged bank, which possesses a monopoly or almost a monopoly of the note issue, and whose antiquity and financial resources, and still more its extraordinary reputation throughout the whole country, give it a unique position. And on the other hand there is a series of rival banks, which have not the right of issue and which, however great their reputation and the confidence in their solvency, are unable to compete in the capacity for circulation of their money substitutes with the privileged bank, behind which stands the state with all its authority.

Different principles apply to the policies of the two kinds of bank. For the banks of the second group, it is sufficient if they keep in readiness for the redemption of those money substitutes which are returned to them a certain sum of such assets as will enable them to command on demand the credit of the central bank.

They extend the circulation of their fiduciary media as far as possible. If in so doing they exceed the issue that their customers can absorb, so that some of their fiduciary media are presented for redemption, then they procure from the central bank the necessary resources for this by rediscounting bills from their portfolio, or by pledging securities. Thus the essence of the policy that they must pursue to maintain their position as credit-issuing banks consists in always maintaining a sufficiently large quantity of such assets as the central bank regards as an adequate basis for granting credit.

The central banks have no such support from a more powerful and distinguished institution. They are thrown entirely upon their own resources, and must shape their policy accordingly. If they have put too many money substitutes into circulation so that holders apply for their redemption, then they have no other way out than that provided by their redemption fund.

Consequently, it is necessary for them to see that there are never more of their fiduciary media in circulation than will meet the requirements of their customers. As has already been said, it is not possible to make a direct evaluation of these requirements. Only an indirect evaluation is practicable. The proportion of the total demand for money in the broader sense that cannot be satisfied by fiduciary media must be determined. This will be the quantity of money that is necessary for doing business with the persons who are not customers of the central bank; that is, the quantity required for purposes of foreign trade.

The demand for money for international trade is composed of two different elements. It consists, first, of the demand for those sums of money which, as a result of variations in the relative extent and intensity of the demand for money in different countries, are transported from one country to another until that position of equilibrium is reestablished in which the objective exchange value of money has the same level everywhere.

It is impossible to avoid the transfers of money that are necessary on this account. It is true that we might imagine the establishment of an international deposit bank in which large sums of money were deposited, perhaps even all the money in the world, and made the basis of an issue of money certificates, that is, of notes or balances completely backed by money. This well might put a stop to the physical use of coins, and might in certain circumstances tend to a considerable reduction of costs; instead of coins being used, notes would be sent or transfers made in the books of the bank. But such external differences would not affect the nature of the process.

The other motive for international transfers of money is provided by those balances that arise in the international exchange of commodities and services. These have to be settled by transfers in opposite directions, and it is therefore theoretically possible to eliminate them completely by developing the clearing process. In foreign-exchange dealings and the related transactions that in recent times have been united with them, there is a fine mechanism which cancels out nearly all such transfers of money. It is only exceptionally nowadays that two ships meet at sea, one of them taking gold from London to New York and the other bringing gold from New York to London.

International transfers of money are controlled as a rule merely by variations in the ratio between the demand for money and the stock of money. Among these variations, those with the greatest practical importance are those which distribute the newly mined precious metals throughout the world, a process in which London often plays the part of a middleman. Apart from this, and provided that no extraordinary cause suddenly alters the relative demand for money in different countries, the transference of money from country to country cannot be particularly extensive.

It may be assumed that, as a rule, the variations that occur in this way are not so great as those variations in stocks of money that are due to new production, or at least that they do not exceed them by very much.

If this is true-and it is supported only by rough estimates-then the movements which are necessary for bringing the purchasing power of money to a common level will consist largely or entirely of variations in the distribution of the additional quantity of money only. It is possible to estimate on empirical grounds that the relative demand for money in a country, that is, the extent and intensity of its demand for money in relation to the extent and intensity of the demand for money in other countries (this phrase being interpreted throughout in the broader sense), will not decrease within a relatively short period to such an extent as to cause the quantity of money and fiduciary media together in circulation to sink below such and such a fraction of its present amount.

Of course, such estimates are necessarily based upon more or less arbitrary combinations of factors and it is obviously never out of the question that they will be subsequently upset by unforeseen events. But if the amount is estimated very conservatively, and if due account is also taken of the fact that the state of international trade may necessitate transfers of money from country to country if only temporarily, then, so long as the quantity of fiduciary media circulating within the country is not increased beyond the estimated amount and no money certificates are issued either, the accumulation of a redemption fund might prove altogether unnecessary.

For so long as the issue of fiduciary media does not exceed this limit, and assuming of course the correctness of the estimate on which it is based, there can arise no demand for redemption of the fiduciary media. If, for example, the quantity of the banknotes, treasury notes, token coins, and deposits at present in circulation in Germany were reduced by the sum deposited as cover for it in the vaults of the banks, the money and credit system would not be changed in any way.

Germany's power to transact business through the medium of money with foreign countries would not be affected. It is only the notes, deposits, and so forth, that are not covered by money that have the character of fiduciary media; it is these only and not those covered by money that have the effects on the determination of prices which it is the task of this part of our book to describe.

If the amount of fiduciary media in circulation were kept at a level below the limit set by the presumable maximum requirements of foreign trade, then it would be possible to do without a redemption reserve altogether, if it were not for a further circumstance that enters into the question. This circumstance is the following: if persons who needed a sum of money for foreign payments and were obliged to obtain it by the exchange of money substitutes could do this only through numerous money-changing transactions, perhaps involving an expenditure of time and trouble so that the procedure cost them something, this would militate against the complete equivalence of money substitutes and money, causing the former to circulate at a discount.

Hence, if only on this account, a redemption fund of a certain amount would have to be maintained, even though the quantity of money actually in circulation was enough for trade with foreign countries. It follows from this that the fully backed note and the fully covered deposit, originally necessary in order to accustom the public to the use of these forms of money substitute, have still to be retained nowadays along with the superficially similar but essentially different fiduciary medium. A note or deposit currency with no money backing at all, that is, one which consists entirely of fiduciary media, still remains a practical impossibility.

If we look at the redemption funds of the self-sufficing banks, we shall observe in them an apparently quite irregular multifariousness. We shall observe that the kind and amount of cover of the money substitutes, especially those issued in note form, are regulated by a series of rules, constructed on quite different lines, partly by mercantile usage and partly by legislation.

It is hardly correct to speak of different systems in this connection; that ambitious designation is little suited to empirical rules that have for the most part been founded on erroneous views of the nature of money and fiduciary media. There is, however, one idea that is expressed in all of them; the idea that the issue of fiduciary media needs to be limited by some kind of artificial restriction since it has no natural limits. Thus the question underlying all monetary policy, whether an unlimited increase of fiduciary media with its ineluctable consequence of a diminution in the objective exchange value of money is a thing to be encouraged, is implicitly answered in the negative.

Recognition of the need for an artificial limitation of the circulation of fiduciary media is, both on strictly scientific grounds and also on grounds of practical expediency, a product of economic inquiry during the first half of the nineteenth century. Its triumph over other views ended decades of such lively discussion as our science has seldom known, and at the same time concluded a period of uncertain experiment in the issuing of fiduciary media. During the years that have since elapsed, the grounds on which it was based have been subjected to criticism, sometimes ill founded, sometimes founded upon real objections.

But the principle of limiting the issue of uncovered notes has not been abandoned in banking legislation. Nowadays it still constitutes an essential element in the banking policy of civilized nations, even if the circumstance that the limitation only applies to the issue of fiduciary media in the form of notes and not to the constantly growing issue in the form of deposits may make its practical importance less than it was some decades ago.

Limitation of fiduciary media also forms part of the money and credit system in India, the Philippines, and those countries that have imitated them, although in a different garb. No direct numerical proportion has been set up between the redemption fund administered by the government and the quantity of fiduciary media in circulation; any attempt to do this would have met with technical difficulties if only because it was impossible to calculate exactly what the quantity of fiduciary media was at the time of the transition to the new standard. But the further issue of fiduciary media in the form of legal-tender coinage is reserved to the state (it mostly requires special legislation) in a similar fashion to that in which the issue of token coinage and the like is regulated elsewhere.

FIDUCIARY MONEY COVER

The expressions solvency and liquidity are not always used correctly when they are applied to the circumstances of a bank. They are sometimes regarded as synonymous; but orthodox opinion understands them to refer to two different states. (It must be admitted that a clear definition and distinction of the two concepts is usually not attempted.) A bank may be said to be solvent when its assets are so constituted that a liquidation would necessarily result at least in complete satisfaction of all of its creditors. Liquidity is that condition of the bank's assets which will enable it to meet all its liabilities, not merely in full, but also in time, that is, without being obliged to ask for anything in the nature of a moratorium from its creditors. Liquidity is a particular sort of solvency.

Every enterprise-for the same is true of any body that participates in credit transactions-that is liquid is also solvent; but on the other hand not every undertaking that is solvent is also liquid.

A person who cannot settle a debt on the day when it falls due has not a liquid status, even if there is no doubt that he will be able in three or six months' time to pay the debt together with interest and the other costs in which the delay is meanwhile involving the creditor. Since ancient times commercial law has imposed on everybody the obligation to have regard to liquidity throughout the whole conduct of his business.

This requirement is characteristically expressed in mercantile life. Anyone who has to approach his creditor for permission to defer the payment of a debt, anyone who allows matters to reach the point of having his bills protested, has imperiled his business reputation, even if he is afterward able to meet all his outstanding obligations in full.

All undertakings are subject to the rule that we have already encountered as the business principle of the credit-negotiating banks, that steps must be taken to permit the full and punctual settlement of every claim as it falls due.

For credit-issuing banks, regard to this fundamental rule of prudent conduct is an impossibility. It lies in their nature to build upon the fact that a proportion-the larger proportion-of the fiduciary media remains in circulation and that the claims arising from this part of the issue will not be enforced, or at least will not be enforced simultaneously.

They are bound to collapse as soon as confidence in their conduct is destroyed and the creditors storm their counters. They, therefore, are unable to aim at liquidity of investment like all other banks and undertakings in general; they have to be content with solvency as the goal of their policy.

This is customarily overlooked when the covering of the issue of fiduciary media by means of short-term loans is referred to as a method that is peculiarly suited to their nature and function, and when the appellation "characteristically banking type of cover" is applied to it, because it is supposed that consistent application of the general rule about liquidity to the special circumstances of the credit-issuing banks shows it to be the system of investment that is proper to such banks.

Whether the assets of a credit-issuing bank consist of short-term bills or of hypothecary loans remains a matter of indifference in the case of a general run. If the bank is in immediate need of large sums of money it can procure them only by disposing of its assets; when the panic-stricken public is clamoring at its counters for the redemption of notes or the repayment of deposits, a bill that has still thirty days to run is of no more use to it than a mortgage which is irredeemable for just as many years.

At such moments the most that can matter is the greater or lesser negotiability of the assets. But in certain circumstances, long-term or even irredeemable claims may be easier to realize than short-term; in times of crisis, government annuities and mortgages may perhaps find buyers more readily than commercial bills.

It has already been mentioned that in most states two categories of banks exist, as far as the public confidence they enjoy is concerned. The central bank-of-issue, which is usually the only bank with the right to issue notes, occupies an exceptional position, owing to its partial or entire administration by the state and the strict control to which all its activities are subjected.

It enjoys a greater reputation than the other credit-issuing banks, which have not such a simple type of business to carry on, which often risk more for the sake of profit than they can be responsible for, and which, at least in some states, carry on a series of additional enterprises, the business of company formation for example, besides their banking activities proper, the negotiation of credit and the granting of credit through the issue of fiduciary media.

These banks of the second order may under certain circumstances lose the confidence of the public without the position of the central bank being shaken. In this case they are able to maintain themselves in a state of liquidity by securing credit from the central bank on their own behalf (as indeed they also do in other cases when their resources are exhausted) and so being enabled to meet their obligations punctually and in full.

It is therefore possible to say that these banks are in a state of liquidity so long as their liabilities as they fall due from day to day are balanced by such assets as the central bank considers a sufficient security for advances. It is well known that some banks are not liquid even in this sense.

The central banks of individual countries could similarly attain a state of liquidity if they only carried such assets against their issues of fiduciary media as would be regarded as possible investments by their sister institutions abroad. But even then it would remain true that it is theoretically impossible to maintain the credit bank system in a state of liquidity. A simultaneous destruction of confidence in all banks would necessarily lead to a general collapse.

It is true that the investment of its assets in short-term loans does make it possible for a bank to satisfy its creditors within a certain comparatively short period. But this would prove adequate in the face of a loss of confidence only if the holders of notes and deposits did not apply simultaneously to the bank for immediate payment of the sums of money owing to them.

Such a supposition is not very probable. Either there is no lack of confidence at all or it is general. There is only one way in which liquidity of status might be at least formally secured with regard to the special circumstances of credit-issuing banks. If such banks made loans only on the condition that they had the right to demand repayment at any time, then the problem of liquidity would of course be solved for them in a simple manner.

But from the point of view of the community as a whole, this is of course no solution, but only a shelving, of the problem. The status of the bank could only apparently be kept liquid at the expense of the status of those who borrowed from it, for these would be faced with precisely the same insurmountable difficulty. The banks' debtors would not have kept the borrowed sums in their safes, but would have put them into productive investments from which they certainly could not withdraw them without delay. The problem is thus in no way altered; it remains insoluble.

SIGNIFICANCE OF SHORT-TERM COVER

Credit-issuing banks as a rule give preference to short-term loans as investments. Often the law compels them to do this, but in any case they would be forced to do it by public opinion. But the significance of this preference has nothing to do with the greater ease with which it is generally, but erroneously, supposed to allow the fiduciary media to be redeemed.

It is true that it is a policy that has preserved the bank-credit system in the past from severe shocks; it is true that its neglect has always avenged itself; and it is true that it still is important for the present and future; but the reasons for this are entirely different from those which the champions of short-term cover are in the habit of putting forward.

One of its reasons, and the less weighty, is that it is easier to judge the soundness of investments made in the form of short-term loans than that of long-term investments.

It is true that there are numerous long-term investments that are sounder than very many short-term investments; nevertheless, the soundness of an investment can as a rule be judged with greater certainty when all that has to be done is to survey the circumstances of the market in general and of the borrower in particular for the next few weeks or months, than when it is a matter of years or decades. The second and decisive reason has already been mentioned. If the granting of credit through the issue of fiduciary media is restricted to loans that are to be paid back after a short space of time, then there is a certain limitation of the amount of the issue of fiduciary media. The rule that it is desirable for credit-issuing banks to grant only short-term loans is the outcome of centuries of experience. It has been its fate always to be misunderstood; but even so, obedience to it has had the important effect of helping to limit the issue of fiduciary media.

INVESTMENTS OF THE CREDIT-ISSUING BANKS

The solution of the problem of soundness is no more difficult for the credit-issuing banks than for the credit-negotiating banks. If the fiduciary media are issued only on good security and if a guarantee fund is created out of the bank's share capital for the purpose of covering losses, for even under prudent management losses cannot always be avoided, then the bank can put itself in a position to redeem in full the fiduciary media that it issues, although not within the term specified in its promises to pay. Nevertheless, the soundness of the cover is only of subordinate importance as far as fiduciary media are concerned. It may disappear entirely, at least in a certain sense, without prejudicing their capacity of circulation. Fiduciary media can even be issued without any cover at all. This occurs, for example, when the state issues token coins and does not devote the seigniorage to a particular fund for their redemption. (Under certain circumstances, the metal value of the coins themselves may be regarded as partial security. And of course the state as a whole has assets that provide far greater security than any sort of special fund could offer) On the other hand, even if the fiduciary media are completely covered by the assets of the issuer, so that only the time of their redemption and not its ultimate occurrence is open to question, this cannot have any sort of influence whatever in support of their capacity for circulation; for this depends exclusively upon the expectation that the issuer will redeem them promptly.

To have overlooked this is the error underlying all those proposals and experiments which have aimed at guaranteeing the issue of fiduciary media by means of funds consisting of nonliquid assets, such as mortgages. If those money substitutes that are presented for redemption are immediately and fully redeemed in money, then, beyond the cash reserve necessary for this redemption, no stock of goods is needed for maintaining equivalence between the fiduciary media and money. If, however, the money substitutes are not fully and immediately redeemed for money, then they will not be reckoned as equivalent to money just because there are some goods somewhere that will at some time be used to satisfy the demands that the holders of the money substitutes are entitled to make on the ground of the claims that the money substitutes embody. They will be valued at less than the sums of money to which they refer, because their redemption is in doubt and at the best will not occur until after the passage of a period of time. And so they will cease to be money substitutes; if they continue to be used as media of exchange, it will be at an independent valuation; they will be no longer money substitutes, but credit money.

For credit money also, that is for unmatured claims which serve as common media of exchange, "cover" by a special fund is superfluous. So long as the claims are tendered and accepted as money, and thus have obtained an exchange value in excess of that which is attributed to them as mere claims, such a fund has no bearing on the matter. The significance of the regulations as to cover and the funds for that purpose lies here, as with fiduciary media, in the fact that they indirectly set a limit to the quantity that can be issued.

11

Trust in Market Liquidity

Market players assume that other players possess or have access to the liquid means they need in order to act on their intentions and obligations. They know, from personal experience, that idle capital tends to dwindle and that the only way to, perhaps, maintain or increase it is to transact with others, directly or through intermediaries, such as banks.

TRUST IN OTHERS' KNOWLEDGE AND ABILITY

Market players assume that other players possess or have access to the intellectual property, technology, and knowledge they need in order to realize their intentions and obligations. This implicitly presupposes that all other market players are physically, mentally, legally and financially able and willing to act their parts as stipulated, for instance, in contracts they sign. The emotional dimensions of contracting are often neglected in economics. Players assume that their counterparts maintain a realistic and stable sense of self-worth based on intimate knowledge of their own strengths and weaknesses. Market participants are presumed to harbor realistic expectations, commensurate with their skills and accomplishments. Allowance is made for exaggeration, disinformation, even outright deception-but these are supposed to be marginal phenomena.

When trust breaks down-often the result of an external or internal systemic shock-people react expectedly. The number of voluntary interactions and transactions decreases sharply.

With a collapsed investment horizon, individuals and firms become corrupt in an effort to shortcut their way into economic benefits, not knowing how long will the system survive. Criminal activity increases. People compensate with fantasies and grandiose delusions for their growing sense of uncertainty, helplessness, and fears. This is a self-reinforcing mechanism, a vicious cycle which results in under-confidence and a fluctuating self esteem. They develop psychological defence mechanisms.

Cognitive dissonance ("I really choose to be poor rather than heartless"), pathological envy (seeks to deprive others and thus gain emotional reward), rigidity ("I am like that, my family or ethnic group has been like that for generations, there is nothing I can do"), passive-aggressive behavior (obstructing the work flow, absenteeism, stealing from the employer, adhering strictly to arcane regulations)-are all reactions to a breakdown in one or more of the four aforementioned types of trust.

Furthermore, people in a trust crisis are unable to postpone gratification. They often become frustrated, aggressive, and deceitful if denied. They resort to reckless behaviour and stopgap economic activities.

In economic environments with compromised and impaired trust, loyalty decreases and mobility increases. People switch jobs, renege on obligations, fail to repay debts, relocate often. Concepts like exclusivity, the sanctity of contracts, workplace loyalty, or a career path-all get eroded. As a result, little is invested in the future, in the acquisition of skills, in long term savings. Short-termism and bottom line mentality rule.

The outcomes of a crisis of trust are, usually, catastrophic: Economic activity is much reduced, human capital is corroded and wasted, brain drain increases, illegal and extra-legal activities rise, society is polarized between haves and haves-not, interethnic and inter-racial tensions increase. To rebuild trust in such circumstances is a daunting task. The loss of trust is contagious and, finally, it infects every institution and profession in the land. It is the stuff revolutions are made of.

THE DISTRIBUTIVE JUSTICE OF THE MARKET

The public outcry against executive pay and compensation followed disclosures of insider trading, double dealing, and outright fraud. But even honest and productive entrepreneurs often earn more money in one year than Albert Einstein did in his entire life. This strikes many-especially academics-as unfair. Surely Einstein's contributions to human knowledge and welfare far exceed anything ever accomplished by sundry businessmen? Fortunately, this discrepancy is cause for constructive jealousy, emulation, and imitation. It can, however, lead to an orgy of destructive and self-ruinous envy. Such envy is reinforced by declining social mobility in the United States. Recent (2006-7) studies by the OECD (Organization for Economic Cooperation and Development) clearly demonstrate that the American Dream is a myth. In an editorial dated July 13, 2007, the New-York Times described the rapidly deteriorating situation thus: "... (M)obility between generations — people doing better or worse than their parents — is weaker in America than in Denmark, Austria, Norway, Finland, Canada, Sweden, Germany, Spain and France. In America, there is more than a 40 percent chance that if a father is in the bottom fifth of the earnings' distribution, his son will end up there, too. In Denmark, the equivalent odds are under 25 percent, and they are less than 30 percent in Britain.

America's sluggish mobility is ultimately unsurprising. Wealthy parents not only pass on that wealth in inheritances, they can pay for better education, nutrition and health care for their children. The poor cannot afford this investment in their children's development — and the government doesn't provide nearly enough help. In a speech earlier this year, the Federal Reserve chairman, Ben Bernanke, argued that while the inequality of rewards fuels the economy by making people exert themselves, opportunity should be "as widely distributed and as equal as possible." The problem is that the have-nots don't have many opportunities either."

Still, entrepreneurs recombine natural and human resources in novel ways. They do so to respond to forecasts of future needs, or to observations of failures and shortcomings of current products or services. Entrepreneurs are professional-though usually intuitive-futurologists. This is a valuable service and it is financed by systematic risk takers, such as venture capitalists. Surely they all deserve compensation for their efforts and the hazards they assume?

Exclusive ownership is the most ancient type of such remuneration. First movers, entrepreneurs, risk takers, owners of the wealth they generated, exploiters of resources-are allowed to exclude others from owning or exploiting the same things. Mineral concessions, patents, copyright, trademarks-are all forms of monopoly ownership. What moral right to exclude others is gained from being the first?

Nozick advanced Locke's Proviso. An exclusive ownership of property is just only if "enough and as good is left in common for others". If it does not worsen other people's lot, exclusivity is morally permissible. It can be argued, though, that all modes of exclusive ownership aggravate other people's situation. As far as everyone, bar the entrepreneur, are concerned, exclusivity also prevents a more advantageous distribution of income and wealth.

Exclusive ownership reflects real-life irreversibility. A first mover has the advantage of excess information and of irreversibly invested work, time, and effort. Economic enterprise is subject to information asymmetry: we know nothing about the future and everything about the past. This asymmetry is known as "investment risk". Society compensates the entrepreneur with one type of asymmetry-exclusive ownership-for assuming another, the investment risk.

One way of looking at it is that all others are worse off by the amount of profits and rents accruing to owner-entrepreneurs. Profits and rents reflect an intrinsic inefficiency. Another is to recall that ownership is the result of adding value to the world. It is only reasonable to expect it to yield to the entrepreneur at least this value added now and in the future.

In a "Theory of Justice" (published 1971, p. 302), John Rawls described an ideal society thus:

"(1) Each person is to have an equal right to the most extensive total system of equal basic liberties compatible with a similar system of liberty for all. (2) Social and economic inequalities are to be arranged so that they are both: (a) to the greatest benefit of the least advantaged, consistent with the just savings principle, and (b) attached to offices and positions open to all under conditions of fair equality of opportunity."

It all harks back to scarcity of resources-land, money, raw materials, manpower, creative brains. Those who can afford to do so, hoard resources to offset anxiety regarding future uncertainty. Others wallow in paucity. The distribution of means is thus skewed. "Distributive justice" deals with the just allocation of scarce resources.

Yet, even the basic terminology is somewhat fuzzy. What constitutes a resource? what is meant by allocation? Who should allocate resources-Adam Smith's "invisible hand", the government, the consumer, or business? Should it reflect differences in power, in intelligence, in knowledge, or in heredity? Should resource allocation be subject to a principle of entitlement? Is it reasonable to demand that it be just-or merely efficient? Are justice and efficiency antonyms?

Justice is concerned with equal access to opportunities. Equal access does not guarantee equal outcomes, invariably determined by idiosyncrasies and differences between people. Access leveraged by the application of natural or acquired capacities-translates into accrued wealth. Disparities in these capacities lead to discrepancies in accrued wealth.

The doctrine of equal access is founded on the equivalence of Men. That all men are created equal and deserve the same respect and, therefore, equal treatment is not self evident. European aristocracy well into this century would have probably found this notion abhorrent. Jose Ortega Y Gasset, writing in the 1930's, preached that access to educational and economic opportunities should be premised on one's lineage, up bringing, wealth, and social responsibilities.

A succession of societies and cultures discriminated against the ignorant, criminals, atheists, females, homosexuals, members of ethnic, religious, or racial groups, the old, the immigrant, and the poor. Communism-ostensibly a strict egalitarian idea-foundered because it failed to reconcile strict equality with economic and psychological realities within an impatient timetable.

Philosophers tried to specify a "bundle" or "package" of goods, services, and intangibles (like information, or skills, or knowledge). Justice-though not necessarily happiness-is when everyone possesses an identical bundle. Happiness-though not necessarily justice-is when each one of us possesses a "bundle" which reflects his or her preferences, priorities, and predilections. None of us will be too happy with a standardized bundle, selected by a committee of philosophers-or bureaucrats, as was the case under communism.

The market allows for the exchange of goods and services between holders of identical bundles. If I seek books, but detest oranges-I can swap them with someone in return for his books. That way both of us are rendered better off than under the strict egalitarian version.

Still, there is no guarantee that I will find my exact match-a person who is interested in swapping his books for my oranges. Illiquid, small, or imperfect markets thus inhibit the scope of these exchanges. Additionally, exchange participants have to agree on an index: how many books for how many oranges? This is the price of oranges in terms of books.

Money-the obvious "index"-does not solve this problem, merely simplifies it and facilitates exchanges. It does not eliminate the necessity to negotiate an "exchange rate". It does not prevent market failures. In other words: money is not an index. It is merely a medium of exchange and a store of value. The index-as expressed in terms of money-is the underlying agreement regarding the values of resources in terms of other resources (i.e., their relative values).

The market-and the price mechanism-increase happiness and welfare by allowing people to alter the composition of their bundles. The invisible hand is just and benevolent. But money is imperfect. The aforementioned Rawles demonstrated (1971), that we need to combine money with other measures in order to place a value on intangibles.

The prevailing market theories postulate that everyone has the same resources at some initial point (the "starting gate"). It is up to them to deploy these endowments and, thus, to ravage or increase their wealth. While the initial distribution is equal-the end distribution depends on how wisely-or imprudently-the initial distribution was used.

Egalitarian thinkers proposed to equate everyone's income in each time frame (e.g., annually). But identical incomes do not automatically yield the same accrued wealth. The latter depends on how the income is used-saved, invested, or squandered. Relative disparities of wealth are bound to emerge, regardless of the nature of income distribution.

Some say that excess wealth should be confiscated and redistributed. Progressive taxation and the welfare state aim to secure this outcome. Redistributive mechanisms reset the "wealth clock" periodically (at the end of every month, or fiscal year). In many countries, the law dictates which portion of one's income must be saved and, by implication, how much can be consumed. This conflicts with basic rights like the freedom to make economic choices. The legalized expropriation of income (i.e., taxes) is morally dubious. Anti-tax movements have sprung all over the world and their philosophy permeates the ideology of political parties in many countries, not least the USA. Taxes are punitive: they penalize enterprise, success, entrepreneurship, foresight, and risk assumption. Welfare, on the other hand, rewards dependence and parasitism.

According to Rawles' Difference Principle, all tenets of justice are either redistributive or retributive. This ignores non-economic activities and human inherent variance. Moreover, conflict and inequality are the engines of growth and innovation-which mostly benefit the least advantaged in the long run. Experience shows that unmitigated equality results in atrophy, corruption and stagnation. Thermodynamics teaches us that life and motion are engendered by an irregular distribution of energy. Entropy-an even distribution of energy-equals death and stasis. What about the disadvantaged and challenged-the mentally retarded, the mentally insane, the paralyzed, the chronically ill? For that matter, what about the less talented, less skilled, less daring? Dworkin (1981) proposed a compensation scheme. He suggested a model of fair distribution in which every person is given the same purchasing power and uses it to bid, in a fair auction, for resources that best fit that person's life plan, goals and preferences.

Having thus acquired these resources, we are then permitted to use them as we see fit. Obviously, we end up with disparate economic results. But we cannot complain-we were given the same purchasing power and the freedom to bid for a bundle of our choice. Dworkin assumes that prior to the hypothetical auction, people are unaware of their own natural endowments but are willing and able to insure against being naturally disadvantaged. Their payments create an insurance pool to compensate the less fortunate for their misfortune.

This, of course, is highly unrealistic. We are usually very much aware of natural endowments and liabilities-both ours and others'. Therefore, the demand for such insurance is not universal, nor uniform. Some of us badly need and want it-others not at all. It is morally acceptable to let willing buyers and sellers to trade in such coverage (e.g., by offering charity or alms)-but may be immoral to make it compulsory.

Most of the modern welfare programs are involuntary Dworkin schemes. Worse yet, they often measure differences in natural endowments arbitrarily, compensate for lack of acquired skills, and discriminate between types of endowments in accordance with cultural biases and fads. Libertarians limit themselves to ensuring a level playing field of just exchanges, where just actions always result in just outcomes. Justice is not dependent on a particular distribution pattern, whether as a starting point, or as an outcome. Robert Nozick "Entitlement Theory" proposed in 1974 is based on this approach.

That the market is wiser than any of its participants is a pillar of the philosophy of capitalism. In its pure form, the theory claims that markets yield patterns of merited distribution-i.e., reward and punish justly. Capitalism generate just deserts. Market failures-for instance, in the provision of public goods-should be tackled by governments. But a just distribution of income and wealth does not constitute a market failure and, therefore, should not be tampered with.

THE AGENT-PRINCIPAL CONUNDRUM

In the catechism of capitalism, shares represent the part-ownership of an economic enterprise, usually a firm. The value of shares is determined by the replacement value of the assets of the firm, including intangibles such as goodwill. The price of the share is determined by transactions among arm's length buyers and sellers in an efficient and liquid market. The price reflects expectations regarding the future value of the firm and the stock's future stream of income-i.e., dividends. Alas, none of these oft-recited dogmas bears any resemblance to reality. Shares rarely represent ownership. The float-the number of shares available to the public-is frequently marginal. Shareholders meet once a year to vent and disperse. Boards of directors are appointed by management-as are auditors. Shareholders are not represented in any decision making process-small or big.

The dismal truth is that shares reify the expectation to find future buyers at a higher price and thus incur capital gains. In the Ponzi scheme known as the stock exchange, this expectation is proportional to liquidity-new suckers-and volatility. Thus, the price of any given stock reflects merely the consensus as to how easy it would be to offload one's holdings and at what price.

Another myth has to do with the role of managers. They are supposed to generate higher returns to shareholders by increasing the value of the firm's assets and, therefore, of the firm. If they fail to do so, goes the moral tale, they are booted out mercilessly. This is one manifestation of the "Principal-Agent Problem". It is defined thus by the Oxford Dictionary of Economics:

"The problem of how a person A can motivate person B to act for A's benefit rather than following (his) self-interest." The obvious answer is that A can never motivate B not to follow B's self-interest-never mind what the incentives are. That economists pretend otherwise-in "optimal contracting theory"-just serves to demonstrate how divorced economics is from human psychology and, thus, from reality.

Managers will always rob blind the companies they run. They will always manipulate boards to collude in their shenanigans. They will always bribe auditors to bend the rules. In other words, they will always act in their self-interest. In their defense, they can say that the damage from such actions to each shareholder is minuscule while the benefits to the manager are enormous. In other words, this is the rational, self-interested, thing to do. But why do shareholders cooperate with such corporate brigandage? In an important Chicago Law Review article whose preprint was posted to the Web a few weeks ago-titled "Managerial Power and Rent Extraction in the Design of Executive Compensation"-the authors demonstrate how the typical stock option granted to managers as part of their remuneration rewards mediocrity rather than encourages excellence.

But everything falls into place if we realize that shareholders and managers are allied against the firm-not pitted against each other. The paramount interest of both shareholders and managers is to increase the value of the stock-regardless of the true value of the firm. Both are concerned with the performance of the share-rather than the performance of the firm. Both are preoccupied with boosting the share's price-rather than the company's business.

Hence the inflationary executive pay packets. Shareholders hire stock manipulators-euphemistically known as "managers"-to generate expectations regarding the future prices of their shares. These snake oil salesmen and snake charmers-the corporate executives-are allowed by shareholders to loot the company providing they generate consistent capital gains to their masters by provoking persistent interest and excitement around the business. Shareholders, in other words, do not behave as owners of the firm-they behave as free-riders.

The Principal-Agent Problem arises in other social interactions and is equally misunderstood there. Consider taxpayers and their government. Contrary to conservative lore, the former want the government to tax them providing they share in the spoils. They tolerate corruption in high places, cronyism, nepotism, inaptitude and worse-on condition that the government and the legislature redistribute the wealth they confiscate. Such redistribution often comes in the form of pork barrel projects and benefits to the middle-class.

This is why the tax burden and the government's share of GDP have been soaring inexorably with the consent of the citizenry. People adore government spending precisely because it is inefficient and distorts the proper allocation of economic resources. The vast majority of people are rent-seekers. Witness the mass demonstrations that erupt whenever governments try to slash expenditures, privatize, and eliminate their gaping deficits. This is one reason the IMF with its austerity measures is universally unpopular. Employers and employees, producers and consumers-these are all instances of the Principal-Agent Problem. Economists would do well to discard their models and go back to basics. They could start by asking:

Why do shareholders acquiesce with executive malfeasance as long as share prices are rising? Why do citizens protest against a smaller government-even though it means lower taxes? Could it mean that the interests of shareholders and managers are identical? Does it imply that people prefer tax-and-spend governments and pork barrel politics to the Thatcherite alternative?

Nothing happens by accident or by coercion. Shareholders aided and abetted the current crop of corporate executives enthusiastically. They knew well what was happening. They may not have been aware of the exact nature and extent of the rot-but they witnessed approvingly the public relations antics, insider trading, stock option resetting, unwinding, and unloading, share price manipulation, opaque transactions, and outlandish pay packages. Investors remained mum throughout the corruption of corporate America. It is time for the hangover.

THE GREEN-EYED CAPITALIST

Conservative sociologists self-servingly marvel at the peaceful proximity of abject poverty and ostentatious affluence in American-or, for that matter, Western-cities. Devastating riots do erupt, but these are reactions either to perceived social injustice (Los Angeles 1965) or to political oppression (Paris 1968). The French Revolution may have been the last time the urban sans-culotte raised a fuss against the economically enfranchised.

This pacific co-existence conceals a maelstrom of envy. Behold the rampant Schadenfreude which accompanied the antitrust case against the predatory but loaded Microsoft. Observe the glee which engulfed many destitute countries in the wake of the September 11 atrocities against America, the epitome of triumphant prosperity. Witness the post-World.com orgiastic castigation of avaricious CEO's.

Envy-a pathological manifestation of destructive aggressiveness-is distinct from jealousy. The New Oxford Dictionary of English defines envy as: "A feeling of discontented or resentful longing aroused by someone else's possessions, qualities, or luck... Mortification and ill-will occasioned by the contemplation of another's superior advantages."

Pathological envy-the fourth deadly sin-is engendered by the realization of some lack, deficiency, or inadequacy in oneself. The envious begrudge others their success, brilliance, happiness, beauty, good fortune, or wealth. Envy provokes misery, humiliation, and impotent rage.

The envious copes with his pernicious emotions in five ways:

1. They attack the perceived source of frustration in an attempt to destroy it, or "reduce it" to their "size". Such destructive impulses often assume the disguise of championing social causes, fighting injustice, touting reform, or promoting an ideology.
2. They seek to subsume the object of envy by imitating it. In extreme cases, they strive to get rich quick through

criminal scams, or corruption. They endeavor to outsmart the system and shortcut their way to fortune and celebrity.

3. They resort to self-deprecation. They idealize the successful, the rich, the mighty, and the lucky and attribute to them super-human, almost divine, qualities. At the same time, they humble themselves. Indeed, most of this strain of the envious end up disenchanted and bitter, driving the objects of their own erstwhile devotion and adulation to destruction and decrepitude.
4. They experience cognitive dissonance. These people devalue the source of their frustration and envy by finding faults in everything they most desire and in everyone they envy.
5. They avoid the envied person and thus the agonizing pangs of envy.

Envy is not a new phenomenon. Belisarius, the general who conquered the world for Emperor Justinian, was blinded and stripped of his assets by his envious peers. I-and many others-have written extensively about envy in command economies. Nor is envy likely to diminish.

In his book, "Facial Justice", Hartley describes a post-apocalyptic dystopia, New State, in which envy is forbidden and equality extolled and everything enviable is obliterated. Women are modified to look like men and given identical "beta faces". Tall buildings are razed. Joseph Schumpeter, the prophetic Austrian-American economist, believed that socialism will disinherit capitalism. In "Capitalism, Socialism, and Democracy" he foresaw a conflict between a class of refined but dirt-poor intellectuals and the vulgar but filthy rich businessmen and managers they virulently envy and resent. Samuel Johnson wrote: "He was dull in a new way, and that made many people think him great." The literati seek to tear down the market economy which they feel has so disenfranchised and undervalued them.

Hitler, who fancied himself an artist, labeled the British a "nation of shopkeepers" in one of his bouts of raging envy.

Ralph Reiland, the Kenneth Simon professor of free enterprise at Robert Morris University, quotes David Brooks of the "weekly Standard", who christened this phenomenon "bourgeoisophobia":

"The hatred of the bourgeoisie is the beginning of all virtue'- wrote Gustav Flaubert. He signed his letters 'Bourgeoisophobus' to show how much he despised 'stupid grocers and their ilk... Through some screw-up in the great scheme of the universe, their narrow-minded greed had brought them vast wealth, unstoppable power and growing social prestige."

Reiland also quotes from Ludwig van Mises's "The Anti-Capitalist Mentality": "Many people, and especially intellectuals, passionately loathe capitalism. In a society based on caste and status, the individual can ascribe adverse fate to conditions beyond his control. In... capitalism... everybody's station in life depends on his doing... (what makes a man rich is) not the evaluation of his contribution from any 'absolute' principle of justice but the evaluation on the part of his fellow men who exclusively apply the yardstick of their personal wants, desires and ends... Everybody knows very well that there are people like himself who succeeded where he himself failed.

Everybody knows that many of those he envies are self-made men who started from the same point from which he himself started. Everybody is aware of his own defeat. In order to console himself and to restore his self-assertion, such a man is in search of a scapegoat. He tries to persuade himself that he failed through no fault of his own. He was too decent to resort to the base tricks to which his successful rivals owe their ascendancy. The nefarious social order does not accord the prizes to the most meritorious men; it crowns the dishonest, unscrupulous scoundrel, the swindler, the exploiter, the 'rugged individualist'." In "The Virtue of Prosperity", Dinesh D'Souza accuses prosperity and capitalism of inspiring vice and temptation. Inevitably, it provokes envy in the poor and depravity in the rich.

With only a modicum of overstatement, capitalism can be depicted as the sublimation of jealousy. As opposed to destructive envy-jealousy induces emulation. Consumers-responsible for two thirds of America's GDP-ape role models and vie with neighbors, colleagues, and family members for possessions and the social status they endow. Productive and constructive competition-among scientists, innovators, managers, actors, lawyers, politicians, and the members of just about every other profession-is driven by jealousy.

The eminent Nobel prize winning British economist and philosopher of Austrian descent, Friedrich Hayek, suggested in "The Constitution of Liberty" that innovation and progress in living standards are the outcomes of class envy. The wealthy are early adopters of expensive and unproven technologies. The rich finance with their conspicuous consumption the research and development phase of new products. The poor, driven by jealousy, imitate them and thus create a mass market which allows manufacturers to lower prices.

But jealousy is premised on the twin beliefs of equality and a level playing field. "I am as good, as skilled, and as talented as the object of my jealousy."-goes the subtext-"Given equal opportunities, equitable treatment, and a bit of luck, I can accomplish the same or more."

Jealousy is easily transformed to outrage when its presumptions-equality, honesty, and fairness-prove wrong. In a paper recently published by Harvard University's John M. Olin Centre for Law and titled "Executive Compensation in America: Optimal Contracting or Extraction of Rents?", the authors argue that executive malfeasance is most effectively regulated by this "outrage constraint": "Directors (and non-executive directors) would be reluctant to approve, and executives would be hesitant to seek, compensation arrangements that might be viewed by observers as outrageous."

12

Nature of Corruption and Anti-corruption Strategies

Pakistan may not be making headlines in the world on corruption these days but contemporary discourse within the country has been focused on the issue in the recent past. In fact there is a discernible pattern over the years where concerns about corruption dominate discourse for some time and then seamlessly other issues take over public imagination. Meanwhile corrupt practices continue in one form or the other, only to raise their head again. It is useful to note that corruption was mentioned as one of the ailments afflicting territories constituting Pakistan by the founder of the country, Mohammad Ali Jinnah, in his first address to the Constituent Assembly on 11 August 1947. He said:

One of the biggest curses from which India is suffering—I do not say that other countries are free from it, but, I think our condition is much worse—is bribery and corruption. That really is a poison. We must put that down with an iron hand and I hope that you will take adequate measures as soon as it is possible for this Assembly to do so. That is exactly what the Constituent Assembly did: an anti-corruption law was one of the first items of legislation enacted by the assembly soon after independence, only to be followed by a myriad of laws. However, the perception of Pakistan as a highly corrupt polity and society persists amongst Pakistanis as well as outsiders even after 62 years of the country's existence.

The obvious question to ask is that in spite of so much concern for so long, why has Pakistan failed to effectively reduce corruption? Is it because of a lack of effective anti-corruption strategies? If that is so, then why can international or regional best practice not be adopted? After all, in some areas—most notably in technologies and strategies related to weaponization and warfare—international best practice has been adopted.

Or is corruption not the cause but the symptom of socio-political imbalances—such as the enduring civil-military divide as well as regional-ethnic imbalances—that Pakistan as a nation-state has been unable to resolve over the years?

One can only attempt to answer the above questions once we discern the nature of corruption prevalent in Pakistan as well as the form and substance of anti-corruption strategies adopted to combat the problem. Section 1 of this article lays out the broad contours of corruption in Pakistan through three different analytical vantage points. Section 2 provides a critical assessment for the success and failures of anti-corruption laws and strategies in the country. Section 3 then provides a tentative way forward for more effective and sustainable anti-corruption policy in Pakistan.

CONTOURS OF CORRUPTION IN PAKISTAN

Corrupt practices and their impact on citizens?welfare can be categorized in numerous ways across time and across countries. For the purposes of this paper, it is important to focus on a succinct definition of corruption. Numerous unethical and illegal practices are termed as corrupt in common parlance. However, there is no perfect overlap between legality and ethics or vice versa.

For these very reasons, the UN Convention Against Corruption itself does not provide a succinct definition of the phenomenon. There are three board analytical areas where the prevalence of corruption needs to be understood in Pakistan. This particular categorization will also help us in assessing the effectiveness or otherwise of anti-corruption mechanisms adopted in the country.

Private Sector-state Collusion

Commonly referred as 'rent-seeking? in economic literature, through a variety of mechanisms, individuals and groups from the private sector interface with the state to transfer public resources to themselves. The most salient of this form of corruption in Pakistan has been allocation of state land to private interests, as well as land transactions. The practice started immediately after partition, when millions of refugees came to Pakistani territory from post-partition India. The state adopted a policy of granting land and housing left behind by Hindus who migrated to India to refugees based on claims of property they left behind in India. There is some documentation on the use of influence and money in granting such claims, as well as some politicians using land as a form of patronage to create constituencies by deliberately driving out those Hindus who had otherwise wished to stay in Pakistan. This particular policy resulted in a class of propertied migrants to the exclusion of others.

The practice of land grabbing—both urban and rural—has continued in different ways over the years. Its modern manifestation is in different arms of the state using the Acquisition of Land Act in ways it was not intended so as to sell acquired land cheaply to mafia-like groups of land developers and builders, who subsequently sell it at a premium to prospective home dwellers or for commercial purposes. Moreover land transactions are a typical way of whitening black money acquired through corruption and criminal activities. Due to taxation loopholes, more than two-thirds of the money paid in land or property taxation is unrecorded. Thus, even if an honest property seller is to claim the market value of her property, she will be handed a large chunk of the money, which is not declared. This particular practice, which is pervasive, results in large amounts of black money circulating and a variety of ingenious methods being adopted to launder that money.

Other forms of private sector-state interface that breed corruption have occurred due to state control over allocation of resources. In the pre-liberalization period, bribery in acquiring industrial and commercial licenses and later in willfully defaulting on loans acquired from state-owned banks and financial institutions frequently hit the headlines in Pakistan. The cost of this type of corruption has been borne by the consumer, in high prices paid for goods and services as a result of inefficiency and monopoly pricing. In the post-liberalization period, a lack of regulation on cartels—particularly in banking services, and the automobile, cement, fertilizer and sugar sectors—has also hit consumers hard.

Corruption and Extortion by State Actors

State personnel across different institutions of the state engage in various forms of corrupt practices. These range from straightforward bribery and extortion of individuals and businesses to various forms of domestic and international kickbacks on procurement of materials and services. For the sake of clarity we will distinguish state-led corruption by civil bureaucrats, the armed forces and politicians. Much of the bribery and extortion carried out by the state is executed through the civil bureaucracy. Ranging from petty bribes to the policeman or building authority clerk to major kickbacks on procurement, civil bureaucrats are the 'deal executors? They are in the loop for the simple reason that they carry out the documentation and are most familiar with rules and regulations, as well as the loopholes and lacunae that exist. However, apart from the petty bribes and extortion, for the most part the civil bureaucrat is not the sole claimant of big-ticket corruption. Over the years, the civil bureaucracy in Pakistan has lost its clout and political power to the executive and legislature, whether military or civilian.

The central protagonists in state-led corruption are the military and politicians. Arguably, civilian politicians are more accountable than the military for three reasons. First, the logic of electoral democracy itself holds politicians accountable for their misdeeds and lack of delivery to the electorate. Although this proposition may be contested in the case of Pakistan, where politicians with tainted reputations are re-elected time and again, the fact that electoral democracy has not had a fair run—in the sense that an incumbent government has not yet gone back to the electorate after completion of its term and been subjected to a largely fair election process—means that this contention has not been put to a robust test. Second, audit and accountability laws apply to politicians, which makes them relatively more susceptible to legal provisions than their uniformed counterparts. Third, their conduct is more in the public eye because of their greater interface with the public as well as the media.

The military, on the other hand, is powerful enough to evade public accountability. The military's budget in Pakistan is neither presented in detail to parliament nor have public representatives so far been able to debate it. Moreover, civilian audit authorities do not audit the military budget, and to top it all, serving military personnel have been exempted from investigation by civilian anti-corruption watchdogs by law. Also, because of the very nature of the civilian-military imbalance in Pakistan, demanding accountability in military scandals is a much more hazardous proposition for an otherwise free media than it is from civilian politicians.

Institutionalized Corruption

There are a number of areas in Pakistan where corruption is institutionalized. As mentioned earlier, enough tax and legal lacunae exist through which black money can be laundered. The most salient in this regard is the 'no questions asked private remittance in foreign exchange. According to law, an individual can get as much foreign exchange into the country tax-free as they wish without being questioned over the source of funds. This is the most-used conduit for laundering money obtained through land transactions, tax evasion, and criminal activity. In addition, the state periodically provides a window through which to 'whiten black money at a nominal rate of taxation by announcing a 'whitener scheme where black money can be declared at a minimal rate of taxation that is lower than for those who earn legitimate taxable income (last time, December 2008, the rate was two per cent). That the state provides this facility every few years creates an incentive to accumulate black money rather than pose any threat of penalization. The other form of institutionalized corruption is land grants given to military personnel.

Officers of the armed forces are entitled to residential, commercial and agricultural land at highly subsidized prices. In the case of residential land, numerous societies developed by the armed forces dot Pakistan's urban landscape where infrastructure is developed (largely at state expense) and land is allotted to military personnel at subsidized rates, who in turn can sell it at the market rate and extract a hefty premium. Similarly, developed agricultural land is provided at subsidized rates and in some cases army personnel are deputed to tend the land at state expense.

Another feature of institutionalized corruption in Pakistan is located in the country's security and foreign policy. For the last three decades, the Pakistani state has been involved in a number of major covert operations as part of its foreign and security policy. Perhaps the most elaborate has been the country's nuclear program. The confession of Dr. A.Q. Khan—one of the main protagonists in Pakistan's nuclear program—in 2004 that he supplied contraband material to other countries in return for cash may be the tip of the iceberg so far as money laundering and clandestine activity for this purpose is concerned. In the formative phase of the program, material and equipment were purchased illegally from the international market. This process would have involved a large number of state and non-state actors laundering state money.

The other major element has been covert warfare conducted in Afghanistan and Kashmir. A large chunk of state resources was diverted to conduct the entire war effort through non-state actors (including training, provision of arms and ammunition as well as logistic support). Much of this money would have made its way back to Pakistan through re-laundering and into land, real estate and other 'legal' activities as well as criminal ones.

The most important implication of institutionalized corruption is that powerful actors—whether state or non-state—cannot be investigated and prosecuted under anti-corruption laws if the entrepreneurial class (in the case of big business) and state personnel (in the case of covert policy operations) have the imperative to protect important state and economic interests against these laws.

ECONOMIC LIBERALIZATION

Another anti-corruption mechanism that was popular in the recent past was to reduce the role of the state in resource allocation, as it was deemed to create rents and lead to corrupt practices. Pakistan has vigorously pursued privatization and deregulation of the economy. This has at best produced mixed results. Some of the sectors privatized have indeed become more efficient and benefited from being out of direct government control, while others—particularly public monopolies—have only turned into private monopolies with no benefits to the consumer. Moreover, the process of privatization itself has been called into question as being less than transparent, and collusive.

Deregulation of the economy has in many cases gone to the other extreme, where regulation that protects public interest has also been dismantled, with results including cartels and market manipulation.

That corruption in Pakistan is pervasive and endemic is without doubt. We have attempted to show in section 1 that it is also multifaceted in character. In section 2, we have seen that in spite of the number of laws enacted and bureaus created to check corruption, they are not perceived as effective and are not broad-based.

While there are issues remaining for the improving of capacity and for better strategizing on anti-corruption mechanisms, corruption is inextricably linked to socio-political imbalances in Pakistan. If the country is to embark on an effective and sustainable anti-corruption drive, some level of agreement among different power wielders is necessary to ensure that accountability will be across the board. Only then will there be broader societal legitimacy for anti-corruption practices. Once such an agreement is reached, a future anti-corruption program requires us to:

1. Bury the past and start anew. Bringing up corruption cases from the past will open a Pandora's box, from which demands for accountability of all manner of powerful sections of the elite will emerge. Not only will this be divisive but it will also consume valuable time. Moreover, those in powerful positions (including formulators of the state's security policy) will resist such a move. If catharsis is needed, then a process of truth and reconciliation, like that in South Africa, should be initiated.
2. Create a constitutional body to oversee all aspects of corruption, with no group or entity outside its ambit. The creation of such an entity would also mean that the duplication in mandates of several agencies could be rationalized.
3. Enhance the capacity and oversight functions of the auditor's office to ensure that corruption in service delivery—which is the most important for the citizen—is minimized.
4. Carry out civil bureaucratic reform to strike a balance between security of tenure and credible penalization for wrongdoing. In this process it is very important to keep in mind that excessive moralizing on corruption does not generate substantive dividends. As with much else, it is advisable to create institutions that will over time reduce the incidence of corruption in society.

A SERIOUS THREAT TO INDIA'S INTERNAL SECURITY

Tulsidas said: "I am troubled by two kinds of people; the good people and the bad people". When asked how the good people troubled him he replied: "The good people trouble me because of their absence and the bad people trouble me because of their presence".

Good people are not absent they are in the shadows and sidelines. Bad people have swamped the stage. Their doings have reduced the faith of people in the Administrative machinery in India. Even intellectuals and ideologues are feeling that with such inefficient and largely dishonest machinery, there is little hope of bringing about any progress or economic development. The preamble to the Indian Constitution says: "We the people of India, having solemnly resolved to constitute INDIA into a Sovereign Socialist Secular Democratic Republic and to secure to all its citizens, Justice, Social, Economic and Political... equality of Status and opportunity... in our Constituent Assembly this Twenty Sixth day of November, 1949, do hereby adopt, enact and give to ourselves this Constitution." In the directive principles of the Constitution, the State shall strive to promote the welfare of the people by securing and protecting a Social order with justice, economic and political, in all Institutions of National life. How difficult it is to achieve this task of reaching these lofty goals set by the founding fathers of our Constitution with corruption prone Administrative machinery?

We believed in 'Simple living and High thinking'. We are seeing now 'High living and simple thinking'. We were taught eating in public and easing in private; it is the opposite now. Newspeak has coined expressions like 'Speed money' 'Hush money' 'Slush money' and so on. A static bureaucracy and a dynamic bureaucracy are both Bureaucracies; the difference lies only in the attitudes; the first is slow motion of Man as a mere functionary, a mere bureaucrat. That is a poor state of man; and that state of mind is prone to end often and succumb to corruption. The second represents Man as inwardly rich in his being, on the strength of citizenship awareness and patriotic impulse, and pouring out that richness into National growth. Such an attitude fosters service and spirit, and contains much innate strength to resist and overcome corrupt influences. In short, attitude plays a great part in running a clean Administration.

Integrity in Administration becomes one of the essential requisites of a Welfare State. With the expansion of the role of the State in every walk of life, with successive five-year plans pouring in crores of rupees for economic growth and development; with discretionary powers given to functionaries in handling large sums of money; with a mania of acquisitive hedonism pervading a permissive society; and an alround lowering of ethics, morals, values, and character in all walks of life, it is but natural that corruption has struck deep roots in our public life. Since corruption has touched the highest seats of power, the governing machinery that is a part of the social milieu could not remain an idle spectator but had to become part of the package. A stage has come where things have gone completely out of control and people are wondering whether it would not be better to put the expanding State in Reverse gear and prohibit further involvement of the State in the People's affairs so that corruption could be contained at the level it is today.

Beginning of Corruption

Corruption always starts from small beginning like cancer. Later, it becomes deep-rooted, widespread, and incurable. It develops immunity and resists easy detection or cure. Being contagious, it is able to spread fast, engulfing more and more parts of the anatomy. The stark tragedy is that corruption has lost the social stigma. People have taken dishonesty in their stride. For survival, human societies get progressively used to certain levels of infirmities, shortcomings and weaknesses in their Institutions. Violations of encroachments on traditional morality are gradually accepted and accommodated up to a point, to avoid irritation and confrontation. Beyond a point it explodes. The message is that corruption leads to compromise and defiance of law, which escalates, into naked violence and weakening of the State. These are seeds of revolution, which get slowly sprouted. The French, Russian, and Chinese revolutions have not taught the privileged, the; 'Haves' and 'Neo-Rich' and the moneybags, any lessons as they are proceeding towards the same fate and destination. History tells us that unless justice, equality and equal opportunities are given to the people, the handful of exploiters will perish; their lives will be in peril. If the State will not punish the guilty and corrupt, the people will.

Causes of Corruption

The Santhanam Committed of 1962 set up to investigate into the causes of corruption and evolving remedies to stem the rising tide observed: "The advance of technological and scientific development is contributing to the emergence of a 'Mass Society' with a large rank and file, and a small controlling elite, encouraging the growth of monopolies, rise of a Managerial class, and intricate Institutional mechanisms. The inability of society to appreciate an honest functioning social, political and economic process results in the emergence and growth of white collar and economic crimes. Corruption is a white-collar crime defying any permanent solution. White-collar crimes have been jeopardizing social and moral values. It is recklessly disrupting norms and rectitude. It has promoted Hedonism, Individualism that has supplanted traditionalism. Detestable competitive sprit to demonstrate affluence, living a life beyond means, living only for today and making the most out of it, an all round breakdown of family, societal, National discipline have all contributed towards mounting corruption, denying the underprivileged their legitimate share, making them poorer than before'.

Growth of Corruption

Corruption crept into the system during the concluding stages of the Second World War. Big contracts, gigantic purchases, speedy disposals, collection of funds for war effort and decentralization of decisions at discretionary nodal points all created a climate of dishonesty, moral degradation and making a quick and easy buck in the bargain. Speed was the criterion; end result was the evaluation; delivering the goods was the ultimate judgment. The means adopted were conveniently lost sight of. Corruption thrived and many became rich overnight. In the bargain, the system was corroded and the beginnings of a lowering of moral and ethical standards at high levels were noticed. Later, after Independence, the increasing involvement of the Sate in people' affairs in the name of Democracy and Socialism loosened many of the joints of the bureaucratic machinery slowly first and rapidly later, and the cancer of corruption struck deep roots. We have now reached a stage of no return. The added tragedy is that corruption has spread to all walks of life like public sector undertakings, local bodies and even philanthropic and charitable

Institutions where embezzlement and misappropriation of funds have become increasingly manifest.

Santhanam Committee's Recommendations

To stem the rot, the Santhanam Committee recommended the creation of a Central Vigilance commission with a role and charter of duties. Being independent, the CVC could call for any records, direct any agency to investigate cases, offer advice to introduce Administrative reforms, and so on. The aim was to have an independent and objective body to advice Government in matters relating to corruption, misconduct, lack of integrity and other malpractices and misdemeanors, on the part of public servants under the Executive control of the Central Government including public sector undertakings and Banks. The then Home Minister said: "The Commission is a unique example of the Government imposing on itself certain extra-constitutional obligations of far-reaching importance of its own free will. These obligations have the practical effect of trammeling its wide discretionary powers.

The CVC was followed by Anti-corruption Bureaus in the States, which unlike the CVC were not independent but under the exclusive and total control of the State Government. Whereas the CVC was only an Advisory Body without any teeth, the ACB of the State had the striking power at targets of its choice. Being non-autonomous, the political bosses could use it more as a weapon against adversaries than against interlopers committing misconduct. The CVC used the CBI for investigation purposes whereas the ACB of the State had its own body, brain and brawn. Like all systems becoming old, stale and routine, the Anti-Corruption Bureaus also did not make any major impact. The honest and dishonest officers both paid respects and homage at its altar for different reasons. The honest for allowing their integrity and morals to remain with them; and the dishonest for getting protection, patronage and cover behind their misdeeds.

The word vigilance connotes 'Caution', 'watchfulness', 'Precaution' and so on. It is mostly preventive. To be effective, vigilance should focus and concentrate on preventive steps and measures. After corruption has occurred and is detected, the investigating machinery has to go in the reverse gear to the occurrence point and travel down to the stage where the detection took place. This is laborious, painstaking, time-consuming and cumbersome. So the Santhanam Committee observed "Corruption cannot be eliminated or reduced unless preventive measures are planned and implemented in a concentrated sustained manner". They divided the preventive area into five zones viz.

i) Administrative;

ii) Legal;

iii) Social;

iv) Economic;

v) Educative.

At the Administrative level they recommended that the cleansing operation should start from the sensitive areas at the TOP, simultaneously giving special attention at the cutting edge level. On the legal plane, they urged the constant review and revision of conduct rules and legal procedures to suit the ever-changing needs. Inspections, surprise checks etc. could reveal more than they could conceal. At the Social level chopping off deadwood, removing the cancer through surgery, giving protection to proven honest officers, setting personal examples, and rewarding the men of integrity were some measures propounded and recommended by them.

At the Economic level they recommended need-based wages and at the Educative level, a social climate of honesty and character. They further observed that vigilance normally should be an internal affair of the organization with external force to step in when the internal system becomes ineffective. Although the Santhanam Committee made very original, useful and revolutionary suggestions, like all systems when introduced in the beginning, it showed spectacular results. Later it sank into sandy bottoms and stayed there. Now CVC, CBI, ACB and so on, only release figures of citadels captured never disclosing what they contained or what happened to them ultimately.

Erosion of Institutions

The CBI (SPE-Special Police Establishment 1946) proved a powerful weapon for a long time. It attained superb stature under a succession of dedicated leaders. The measure of its credibility can be gauged when ruling and opposition parties both clamoured for its interference, indulgence and involvement to tackle complicated cases. An Institution accepted by all, remains on an envious pedestal like the judicial courts at one time before they also joined the mundane gang of human beings. As time passed, as politicians got more and more insight into their working style; as immature leaders and equally puerile advisors got around governing the country, these credible Institutions like CBI and judicial courts also lost their sanctity. Ultimately people realized that justice is available only in people's courts or in God's Durbar. Those who believed in the strength of the people took to the streets to straighten out things through violence, Terrorism, and other dehumanized techniques; those who believed in the DIVINE court became philosophers philosophizing about their inevitable predicament.

Spread of Corruption

Corruption has now assumed global dimensions. Corrupt politicians and corrupt civil servants joined hands with a network of power brokers, commission agents, and Middlemen to suck the Taxpayers money through ingenious conduits never imagined or thought of before. For the first time people started hearing about non-existent front companies, winding up charges, Swiss Accounts and so on. Administrative pollution reached the Top. Large-scale corporate corruption crossed all barriers and breached the dams erected so far; it inundated vast areas of the Administration; individual corruption became a Lilliput; corporate corruption became the Gulliver. It created inflation as rules were bent, modified, scrapped or ignored. Corruption created a new class of liars, Lever Pullers, defenders, and spokesmen of untruth who paraded as the guardians of rectitude and propriety. The whole game of corruption went out of the domain of small time operators to big time Godfathers who could hold a Government to ransom and give protection to a whole group of gangsters who formed a powerful syndicate. The cinema Industry has now come under the threat of Godfathers and Dons who extract enormous sums for the personal safety of popular artists. The killing of Gulshan Kumar, the architect of the T-Series of Audio and Video Cassettes on the 'spiritual and divine' marketing industry was a case of gang power used to eliminate an up-and-coming climber in the new and promising territory of expanding religious sentiments of a section of the population.

Concept of Vigilance

Vigilance is concerned with man and his human qualities and not with rules, regulations, court procedures, and punitive measures. It relates to the environment where man works. It concerns and refers to values in public service. It should inculcate ethics, norms, standards, and morals. To achieve Excellence in work, man behind the work has to be pure and his conscience has to be refined and cleaned. The man at work had to be provided with adequate salary or emoluments to fight temptations and reject adventurism, careerism, affluence and false security.

Raising the level of the human being from the abysmal depths of temptation and surrender to corruption cannot be accomplished in one day. The top has to be cleaned first to set the trend. That cleanliness, and hygiene is mostly self-imposed. If the rule maker himself becomes the culprit, if the Police Officer himself becomes the thief, if the gamekeeper himself becomes the poacher, if the Minister himself becomes a perpetrator of malpractices, the ordinary citizen can look nowhere. He will rally round others and pull down the system. He will erect a new system to protect himself. That is what we are seeing now when we look around.

Smt. Indira Gandhi speaking at the National Joint Conference of ACB Officers in March 1981 said: "If India is to progress and be strong enough to face her external threats and solve her internal problems, the containment of corruption is a basic need. Otherwise, the fabric of our country is likely to be damaged."

On another occasion she said, "The General Administrator is basically a Status-Quo man. He lives by rules, which are the outcome of precedence and past experience. Scientists, Managers, and politicians should have a keen perception of the future and be sensitive to change.

Most people still tend to judge the Government by the static norms of the Revenue dominated, and law and order administration of older days, little appreciating how complex the process of Governance has become... it involves not only the skill of production and maintenance, but also of bringing projects to fruition within stipulated time schedules and monetary allocations. It involves a knack of forward planning and heightened awareness of social responsibilities".

The Prime Minister Shri Atal Bihari Vajpayee addressing the Nation after the elections said, "One of our immediate tasks will be to firmly put down Terrorism. We will be guided by 'Zero Tolerance'. The same principles of zero tolerance will apply while dealing with corruption that has bred contempt of the Law. One of the fist legislations we will take up is the Lok Pal Bill so that the rot can be checked from the Top.... We propose electoral reforms".

In spite of these assurances corruption has increased. Black Money circulation is estimated around Rs. 1,00,000 crores. Industries depend on Black money for survival. Our CVC Shri N. Vittal says "Corruption today is a low-risk, high profit Business. There are five key players on our corruption scene; the Neta, The Babu, Lala, Jhola and the Dada. There are five reasons why our system encourages corruption. i) the lack of transparency, ii) scarcity of goods and services iii) red tape, obsolete rules, Time-consuming procedures and speed money. (iv) Protection to the guilty; the Law classifying everyone as innocent until proved otherwise v) Tribalism of corruption protecting the corrupt.

The CVC also observed that India finds itself at the Bottom of the Nations of the World (Position 72 out of 76) in the list where corruption is less or more as published by TRANSPARENCY INTERNATIONAL an organization based in Germany which undertakes survey of the level of corruption in major countries of the world.

What we need to do is to make corruption a high-risk activity, instead of Low risk affair with high profits. The CVC has recommended a 13-point 'action plan' to implement zero tolerance of corruption. Apart from making corruption a high-risk activity what is urgently required is rearming the growing generation with character, ethics, morals, integrity and love for the community and Nation; otherwise called Patriotism. This can be done through special education in Schools, Colleges, Universities and training Institutions. It should be part of the curriculum and syllabus.

The other front to be opened is strengthening of social intuitions which are doing good work but whose voice is wasted in wilderness. The media can play an important role in this respect. Instead of focusing on Pop Music, fashion parades, cinema, crime and sensationalism, the print and visual media could devote more attention to incidents and activities where humanism, Honesty and martyrdom have occurred and are still occurring. KAHILL GIBRAN, the Lebanese Poet, Painter and sage wrote in his Masterpiece 'The Prophet' *"Turtles can tell more about the road than the Hares" and "Faith is an oasis in the Heart"*.

We should increase faith in the system of living, governance, human relations, emotions and hope that better days could definitely be created. The first step is the most difficult; the second is easier; the subsequent steps are the easiest. It is the people's will that should prevail. It will prevail only if the individuals assert, discard; derail the present and work for a better future. There is nothing that the people cannot achieve. After all, we are a democracy. People should run the country and not surrender their rights to vested interests!

The Real Threat

So the threat of instability is from inside the country; not from outside. Corruption not only concentrates wealth in the hands of a few, but it widens the divide between the 'Haves' and 'Have-nots'. It undermines efficiency and morale of Honest Officers. It weakens Institutions and Organisations. It saps National energy and vitality. It retards growth and development. It prevents sharing of gains between the people. It is like filling a leaking vessel.

The more you fill up the more it drains out. Ultimately, the Nation may have nothing to pour into the vessel, having drained out all the resources. The last resource i.e., man himself will be left alone. He will collect others, remove the leaking vessel and replace it with a leak-proof container, where he can put his resources in safety.

As time passes by, the new vessel will become old, develop leaks and repeat the same old story. This is the story of all civilizations, which flourished and perished. Corruption has been the deciding factor in all civilizations like Greek, Roman, Turkish and so on. No state could survive with corruption. The lesson of history is loud and clear.

Problem and Remedy

Gresham's law says that Bad money drives out good money. At considerable public cost to the Exchequer, one cannot tackle a symptom not knowing the disease. The disease has to be cured. So firstly, man and woman should be strengthened morally and spiritually. The fortified defences, which prevented degradation, have to be re-erected.

The individual and the family should become primary. Education has to spread to revive and restore the lost ethics and morals. The media has to be used to tell the people about the advantages of honesty, integrity, happiness and peace of mind. Instead of dishing out mindless entertainment, let it be mixed with stories – real stories of characters that lived, practiced, and sacrificed their lives for preserving the truth. Let Organisations and Institutions spreading light are encouraged, instead of Institutions spreading darkness through concepts borrowed from abroad. The moral fibre of man and woman should be made strong; respect for each other should grow; and a social climate of honesty should be created. Corrupt politicians, Bureaucrats should be looked upon as untouchables and socially ostracized. Respectability gained through wealth should be denounced.

The people should hound ostentatious display of filthy lucre out. While the Industrial worker may clamour for need-based wages, the public servant should be compelled to practice 'Wage-based needs'. In short, Vigilance should spring from within and not imposed form outside.

A three pronged strategy should be adopted to deal with corruption:-

I. Preventive

- Identification of corrupt prone and sensitive areas.
- Simplification of Rules and procedures to cut down delays
- Reducing the area of discretion and patronage particularly at lower levels
- De-regulation wherever possible to reduce the points of corruption and harassment to public
- Introduction of Public Information and assistance counters in departments and places having public dealings.
- Surprise Inspections by Seniors
- Monitoring disposal of cases with a view to check delays
- Including white collar crimes under IPC
- Shifting the burden of onus of proof of innocence on the accused.
- Rewards, Incentives, Honors and Decorations for honesty to Individuals rendering public and community services.

II. Surveillance and Detection

- Greater surveillance in corruption-prone areas particularly at public contact points.
- Closer watch on persons of doubtful integrity. Their income Tax returns should be checked thoroughly.

- A closer liaison should be maintained between CVC, CBI, ACB and Vigilance Cells.

III. Punitive Action

- Investigation/inquiry of cases detected should be speeded up according to a Time-bound schedule.
- Persons of doubtful integrity should be prematurely retired so that corrupt and inefficient elements are weeded out.
- A close watch should be kept for monitoring all anti-corruption measures; and
- Wide publicity should be given regarding punishments awarded to guilty persons.

13

Definition and Measurement of Criminal Behaviour

To fully understand the nature of how genes and the environment influence criminal behaviour, one must first know how criminal behaviour is defined. Law in our society is defined by social and legal institutions, not in biology (Morley & Hall, 2003). Therefore determining what constitutes criminal behaviour can envelope a wide variety of activities and for that reason, researchers tend to focus on the wider context of antisocial behaviour. Authors Morley and Hall (2003), who have investigated the genetic influences on criminal behaviour, point out three different ways to define antisocial behaviour. First is equating it with criminality and delinquency, which both involve engaging in criminal acts.

Criminality can lead to arrest, conviction, or incarceration for adults, while delinquency is related to juveniles committing unlawful acts (Rhee & Waldman, 2002). Information can be collected using court and criminal records, as well as self report surveys to analyse the influences that were present. Secondly, they advise individuals to define antisocial behaviour is through criteria used to diagnose certain personality disorders. More specifically, they mean those personality disorders, such as Antisocial Personality Disorder, which is associated with an increased risk in criminal activity. A final measure suggested for defining antisocial behaviour is by examining personality traits that may be influential in the criminal behaviour of individuals. Traits such as aggressiveness and impulsivity are two traits that have been investigated the most (Morley & Hall, 2003). Further details of disorders and personality traits associated with criminal behaviour will be discussed later in the paper.

With regards to determining the effects the environment plays in criminal behaviour there are fewer resources available. Observational studies and reports submitted by parents are two sources, but not everyone agrees on the validity of information collected from these sources. Three additional sources that most researchers cite when gathering information about both genetic and environmental influences are twin, family, and adoption studies (Tehrani & Mednick, 2000).

Twin, Adoption, and Family Studies

There has been great debate between researchers regarding the outcomes of twin, adoption, and family studies. Some claim that these studies support the notion of a genetic basis to criminal behaviour (Tehrani & Mednick, 2000). On the other hand, some have concluded that there is not enough evidence from these twin, family, and adoption studies to profess that genetics do play a role in antisocial or criminal behaviour (Lowenstein, 2003). To understand why there are such conflicting opinions, one must first look at the available studies that have been conducted.

Twin studies are conducted on the basis of comparing monozygotic (MZ) or identical twins and their rates of criminal behaviour with the rates of criminal behaviour of dizygotic (DZ) or fraternal twins. Ordinarily these studies are used to assess the roles of genetic and environmental influences. If the outcomes of these twin studies show that there is a higher concordance rate for MZ twins than for DZ twins in criminal behaviour, then it can be assumed that there is a genetic influence. A study conducted looked at thirty two MZ twins reared apart, who had been adopted by a non-relative a short time after birth. The results showed that for both childhood and adult antisocial behaviour, there was a high degree of heritability involved (Joseph, 2001). This study was of particular importance because it examined the factor of separate environments.

Another researcher studied eighty-five MZ and one hundred and forty-seven DZ pairs and found that there was a higher concordance rate for the MZ pairs. Ten years later after checking police records of these same twins, two other researchers concluded that there was a fifty-four percent heritability of liability to crime (Joseph, 2001). Around the same time of the study just mentioned, two researchers studied forty-nine MZ and eighty-nine DZ pairs, but found no difference in the concordance rates. They concluded therefore that in respect to common crime, hereditary factors are of little significance (Joseph, 2001). Many other twin studies have been conducted, but there is concern over the validity of those studies and their ability to separate out the nature and nurture aspects; therefore other sources of information should be examined.

Adoption studies are critical in examining the relationship that exists between adopted children and both their biological and adoptive parents because they assume to separate nature and nurture. Studies have been conducted that test for the criminal behaviour of the adopted-away children, if their biological parents had also been involved with criminal activity. In Iowa, the first adoption study was conducted that looked at the genetics of criminal behaviour. The researchers found that as compared to the control group, the adopted individuals, which were born to incarcerated female offenders, had a higher rate of criminal convictions as adults.

Therefore this evidence supports the existence of a heritable component to antisocial or criminal behaviour. Another study in Sweden also showed that if a biological background existed for criminality, then there was an increased risk of criminal behaviour in the adopted children. In Denmark, one of the largest studies of adopted children was conducted and found similar results to the previous studies. The defining feature of the Denmark study was that the researchers found a biological component for criminal acts against property, but not for violent crimes (Joseph, 2001). Children whose biological fathers had been convicted of property crimes were more likely to engage in similar behaviour, when compared to those biological fathers who had been convicted of violent crimes.

According to an article by Jay Joseph (2001), who studied all of the minor and major adoption studies, the majority of researchers have found and agreed upon the non-significance of genes in violent crime. This reestablishes the findings from the studies mentioned already in that there may be a genetic component to antisocial behaviour or that genes influence criminal behaviour, but specifically for property offenses.

Family studies are the third type of instrument used to assess the relationship between genetics and environmental influences on criminal or antisocial behaviour. Research in this field has probably been the least accepted by psychologists and other scholars because of the degree of difficulty in separating out nature and nurture in the family environment. Children experience both the influence of their parents' genes and also the environment in which they are raised, so it is difficult to assign which behaviours were influenced by the two factors. Twin studies have this flaw, as stated earlier, but it is more prevalent in family studies. An additional concern with family studies is the inability to replicate the results, therefore leading to a small number of studies. Regardless of these drawbacks, one family study in particular should be acknowledged for its findings.

Brunner, Nelen, Breakefield, Ropers, and van Oost (1993) conducted a study utilizing a large Dutch family. In their study they found a point mutation in the structural gene for monoamine oxidase A (MAOA), a neurochemical in the brain, which they associated with aggressive criminal behaviour among a number of males in that family (Alper, 1995). These males were reported to have selective MAOA deficiency, which can lead to decreased concentrations of-hydroxyindole-3-acetic acid (5-HIAA) in cerebrospinal fluid. Evidence suggests that low concentrations of-HIAA can be associated with impulsive aggression. These results have not been confirmed in any additional family studies, which lead to a need for more studies to determine if other families share similar results. However, this one family study does seem to suggest that genetics play an important role in antisocial or criminal behaviour.

Neurochemicals in Criminal and Anti-Social Behaviour

Neurochemicals are responsible for the activation of behavioural patterns and tendencies in specific areas of the brain (Elliot, 2000). As seen in the Brunner et al. study, there have been attempts to determine the role of neurochemicals in influencing criminal or antisocial behaviour. Included in the list of neurochemicals already cited by researchers are monoamine oxidase (MOA), epinephrine, norepinephrine, serotonin, and dopamine.

Monoamine oxidase (MAO) is an enzyme that has been shown to be related to antisocial behaviour. Specifically, low MAO activity results in disinhibition which can lead to impulsivity and aggression (Elliot, 2000). The Brunner et al. study is the only one to report findings of a relationship between a point mutation in the structural gene for MAOA and aggression, which makes the findings rare. However, there has been other evidence that points to the conclusion that deficiencies in MAOA activity may be more common and as a result may predispose individuals to antisocial or aggressive behaviour (Brunner et al., 1993). MAO is associated with many of the neurochemicals that already have a link to antisocial or criminal behaviour. Norepinephrine, serotonin, and dopamine are metabolized by both MAOA and MAOB (Elliot, 2000). While, according to Eysenck (1996), MAO is related to norepinephrine, epinephrine, and dopamine, which are all related to the personality factor of psychosis.

Serotonin is a neurochemical that plays an important role in the personality traits of depression, anxiety, and bipolar disorder. It is also involved with brain development and a disorder in this system could lead to an increase in aggressiveness and impulsivity. As Lowenstein (2003) states, "studies point to serotonin as one of the most important central neuro-transmitters underlying the modulation of impulsive aggression". Low levels of serotonin have been found to be associated with impulsive behaviour and emotional aggression. In addition, children who suffer from conduct disorder (which will be discussed later), have also been shown to have low blood serotonin (Elliot, 2000). Needless to say, there is a great deal of evidence that shows serotonin is related to aggression, which can be further associated with antisocial or criminal behaviour.

Dopamine is a neurotransmitter in the brain that is associated with pleasure and is also one of the neuro transmitters that is chiefly associated with aggression. Activation of both affective (emotionally driven) and predatory aggression is accomplished by dopamine (Elliot, 2000). Genes in the dopaminergic pathway have also been found to be involved with Attention Deficit Hyperactivity Disorder (ADHD). In one study cited by Morley and Hall (2003), a relationship was found between the genes in the dopaminergic pathway, impulsivity, ADHD, and violent offenders. Obviously, from this list of neurochemicals it seems plausible that there is a genetic component to antisocial or criminal behaviour.

Personality Disorders and Traits

Personality traits and disorders have recently become essential in the diagnosis of individuals with antisocial or criminal behaviour. These traits and disorders do not first become evident when an individual is an adult, rather these can be seen in children. For that reason it seems logical to discuss those personality disorders that first appear in childhood. Attention Deficit Hyperactivity Disorder (ADHD), Conduct Disorder (CD), and Oppositional Defiance Disorder (ODD) are three of the more prominent disorders that have been shown to have a relationship with later adult behaviour.

ODD is characterized by argumentativeness, noncompliance, and irritability, which can be found in early childhood (Holmes et al., 2001). When a child with ODD grows older, the characteristics of their behaviour also change and more often for the worse. They start to lie and steal, engage in vandalism, substance abuse, and show aggression towards peers. Frequently ODD is the first disorder that is identified in children and if sustained can lead to the diagnosis of CD.

It is important to note however that not all children who are diagnosed with ODD will develop CD.

ADHD is associated with hyperactivity-impulsivity and the inability to keep attention focused on one thing (Morley & Hall, 2003). Holmes et al. (2001) state that, "impulse control dysfunction and the presence of hyperactivity and inattention are the most highly related predisposing factors for presentation of antisocial behaviour". They also point to the fact that children diagnosed with ADHD have the inability to analyse and anticipate consequences or learn from their past behaviour. Children with this disorder are at risk of developing ODD and CD, unless the child is only diagnosed with Attention Deficit Disorder (ADD), in which case their chances of developing ODD or CD are limited. The future for some children is made worse when ADHD and CD are co-occurring because they will be more likely to continue their antisocial tendencies into adulthood.

Conduct Disorder is characterized with an individual's violation of societal rules and norms (Morley & Hall, 2003). As the tendencies or behaviours of those children who are diagnosed with ODD or ADHD worsen and become more prevalent, the next logical diagnosis is CD. What is even more significant is the fact that ODD, ADHD, and CD are risk factors for developing Antisocial Personality Disorder (ASPD). This disorder can only be diagnosed when an individual is over the age of eighteen and at which point an individual shows persistent disregard for the rights of others (Morley & Hall, 2003). ASPD has been shown to be associated with an increased risk of criminal activity. Therefore, it is of great importance that these early childhood disorders are correctly diagnosed and effectively treated to prevent future problems.

Another critical aspect that must be examined regarding antisocial or criminal behaviour is the personality characteristics of individuals. Two of the most cited personality traits that can be shown to have an association with antisocial or criminal behaviour are impulsivity and aggression. According to the article written by Holmes et al. (2001), antisocial behaviour between the ages of nine and fifteen can be correlated strongly with impulsivity and that aggression in early childhood can predict antisocial acts and delinquency. One statistic shows that between seventy and ninety percent of violent offenders had been highly aggressive as young children. These personality traits have, in some research, been shown to be heritable.

Environmental Influences

Thus far it has been established through research and various studies that genetics do influence criminal or antisocial behaviour. Researchers agree on the point that genes influence personality traits and disorders, such as the ones just mentioned. However, researchers also agree that there is an environmental component that needs to be examined. Environmental influences such as family and peers will be discussed, as well as a look into the social learning theory.

The family environment is critical to the upbringing of a child and if problems exist then the child is most likely to suffer the consequences. We have seen the problems associated with a child who is diagnosed with ADHD and how that can influence antisocial or criminal behaviour. In relation to that, some researchers have claimed that it is the family environment that influences the hyperactivity of children (Schmitz, 2003).

The researchers in this article specifically identify family risk factors as poverty, education, parenting practices, and family structure. Prior research on the relationship between family environment and child behaviour characterizes a child's well being with a positive and caring parent-child relationship, a stimulating home environment, and consistent disciplinary techniques (Schmitz, 2003). Families with poor communication and weak family bonds have been shown to have a correlation with children's development of aggressive/criminal behaviour.

Therefore it seems obvious to conclude that those families who are less financially sound, perhaps have more children, and who are unable to consistently punish their children will have a greater likelihood of promoting an environment that will influence antisocial or delinquent behaviour. Another indicator of future antisocial or criminal behaviour is that of abuse or neglect in childhood. A statistic shows that children are at a fifty percent greater risk of engaging in criminal acts, if they were neglected or abused (Holmes et al., 2001). This has been one of the most popular arguments as to why children develop antisocial or delinquent behaviours.

One additional research finding in the debate between genetic and environmental influences on antisocial or criminal behaviour has to deal with the age of the individual. Research seems consistent in recognizing that heritability influences adult behaviour more than environmental influences, but that for children and adolescents the environment is the most significant factor influencing their behaviour. As an adult, we have the ability to choose the environment in which to live and this will either positively or negatively reinforce our personality traits, such as aggressiveness. However, children and adolescents are limited to the extent of choosing an environment, which accounts for the greater influence of environmental factors in childhood behaviours.

Another significant factor in the development of antisocial or delinquent behaviour in adolescence is peer groups. Garnefski and Okma (1996) state that there is a correlation between the involvement in an antisocial or delinquent peer group and problem behaviour. One of the primary causes as to why this occurs can be traced back to aggressive behaviour in young children. When children are in preschool and show aggressive tendencies towards their peers, they will likely be deemed as an outcast. This creates poor peer relationships and relegates those children to be with others who share similar behaviours. A relationship like this would most likely continue into adolescence and maybe even further into adulthood. The similar tendencies of these individuals create an environment in which they influence one another and push the problem towards criminal or violent behaviour (Holmes et al., 2001).

Social learning theory has been cited as way to explain how the environment can influence a child's behaviour. Using this theory to explain the aggressive or antisocial behaviour of a child means that a child observes aggressive behaviour between parents, siblings, or both. As a result, the children believes that this aggressive behaviour is normal and can therefore use it themselves because they do not see the harm in acting similar to their parents (Miles & Carey, 1997). As stated earlier, interaction between family members and disciplinary techniques are influential in creating antisocial behaviour. Using the social learning theory these two factors are also critical in the development of aggression.

Children who are raised in an aggressive family environment would most likely be susceptible to experiencing a lack of parental monitoring, permissiveness or inconsistency in punishment, parental rejection and aggression. The exposure to such high levels of aggression and other environmental factors greatly influences and reinforces a child's behaviour. A significant point that should be known however is the fact that other research has supported the notion that genetics do influence levels of aggression, which stands in opposition to the social learning theory (Miles & Carey, 1997).

Gene-Environment Interactions

There are theories, however, concerning genetic and environmental influences, which seem to suggest an interaction between the two and one such theory is the general arousal theory of criminality. Personality psychologist Eysenck created a model based on three factors known as psychoticism, extraversion, and neuroticism, or what is referred to as the PEN model (Eysenck, 1996). Psychoticism was associated with the traits of aggressive, impersonal, impulsive, cold, antisocial, and un-empathetic. Extraversion was correlated with the traits of sociable, lively, active, sensation-seeking, carefree, dominant, and assertive.

Finally, neuroticism was associated with anxious, depressed, low self-esteem, irrational, moody, emotional, and tense (Eysenck, 1996). Through research and surveys, Eysenck found that these three factors could be used as predictors of criminal behaviour. He believed this to be especially true of the psychoticism factor and that measuring it could predict the difference between criminals and non-criminals. Extraversion was a better predictor for young individuals, while neuroticism was a better predictor for older individuals (Eysenck, 1996). An important point about these factors and the personality traits associated with them is that most of them have already been found to be heritable (Miles & Carey, 1997). Understanding Eysenck's original model is critical to assessing the general arousal theory of criminality, which suggests an interaction between factors. Research has shown that criminality is strongly correlated with low arousal levels in the brain. Characteristics related to low arousal levels include lack of interest, sleepiness, lack of attention, and loss of vigilance. Eysenck (1996) believed that these characteristics were similar to the personality factor of extraversion. Individuals with low arousal levels and those who are extraverts need to seek out stimulation because they do not have enough already in their brains.

Therefore, the premise of the general arousal theory of criminality is that individuals inherit a nervous system that is unresponsive to low levels of stimulation and as a consequence, these individuals have to seek out the proper stimulation to increase their arousal. Under this theory, the proper stimulation includes high-risk activities associated with antisocial behaviour, which consists of sexual promiscuity, substance abuse, and crime (Miles & Carey, 1997). A significant fact that must be pointed out though is that not every individual with low arousal levels or those who are extraverts will seek those high risk activities just mentioned. It takes the right environment and personality to create an individual with antisocial or criminal tendencies and that is why this theory can be considered to take into account both factors of genetic and environmental influences.

Conclusion

There cannot be enough possible evidence to conclude the point that genetics play the most important role in the outcome or behaviour of an individual. The opposing viewpoint of environmental factors is not without its doubts either as to being the prominent factor influencing antisocial or criminal behaviour of an individual. In this paper, there is more evidence supporting the genetics viewpoint, but that does not mean it is more important. With the research and studies having numerous flaws and the inability to adequately separate nature and nurture, there is still a great debate between genetic and environmental factors.

Researchers, however, have certainly come far in their progression, to the point where there is a large consensus of the fact that genes do influence behaviour to a certain extent. Although not as widely publicized, it is the belief of the author that these same researchers also believe that environmental factors account for what cannot be explained by genes. Therefore it seems obvious to reach the conclusion that an individual's antisocial or criminal behaviour can be the result of both their genetic background and the environment in which they were raised.

One researcher has proposed a theory relating to sociopaths and their antisocial behaviour. According to the theory, a primary sociopath is lacking in moral development and does not feel socially responsible for their actions. This type of sociopath is a product of the individual's personality, physiotype, and genotype. A secondary sociopath develops in response to his or her environment because of the disadvantages of social competition. Living in an urban residence, having a low socioeconomic status, or poor social skills can lead an individual to being unsuccessful in reaching their needs in a socially desirable way, which can turn into antisocial or criminal behaviour.

The first type of sociopath is dependent on their genetic makeup and personality, while certain factors of the second type can also be heritable. Notwithstanding, the second type has a greater dependence on environmental factors (Miles & Carey, 1997). Perhaps from this review of both genetic and environmental factors, it seems clear to support the idea of the secondary sociopath type. An individual can inherit certain genes and when combined with the right environmental factors can lead them to engage in antisocial or criminal behaviour.

Although not mentioned extensively in the text of the paper, there is a great need to try and identify those individuals, especially children, who may become susceptible to certain disorders or personality traits that can lead into antisocial, delinquent, or criminal behaviour. Society should not try to imitate the era of controlled breeding, but rather focus on the treatment and rehabilitation of those individuals in need. Certain educational, environment enrichment programs have been shown to have a lasting effect on children if given by a certain age. If more of these programs could be developed, society could help prevent the future antisocial or criminal behaviour of children.

Criminal Behaviour and Personality Disorders

In addition to the research showing that the gene responsible for production of monoamine oxidase has a possible link to criminality, some evidence has also shown a possible link between other genes. One area of personality research in molecular genetics that has received a lot of attention is the trait of novelty-seeking, and novelty seeking is a personality trait often associated with criminality. Research has indicated that the single DRD4 gene may account for 10% of the genetic variance in relation to novelty-seeking (Sloan, 2000). This conclusion is highly controversial because in subsequent studies there has been both replication of the original findings, and failure to replicate in other studies. It seems most molecular genetic approaches in relating heritability of personality characteristics such as criminality to a single gene frequently suffer from failures in replication.

Some studies have demonstrated a genetic link between ADHD, CD, and ODD and criminality. However, there are possible alternate explanations for a greater rate of criminality for those who have suffered from these disorders that the paper failed to mention. It has been shown that people evoke certain responses from their environment. It is plausible that children suffering from these disorders are treated in a different manner than normal children due to the responses that they evoke, and it is because of these environmental differences that they are more prone to criminal behaviour. Say a child suffering from ADHD is having problems in school, they may be placed in a remedial class in which there is a greater rate of delinquency.

This would be a very important environment difference that could contribute greatly to future criminality. Other children may also socialize less with children with these disorders, which could plausible lead to anti-social behaviour.

While it is possible that in some cases the relationship between these disorders and criminality is not direct byproduct of genes, but rather as a byproduct of the same environment. There have been studies on ADHD in relation to a multitude of environmental factors, including everything from nutrition to environmental toxins.

For example, a studies have been done that indicate an increased time spent viewing television in children was related to a decreased attention span and ADHD. There '.ave also been studies showing a relationship between television viewing and desensitization to violence, which could influence criminal behaviour. I am not proposing that it is watching TV that is the major factor in these disorders, or in criminality, I am just trying to illustrate that perhaps there is some environmental factor that could influence criminality as well as disorders such as ADHD.

In addition to ADHD, CD, and ODD, other disorders have shown to influence criminality as well. Studies have shown that there is a higher occurrence of disorders such as schizophrenia, major depressive disorder, bipolar disorder, just to name a few. It is possible that having these personality disorders gives one a greater predisposition toward criminal behaviour. A Swedish study found that the occurrence of major mental disorders in prisoners to be%, as well as a 20% occurrence of personality disorders (Rasmussen, 1999). Other studies have given different values for the occurrence, but in most cases the research agrees that there is a much higher incidence of these mental disorders in those who commit crimes.

Genetics has shown to be a major factor in the occurrence of many of these disorders. There have been studies that examine the rate of personality disorders such a schizophrenia, psychosis, and manic? depressive illness in adopted children. We can hypothesize that if adopted children are more likely to suffer from such disorders if their biological parents are or were afflicted, it would be indicative of a genetic basis for the disorder.

Research done by Leonard Heston in 1960 examined children of schizophrenic mothers that were removed after birth and raised by foster parents. Out of a total of 47 children examined, Heston found that nine of them were diagnosed with sociopathic personalities and antisocial behaviour, and four of the 47 children developed schizophrenia. Heston also found behavioural abnormalities in many of the other children (Eysenk, 1982).

This study shows a significant increase in the rate of personality disorders in the progeny of an affected parent, in comparison to population statistics on these mood disorders. In fact, when both parents are affected by a personality disorder the rate of occurrence in their offspring is even higher.

Not only do adoption studies support a genetic basis for personality disorders that are shown to have a relation to criminality, but twin studies as well. Statistics show a high concordance between identical and non-identical twins for schizophrenia and manic depression.

Analysis of the statistics clearly show the genetic basis for these disorders: For schizophrenia the concordance in identical twins was 60%, compared to only 10% in non-identical twins, and the normal frequency being 1% in northern European populations. Similarly, manic depression showed a 70% concordance between identical twins, a 15% concordance between non-identical twins, and again only a 1% frequency in the normal population (Russo & Cove, 1995). This research supports the theory that genetics play a crucial role in these personality disorders.

Criminality is a Product of Genes and Environment

In considering the roles of genetics and environment on criminal behaviour, or any behaviour for that matter, I think the best explanation is that there is a complex interaction between one's inherited traits and the environment in which he or she lives. Although the idea of environmental influences seems rather intuitive, regardless of knowledge regarding heredity and biological factors, it is surprising that some may have considered criminal behaviour to be solely a result of genetics. I propose that the debate of nature versus nurture now is not whether genetics or environment influence behaviour, but how complex the interaction between these factors is.

Despite the relative lack of reliability and validity in twin, adoption, and family studies, they still provide valuable insight into the roles of heredity and environment in criminal behaviour. However, it seems that most studies of this kind focus on the role of heredity in influencing behaviour.

It would be interesting to see whether any studies with adopted children have examined the role of environment in criminal behaviour. Most adoption studies examine the correlation between criminality in the biological parents of adopted children, but what about the correlation between the children and their adopted parents who are crucial to their environment?

The influence of neurochemicals on criminal and antisocial behaviour are indicative of a genetic component to such behaviours. However, a more complete explanation of neurochemical influences is that they reflect the complex interactions between genetics and environment. There is evidence that the expression of genes is influenced by a wide variety of environmental factors.

Therefore, it is very possible that disorders relating to such chemicals as serotonin and dopamine could be caused by stressful environmental situations. If environment affects the regulation of gene expression and, in turn, the activity of neuro transmitters that modulate behaviour, this kind of interaction may be a significant factor in the development of criminal and antisocial behaviour.

Environmental and genetic factors influence antisocial and criminal behaviour in childhood versus adulthood seems somewhat incomplete. While it is true that adults have more control of their environment than children, I do not think that children are necessarily affected more by environment and adults are influenced more by heredity. Inherited traits provide the foundation by which people are able to learn and respond to their environment.

An adult's personality is the combination of traits and learned behaviour patterns that have been established throughout childhood. Thus, although it is true that adults have more control over their current environment, They are still heavily influenced by both their current environment and by past exposure to environmental factors.

The social learning theory is a good way to explain the influence of environment on antisocial behaviour in children, and does not necessarily have to oppose the notion of genetic influence on behaviour as well. Rather, it should be considered part of a larger theory or model that could describe how environment and genetics interact. Eysenck's general arousal theory, which suggests such an interaction, could be modified to encompass the social learning theory, providing a more complete model to explain how upbringing and inherited traits interact to influence criminal behaviour.

Genetics and environmental factors are so intertwined, that it seems impossible to separate them in explaining how people are caused to engage in criminal acts. It is important for society as a whole to take responsibility in preventing the advent of criminal and antisocial behaviour in children via programs to provide children with healthy, enriching environments. A eugenic approach to preventing antisocial behaviour is immoral and impinges on human rights, but taking an active approach to ensure positive environmental influences would be appropriate.

THE CRIMINAL BEHAVIOUR OF THE SERIAL RAPIST

From 1984 to 1986, FBI Special Agents assigned to the National Centre for the Analysis of Violent Crime (NCAVC) interviewed 41 men who were responsible for raping 837 victims.

Previous issues of the FBI Law Enforcement Bulletin provided an introduction to this research (1) and the characteristics of the rapists and their victims. (2) This article, however, describes the behaviour of these serial rapists during and following the commission of their sexual assaults. The information presented is applicable only to the men interviewed; it is not intended to be generalized to all men who rape.

Premeditation

The majority of the sexual attacks (55-61%) committed by these men were premeditated across their first, middle, and last rapes, while fewer rapists reported their crimes as being

impulsive (15-22%) or opportunistic (22-24%). Although no comparable data on serial rape are available, it is probable that the premeditation involved in these crimes is particularly characteristic of these serial rapists. It is also probable that this premeditation is reflective of their preferential interest in this type of crime and largely accounts for heir ability to avoid detection.

Methods of Approach

There are three different styles of approach rapists frequently use: The "con," the "blitz," and the "surprise." (3) Each reflects a different means of selecting, approaching and subduing a chosen victim.

CONCEPTS OF CRIME AND PUNISHMENT

In sociology, the concept of social control has undergone various transformations. In contemporary sociology, social control is primarily understood in the context of the enforcement of law and/or the control of crime and deviance. Historically, however, the concept of social control enjoyed a much more expansive meaning.

In this chapter, I review the conceptual transformation of social control in sociology as well as its implications in empirical research in the social sciences. Separate attention will go to historians' reliance on various under standings of social control, including the use of social control in research on charitable work and organizations.

Social Control as Social Order

Among the oldest concepts in sociology, social control has historically undergone important transformations in terms of the concept's understanding within different theoretical frameworks. From the late nineteenth century onwards, social control was used primarily in American sociology to refer to a society's capacity to regulate itself without resource to force. This broad concept of social control was understood in a benign sense of self-governance that emphasized a society's continued need for social integration through socialization into common value systems despite trends of increasing individualism. Social control thus characterizes societal integration to the extent that a society does not need to rely on coercion to command conformity. This concept of social control, implying harmony and progressivism, remained en vogue until World War II, especially in US sociology.

The broad consensual notion of social control finds its sharpest expression in the works of George Herbert Mead (1934) and Edward Alsworth Ross (1901). Mead conceived of social control in voluntaristic terms as the ability of individuals to modify their behaviour by taking into account others' expectations, thus harmonizing one's self control and the social control exerted by others.

Social control depends on the ability of individuals "to assume the attitudes of the others who are involved with them in common endeavor" (Mead 1925:275). The implied consensual perspective of the relation between the individual and society is most clearly phrased by Mead by arguing that social control overlaps with self control: "self-criticism is essentially social criticism, and behaviour controlled by self-criticism is essentially behaviour controlled socially. Hence social control, so far from tending to crush out the human individual or to obliterate his self-conscious individuality, is, on the contrary, actually constitutive of and inextricably associated with that individuality" (Mead 1934:255).

The most important representative of the consensual understanding of social control as social order, Edward Ross articulated the role played by society's institutions in fostering social control and identified law as one dimension of social control, next to other institutions such as education, public opinion, and religion.

As a constant function in society, this conception of social control Ross understood to apply to all the members of a society, not just to those who violate normative expectations. Consensus, Ross argued, is the very foundation of social order. Social control is thus opposed to coercive control.

The association of people with one another through various mechanisms of social control applies especially to organic societies, i.e., societies in which (as Durkheim formulated) people are essentially different from one another, perform different functions (division of labour), and have different belief systems.

It is especially under these conditions of increased individualism that societies have to take special efforts to ensure their members to become social beings. Social control also transcends mere social influence. Whereas social influence refers to the ascendancy over individuals by the group to which they belong as a mere effect, social control ensures such ascendancy on behalf of the group in a directed and purposeful manner oriented at harmonizing clashing interests and activities.

The study of social control, Ross further maintained, is part of static sociology because social control is always needed in society, not just at certain times. All possible social institutions, such as art, law, beliefs, public opinion, religion, education, and custom, serve social control functions. Therefore, based on Ross's work, it is not possible to categorize institutions in order to study their social control functions (e.g., a study of education as an institution of social control). Instead, with Ross, attention turns to the study of social control as a societal foundation which is secured through multiple institutions of social control (e.g., education is an institution of social control).

While clearly conservative in its bias towards assumptions on the consensual nature of modern society, Ross's work was developed in the background of an attention for social problems, such as urbanization, poverty, alcoholism, and prostitution.

The solution the early American sociologists typically favoured towards these problems were liberal (in the traditional sense). As Spierenburg (2004) argues, social control was conceived of as a contribution to the creation of a social order that is based on peaceful social relations and collective harmony. Ross's concept of social control also implied a plea for state intervention, especially of uncontrolled capitalism, a notion that was much admired by US President Theodore Roosevelt.

An important theoretical shift in the sociology of social control came about in the period following World War II, when the model of a consensual society could no longer be easily accepted, especially in the wake of the rise of fascism and Nazism, the atrocities of the war, and the build-up towards the cold war and the nuclear arms race.

The concept of social control was now employed to refer to the more repressive and coercive forms of control that are instituted, not by socialization into norms, but on the basis of power and force. The emphasis in this concept of social control is thus on control.

Importantly, from the viewpoint of the coercive conception of social control, attention also goes to social institutions that are not traditionally understood in terms of coercion and power. From this perspective, for instance, sociologists Frances Fox Piven and Richard Cloward investigated the social control functions of welfare in their landmark study, Regulating the Poor: The Functions of Public Welfare (Piven and Cloward 1971). In this work, welfare is conceived as an effort to exert control over certain classes of people, such as the poor and the unemployed, in order to pacify the economically deprived classes and prevent social rebellion.

Conversely, poor relief is constrained with the workforce needs to be expanded. As van Krieken (1991) argues, this use of the social control concept in historical-sociological studies of social welfare owes much to the Marxian instrumentalist theories of ideology and the state. By extension, this perspective of social control can also be applied to various special categories of people, such as the physically and mentally ill, the young and the old, and the deviant and the criminal. With this conception of social control, then, not all members of society, but only certain special and often suspect categories are subject to social control.

The Control of Crime and Deviance

Extending from the concept of social control focused on certain classes, social control has from the 1950s onwards been conceived more narrowly in relation to deviance and/or crime. Social control now refers to those institutions and mechanisms that define and respond to crime and/or deviance. Corresponding to the dominant theory groups in criminological sociology (the perspectives of crime causation, crime construction, and critical sociology), social control is now conceptualized as a functional response to crime, the societal reaction to deviance, or the reproduction of a social order beyond a mere focus on crime.

First, from the perspective of crime causation theories, such as Edwin Sutherland's (1973) theory of differential association, social control is conceived as a dependent variable which functions, in response to crime, as a mechanism of redress. Crime takes centre stage in such a perspective as criminal behaviour, which needs to be causally explained, is observed to be sanctioned by the forces of social control in order to prevent the disintegration of society.

This perspective of social control can theoretically rely on the functionalist sociology of Talcott Parsons (1951), who developed a perspective of social control as a corollary to a theory of deviance and crime.

Whereas crime is seen as creating a tension in an otherwise stable system, social control is understood as a re-integrative attempt to stabilize the functioning of a society. The mechanisms of social control thus function to fulfill society's integrative needs in the societal community. It is to be noted that this conception of social control is not to be confused with the so-called social control theory of crime, which was developed by

Travis Hirschi (1969). In Hirschi's theory, which is mostly an extension to Durkheim's theory of a society's need for integration and regulation (and what happens in the absence thereof), criminal behaviour is accounted for as the result of a weakening of the bonds with society. As a function of social control, conversely, society offers restraints on people's drives and desires.

Second, from the viewpoint of labelling or societal reaction theories, popularized by Howard S. Becker (1963) and Edwin Schur (1965), crime is viewed as a societal construction on the basis of a process of the criminalization of deviance. Whereas an act of deviance is seen as motivated by an actor, its subsequent criminalization is conceived as a function of the societal conditions that define and respond to deviance. Social control is thus constructive of crime through a process of labelling.

From the perspective of crime construction theories, social control mechanisms are not a functional response to crime, but instead determine crime.

This occurs through two processes of criminalization: through primary criminalization, some acts are defined as criminal; and through secondary criminalization, this definition is applied to specific acts. The formal treatment of crime through the processes of social control, furthermore, is typically observed to not take into account the needs and motives of the deviant actor, but instead imposes a system of control that serves societal goals of retribution and punishment.

Third and finally, from the viewpoint of sociological conflict theory, the interactionist focus of labelling theory is transcended with a structural perspective that situates the labelling processes of social control within the broader society in which they take place (e.g., Quinney 1973). Instead of analysing the interactionist order of rule-violator and rule-enforcer, a critical sociology focuses on social control in terms of the historically grown socio-economic conditions of society and its mechanisms and institutions that are mobilized to maintain order. Marxist perspectives, for instance, focus on the norms of enforcement as representing the interests of a class, the elite, which try to have their interests accepted as general norms. Non-Marxist critical perspectives more broadly focus on a variety of groups and inequalities (classism, racism, sexism, ageism).

To end this review of the concept of social control in relation to crime and deviance, it is to be noted that there have been continued attempts in modern sociology to redefine social control broadly, specifically in the works of Morris Janowitz and Jack Gibbs. Morris Janowitz (1975, 1978) uses the concept of social control to denote a society's capacity to regulate itself within a moral framework that transcends self-interest. He argues that social control has been drastically weakened in advanced industrial societies, and wonders why this is the case and how social control can be re-strengthened.

Jack Gibbs (1989, 1994) has developed a scientific theory with a high degree of predictive power (accuracy, testability, scope, range, intensity, discriminatory power, and parsimony). He defines (attempted) control as "overt behaviour by a human in the belief that (1) the behaviour increases or decreases the probability of some subsequent condition and (2) the increase or decrease is desirable" (Gibbs 1994:27). Distinguished on the basis of the target of control are inanimate, biotic, and human control, pertaining to control over objects, nonhuman organisms, and humans, respectively. Control over human behaviour comprises self-control, proximate, sequential, and social control, relative to how many and how other humans are involved.

Turning to contemporary theories of social control in relation to deviance, at least two very different strands of theorizing can be highlighted: the general theory of social control developed by Donald Black; and the revisionist perspective of social control that builds on the work of Foucault.

A General Theory of Social Control

Originally conceived by Donald Black, the general theory of social control aims to provide a scientific theory of social control that is based on the principles of natural science (Black 1976, 1997). Black is interested in formulating a general theory of law and social control that can account for empirical variation irrespective of any value judgments or policy claims. Conceiving of law as governmental social control, Black's pure sociology is oriented at a general theory of all forms of social control, defined as the handling of right and wrong by defining and responding to deviant behaviour.

The epistemological orientation that underlies Black's pure sociology is scientific in its ambition to formulate a general theory, whereby the ordering of variation in empirical reality is seen as the goal of theory. The paradigmatic framework in which Black's theory is situated is distinctly sociological. Rejecting teleological and anthropocentric premises that take into account, respectively, normative and subjective dimensions, Black's approach is radically anti psychological in developing a multi dimensional perspective of social life, including law, as a function of structural characteristics of social space.

On the basis of this paradigm, Black has developed a number of propositions on the behaviour of law and other forms of social control. Social control is generally conceived of as a reality that appears in variable forms of quantity and style. The quantity of social control refers to the amount of social control that is available, for instance whether or not a particular kind of human conduct is regulated by law and whether or not a legal sanction is applied. The styles of social control can be of various kinds, such as penal, compensatory, therapeutic, or conciliatory. In seeking to account for variations in social control in terms of quantity and style, Black studies the geometry of social control on the basis of variations in social space in terms of such characteristics as stratification, differentiation, integration, and culture.

For instance, stratification refers to the vertical structure of society in terms of the inequality of wealth. Vertical space can be high or low in terms of position or downward or upward in direction. Morphology refers to the horizontal aspect of society, including the division of labour (differentiation) and the relative degrees of intimacy and distance (integration). Culture is the symbolic dimension of social life, including expressed ideas about truth, beauty, and ethics, such as in science, art, and religion. Culturally, societies and social groups can vary from being closely related to extremely distant.

On the basis of the suggested model, Black develops various testable propositions. Among them is the thesis that social control varies directly with stratification: societies with higher degrees of stratification have more social control. Law and social control also vary directly with culture: simpler societies have less law and social control than more differentiated societies. On the basis of such propositions, pure sociology seeks to explain and predict the behaviour of social life in terms of social space in value-neutral terms. Irrespective of the intrinsic merits of Black's approach, it is striking that the sharpness of his formulations has enabled much theoretical debate and empirical research.

Bibliography

Adams, Patricia: *Odious Debts: Loose Lending, Corruption and the Third World's Environmental Legacy*, London, Earthscan, 1991.

Campbell, J.Y., Lo, A.W.: *The Econometrics of Financial Markets,* Princeton University Press, 1996.

Chaudhuri, Pramit: *The Indian Economy: Poverty and Development*, New York, St. Martin's Press, 1979.

Christopher J.: *An Indian Rural Economy: The Tamiland Countryside*, Oxford, Clarendon Press, 1984.

Dhingra, C.: *The Indian Economy: Resources, Planning, Development, and Problems*, Delhi, Sultan Chand, 1983.

Dwivedy, Surendranath; Bhargava, G. S.: *Political Corruption in India*, Bharti, Lucknow, 1967

Goldsmith, W.: *The Financial Development of India, 1860-1977*, New Haven, Yale University Press, 1983.

Guha, Sumit: *The Agrarian Economy of the Bombay Deccan, 1818-1941*, Delhi, Oxford University Press, 1985.

Guhan, Sanjivi; Paul, Samuel: *Corruption in India: Agenda for Action*. Vision Books, Delhi, 1997.

Gupta, K. N.: *Corruption in India*. Anmol Publications Pvt Ltd., Delhi, 2001.

Halayya, M.: *Corruption in India*, Affiliated East-West Press, 1985.

Hart, Oliver: *Firms, Contracts, and Financial Structure,* Clarendon Press, Oxford, 1995.

Huang, Chi-fu: *Foundations of Financial Economics,* Prentice-Hall, 1988.

Jeffrey G.: *American Inequality: A Macroeconomic History,* New York, Academic Press, 1980.

Jha, P.R.: *Agriculture and Economic Development*, New Delhi, Ashish, 1988.

Kohli, Suresh: *Corruption in India: The Growing Evil*. India: Chetana Pvt.Ltd., 1975.

MacKinley, A.C.: *The Econometrics of Financial Markets,* Princeton University Press, 1996.

Martin, Justin: *The Man Behind Money*, Perseus Book Group, 2000.

Martin, L. J. and Hiebert, R. E.: *Current Issues in International Communication*, White Plains, NY: Longman, 1990.

Mishra, Jayashri: *Social and Economic Conditions under the Imperial Rashtrakutas*, New Delhi, Commonwealth, 1992.

Muthiah, S.: *A Social and Economic Atlas of India*, Oxford, Oxford University Press, 1987.

Pandian, M. S. S.: *The Political Economy of Agrarian Change: Nachilnadu, 1880-1939*, New Delhi, Sage Publications, 1990.

Paul, Kegan : *Money and the Mechanism of Exchange,* London, 1890.

Prem Shankar: *India: A Political Economy of Stagnation*, Bombay, Oxford University Press, 1980.

Robert Smith: *Modern Labor Economics,* Harper Collins, 1994.

Romer, David: *Advanced Macroeconomics,* McGraw-Hill, 1996.

Rothermund, Dietmar: *An Economic History of India: From Pre- Colonial Times to 1986*, New Delhi, Manohar, 1988.

Schall and Haley: *Introduction to Financial Crime*, McGraw-hill, 1988.

Somiah, C.G.: *The Honest always Stand Alone*. New Delhi: Niyogi Books, 2010.

Subrahmanyam, Sanjay: *The Political Economy of Commerce: Southern India, 1500-1650*, Cambridge, Cambridge University Press, 1990.

Vittal, N.: *Corruption in India: The Roadblock to National Prosperity*. Academic Foundation, 2003.

Index

□□□